HARRODS
Guide to
LONDON

HARRODS
— Guide to —
LONDON

Lydia Greeves

ILLUSTRATED BY CECILIA EALES

PAVILION

First published in 1992 by
PAVILION BOOKS LIMITED
196 Shaftesbury Avenue, London WC2H 8JL

A CIP record for this book is available from the British Library.

ISBN 1 85145 6082
10 9 8 7 6 5 4 3 2 1

Printed and bound in Italy by Arnoldo Mondadori

Contents

———— • ————

INTRODUCTION

———— • ————

L
ONDON IS A huge city, one of the biggest in the world. It has numerous
attractions of every kind for visitors and residents alike. This book does not
aim to be comprehensive; rather, it is a selection of the best and most popular
places, all of which are accessible by public transport from the centre of the
city. All the great museums, art galleries and historic buildings are here, and
so too are many lesser-known sights which are equally rewarding to visit.
Most are concentrated within the central area, but I also wander south to Greenwich
and Dulwich, north to Hampstead and Highgate and twenty miles west along the
Thames to Windsor and Eton.

The text is intended to work on two levels. First, it is a guide to where to go and
what to see, with descriptions of places of interest arranged in thematic chapters
which point up aspects of the city. Each vignette is a self-contained piece, but each
is also woven into broader and deeper strands running through the book which
together give an overall view of the shape of London and
its history, and introduce the principals in that fascinating
cast of characters who, consciously or unconsciously, have
moulded Britain's capital. Most of these
themes appear in the outline of
London's history which starts the book
('The First 2,000 Years') and they are
taken up again and developed in the
introductions to each chapter and in the
section on the city's villages,
ancient settlements which once
lay among green fields and
orchards and which can still be
traced within the sea of bricks
and mortar which now sur-
rounds them. There are many
cross-references between sections, with places for which
there is a separate entry
elsewhere in the book shown
in italic type.

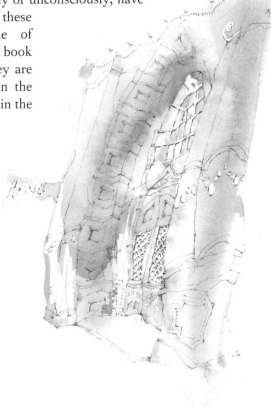

Taken as a whole, London
can be bewildering. But there
is no need to take it as a whole.
More than most capital cities,
London breaks down into

separate neighbourhoods and districts, each of which is small enough soon to become familiar ground. In the central area, the major division is between the City and Westminster, between the sober-suited, bowler-hatted financiers and bankers and the more frivolous fashion shops and stores of the West End. Travelling from Oxford Street to St Paul's, you need to take a tube (see p. 180), but within the West End or the City the simplest and quickest way to get from one destination to another is often on foot. Moreover, only by walking will you really get to know the pattern of the streets and to feel you have London in your bones.

Like all great cities, London has many moods, sometimes seeming warm and welcoming, at others remote and aloof. The weather is rarely blisteringly hot or achingly cold, but it can be oppressively humid in summer and – despite the evidence to the contrary in recent years – rain should be expected. For many, the city is at its best in spring or autumn, when there are often clear, sunny days with a nip in the air which are just right for sightseeing, and for holiday photographs. In winter, after the clocks go back in October, you will be faced with long dark evenings and most attractions will shut earlier. July and August are the height of the tourist season, when everywhere will be at its most crowded, and these are also the weeks when the parks and squares, which add so much to London's attractiveness, start to look tired.

The opening times (for which the 24-hour clock is used) and other details given in the text are correct at the time of writing, but all such information is liable to change, and anyone who is set on visiting somewhere far afield would be wise to check first. Almost everywhere will be closed over the Christmas holiday (24, 25 and 26 December) and on 1 January (New Year's Day), and many places also close on other public holidays (see p. 182). Some attractions, in particular those run by English Heritage, will be shut 13–14 for lunch.

As in so many other things, the admission fees charged for entrance to museums, galleries and historic houses are not necessarily an indication of value for money. Some of the most rewarding attractions in London, such as the *British Museum* and the *National Gallery*, are still free, and long may they remain so. Conversely, exorbitant entrance fees are charged by a number of pretentious establishments. So beware.

Finally, what could be more appropriate than a guide to London endorsed by one of the city's great institutions. Harrods, which has given its name to this book, is both London's most famous shop and a tourist attraction. Indeed, like Tower Bridge or Buckingham Palace, it has become part of London's image, a byword for quality that is recognized all over the world.

Henry Charles Harrod, who started the business by taking over a small grocer's shop in 1853, would surely be amazed if he could see the store that now carries his name. The impressive six-storey building in Knightsbridge with its turn-of-the-century terracotta facade has 20 acres of selling space on five floors, with fifty lifts to carry customers from one level to another, and its own water and power supply. Although you can no longer buy an aeroplane here, and an elephant would tax the resources of the pet department, the range and variety of what is on offer has to be seen to be believed. At Harrods you can pick up a fishing rod or a Celtic harp, purchase a theatre ticket or a weekend break in Budapest, and even buy a house – as well as a brass knocker for the front door and everything you need in the way of furniture. Not for nothing is the telegraphic address 'Everything, London' and the trademark *Omnia, omnibus, ubique* (all things, for all people, everywhere) is no idle boast.

Harrods' reputation for reliability has never been more severely tested than in 1883, when a disastrous fire destroyed both buildings and stock at the start of the Christmas season. Nothing daunted, Henry's son, Charles Digby, made alternative arrangements to fill the flood of orders and wrote to every customer explaining 'your order will be delayed in the execution a day or two. I hope, in the course of Tuesday or Wednesday next, to be able to forward it.' The Christmas trade that season beat all previous records, and a couple of years later the general increase in business led to the first account customers, among them Oscar Wilde, the beautiful Lillie Langtry, who captured the heart of the Prince of Wales, and the actress Ellen Terry.

Today, anyone who is anyone shops at Harrods, and the store is a supplier to Her Majesty the Queen, Elizabeth, the Queen Mother, HRH the Prince of Wales, and the Duke of Edinburgh. The business with an international reputation now also has a presence overseas. There are Harrods shops in Tokyo and at Toronto and Frankfurt airports, there is a Harrods on board the QEII, and the distinctive name and olive-green packaging can even be found on board the *Queen Mary* moored at Long Beach, California. In other ways, too, Harrods' recent history reflects its world-wide appeal. Taken over by the House of Fraser in 1959, Harrods, together with the rest of the group, is now part of the empire controlled by the Al-Fayed brothers, who see themselves as continuing the long tradition of family ownership.

1

THE FIRST 2,000 YEARS

—— • ——

Forget six counties overhung with smoke,
Forget the snorting steam and piston stroke,
Forget the spreading of the hideous town,
Think rather of the pack-horse on the down,
And dream of London, small, and white and clean.

William Morris: *The Earthly Paradise*

L ONDON IS BOTH very old and very new. Although not the most ancient city in Britain – both Winchester and Colchester are earlier foundations – London has been the capital since Roman times and, as centre of both court and government, has seen a concentration of wealth and power which flowered in magnificent palaces and sumptuous mansions. To the casual visitor, however, the city does not feel very old. The vast urban agglomeration sprawling across the Thames valley with long tentacles reaching out into Essex, Hertfordshire, Kent and Surrey is largely a creature of the late nineteenth and twentieth centuries, made possible by the development of an extensive rail and tube network. Even in the Square Mile of the City, site of the Roman foundation and of the walled medieval town, vast modern office blocks dominate the skyline, turning narrow streets beneath them into Manhattan-like canyons.

On the other hand, for those who look, the skeleton of a much older place still shows through the relatively recent skin. Until the building of modern traffic arteries, the chief roads into London were nearly all of Roman origin; the wall which contained the medieval town for centuries and which still stands in places to a height of 35 feet incorporates Roman defences; and the cobbled lanes and alleys which still thread the City and run steeply down to the river reflect the medieval street pattern, names such as Milk Street, Fish Street Hill, Lombard Street and Poultry indicating places where certain trades were practised, or particular goods sold.

For hundreds of years the key to London was the Thames, a watery highway running east towards the Continent and Scandinavia and west through some of England's most fertile and productive countryside. The little trading post established by the Romans in the years after the invasion of AD 43 grew up at the river's lowest crossing point, where the well-drained gravel terrace on the north bank was matched by a tongue of sand rising out of the tidal marshes on the south. Here, very close to what is now London Bridge, the army's engineers built a wooden structure across the Thames. Although destroyed in AD 61 in the savage rebellion led by Queen Boudicca, whose Amazon-like figure, accompanied by her two daughters, still rides furiously towards the Houses of Parliament in a bronze statue at the north end of Westminster Bridge, Londinium soon rose again, with imposing buildings along paved main streets. The remains of a vast palace have been found under what is now Cannon Street Station, and the largest basilica north of the Alps was constructed on one of the two hill-like gravel spurs divided by the valley of the Walbrook.

This civilized city, the largest in Britain, and with a population that may have approached fifty thousand at its height, flourished for four centuries, the same length of time that separates twentieth-century London from the Middle Ages, but has left only shadows behind. Incongruously surrounded by skyscrapers on Queen Victoria Street, just west of the Mansion House, are the foundations of the Temple of Mithras, a three-aisle brick and stone building discovered during excavations along the Walbrook in 1954. The former river valley, now 18 feet below street level, also yielded the finely crafted sculptures in the *Museum of London*, while other Roman remains displayed here include perfectly preserved metal tools, beads of emerald and amber imported from Egypt and the Baltic, and red tableware brought over from France. Early London was a cosmopolitan place with links throughout the civilized world.

In the late fourth century, as the Empire slowly faded, Londinium too crumbled, its large public monuments demolished to provide material for a defensive wall along the river. Nobody knows how long its inhabitants managed to cling to their former lifestyle in the face of Saxon raids, or whether the city soon lay desolate, weeds thick between the paving in the streets, young saplings cracking open mosaic floors and bath suites. A blank in the record for almost two centuries ended when St Augustine, sent from Rome by Pope Gregory in 597, converted the Saxon King Ethelbert, and seven years later appointed the monk Mellitus bishop of London. The first *St Paul's Cathedral* was built on the site of the present church, and early Saxon London grew up a mile west of the ruins of the Roman city, along what is now the Strand. By the eighth century the Venerable Bede could describe London as '*multorum emporium populorum*' ('market of many peoples'), but only a few years later disaster struck once again. In 851 Vikings raided far into England, reducing London to ruins. A faint echo of the town re-established by King Alfred (he who burnt the cakes) on the site of the Roman city can still be sensed in the little inlet of Queenhithe, off Upper Thames Street. As a plaque on the wall records, this mysterious deserted place, where water slaps against wooden quays, was where he built his new harbour, a crucial element in restoring London's former prosperity. Not far away, in All Hallows by the Tower, is a substantial Saxon arch, partly built with red Roman bricks.

So far, political power and commercial interests had both been concentrated in the same place, but in the mid eleventh century began the division between government and City, between the administrators and the wealth-producers, which is such a marked feature of London today. Round a great bend in the Thames, on a marshy island on the edge of the river, Edward the Confessor began a new palace and a great new abbey – his minster in the west, Westminster (see p. 165). Only days after his abbey was consecrated, on a cold January night in 1066, the saintly Edward died, and his childlessness unleashed a struggle for the Crown which ended with the invasion by William of Normandy and his victory at the Battle of Hastings.

From the Conqueror's time date two of the greatest buildings in the London area. On the eastern edge of the city he erected the White Tower, the palace-keep at the heart of the *Tower of London*, while away to the west, on a chalk spur overlooking the Thames, he constructed the motte-and-bailey fortress which grew into *Windsor*

Castle, originally one of nine strongholds ringing the capital. With these symbols of royal authority to subdue the 'vast and fierce populace', William ensconced himself in Edward's palace at Westminster.

So the medieval city grew around two centres, one confined within the old walls, the other upstream at Westminster, while at the south end of London Bridge the suburb of Southwark developed to cater for travellers converging on the capital. As in Roman times, the walls ran for some two miles, north from the Tower, west along what is now London Wall, and south to the river at Blackfriars, enclosing a semi-circular area of over 330 acres. Fragments of the defences survive all along the route, but two of the most impressive stretches are on Tower Hill, where both Roman and medieval stonework can clearly be seen, and in the gardens east of the *Museum of London*, where there are substantial remains of two bastion towers. The gates which once guarded the entrances to the city, and where undesirables such as lepers would be turned away, have all disappeared, but their names live on in Aldersgate, Aldgate, Moorgate, Bishopsgate, etc. The medieval and Tudor city, dominated by the great Gothic cathedral which had developed from the church founded by Mellitus, was a place of dark alleys and narrow winding streets, ankle deep in mud and refuse and lined with houses of lath and timber, or half of timber and half of brick, the upper floors jettied out over the lower in crazy, top-heavy constructions which sometimes collapsed on to passers-by. In among them were the great mansions of the merchant princes, set round interconnecting courtyards, while huge acreages both in and outside the walls were taken up by the precincts of monastic houses. Disease and fire were constant hazards, the Black Death of 1348–9 carrying off perhaps two-thirds of a population which had become as great as it had been under the Romans.

Everywhere was within walking distance of the river, where hundreds of little boats ferried those who could afford them up and downstream, or from one bank to the other. London Bridge, rebuilt in stone between 1176 and 1209, was still the only bridge across the river, the roadway constricted to a narrow 12-foot passage by bulging houses which overhung the water on either side. The Thames was also the main route to Westminster, its banks and the two link roads to the north – one leading along Holborn from Newgate, the other from Ludgate along the Strand – lined by the estates of courtiers and nobles, their names recorded in Buckingham and Savoy Street, Somerset House and Essex Street. Just west of the City walls, a wedge of secluded courtyards and gardens formed a separate legal quarter, which still stretches north from the river for three-quarters of a mile. These Inns of Court, where gowned figures clutching ribboned briefs hurry past, even now have a medieval flavour, the Tudor brick gateway to Lincoln's Inn leading into a courtyard closed by a hall of 1490–2, with stone mullioned windows and linenfold panelling. So does the riverside palace built for the Archbishop of Canterbury at Lambeth, across the Thames, where the castellated brick gateway dates from 1495, while in the City itself the *Charterhouse* is a miraculous survival of one of the courtyard houses of the nobility. The great hall of another, built in the fifteenth century for the wealthy wool merchant Sir John Crosby and later owned by the scholarly Sir Thomas More, Henry VIII's Lord Chancellor, was re-erected in 1910 on More's Chelsea estate (see p.172); the lofty, balconied room, with a five-sided oriel window in stone lighting the high-table end, is now appropriately used as a dining hall for postgraduate students at London University. Even more evocative, though much restored, is the long, half-timbered, three- and four-storey façade of Staple Inn on Holborn, a jumble of beams and gables, overhangs and small-paned casement windows conjuring up the London of Elizabeth I.

The city was by now bursting its bounds and, despite an edict of 1580, the first of many, which prohibited the building of any new houses within three miles of one of the gates, the antiquary John Stow (1525–1605) reported that the pleasant fields he had known to the east of the city, 'with fayre hedgerowes and Elme trees, with Bridges and easie stiles to passe over', had disappeared under small tenements and cottages. Well before the disasters of the mid seventeenth century, when the Plague of 1665 may have claimed as many as a hundred thousand victims and the Great Fire of 1666 destroyed four-fifths of the City, the rich were moving westwards, and these decades also saw the beginnings of an architectural revolution. Renaissance influences had begun to seep into England a hundred years before, in the Italianate decoration of Henry VII's tomb in *Westminster Abbey*, or in the terracotta roundels which Henry VIII added to his palace at *Hampton Court*, but London's first wholly classical buildings were the work of the architect Inigo Jones, the son of a Smithfield clothworker, who was a genius far ahead of his time. His *Queen's House* at Greenwich (begun 1616) and *Banqueting House* in Whitehall (1619–22) are now among other Italianate buildings, but his Queen's Chapel in St James's (1623–5) is still seen juxtaposed with the red brick of the old Tudor palace, showing how revolutionary the stone façades, pediments, pilasters and other Palladian features would have originally seemed amongst the gables, mullions and bargeboards of the old city.

Inigo Jones was also responsible for London's first square, laid out from 1631 on the Earl of Bedford's Covent Garden estate. He designed it in the style of an Italian piazza, with two ranges of arcaded houses, a Tuscan church filling the west side, and the fourth open to the river. Architectural spaces such as this were to characterize London's development over the next two hundred years and are a principal reason why much of the West End is now such a joy to walk through. Apart from his restored church, Jones's Covent Garden has largely disappeared, although the reconstructed colonnaded range in the north-west corner gives some idea of how it might have looked. The centre, where painted benches and trees once surrounded a sundial, is now filled by Charles Fowler's attractive arcaded buildings of 1828–32, designed to house the fruit and vegetable market which began here in 1654. Since the market moved south of the river, Covent Garden has become one of London's greatest tourist attractions, filled with highly-priced boutiques, wine bars and

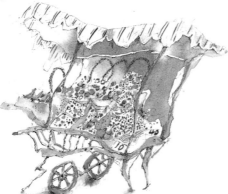

restaurants, and a favourite place for street entertainment.

Inigo Jones, who was only nine years younger than Shakespeare, died in 1652, so never saw the devastation wrought by the Great Fire, which started in the early morning of 2 September 1666, in a baker's shop near the north end of London Bridge. The diarist Samuel Pepys, who then lived in Seething Lane just west of the Tower, at first thought the fire was no danger, but by the end of that day the extent of the disaster was only too apparent: ' . . . we to a little ale-house on the Bankside, over against the Three Cranes, and there stayed till it was dark almost, and saw the fire grow; and as it grew darker, appeared more and more, and in corners and upon steeples, and between churches and houses, as far as we could see up the hill of the City, in a most horrid malicious bloody flame, not like the fine flame of an ordinary fire.' People stayed in their houses 'as till the very fire touched them, and then running into boats or clambering from one pair of stairs by the waterside to another. And among other things, the poor pigeons, I perceive, were loath to leave their houses, but hovered about the windows and balconies, till they burned their wings, and fell down.' Early the next morning Pepys drove in his nightshirt to a friend's house in Bethnal Green, where he left his valuables. He then buried his wine and Parmesan cheese in the garden, and found a boat to ferry his furniture downstream. For four days the fire raged unchecked, until a change of wind, coupled with the determined actions of Charles II and his brother the Duke of York, who blew up buildings to create firebreaks, brought the flames under control. Pepys's house was spared, but over 13,000 houses and 89 churches, among them the great Gothic cathedral, had been destroyed, and some quarter of a million people were homeless.

Designs for an orderly, planned city, such as Charles II would have liked, poured in. The diarist John Evelyn and the 33-year-old Christopher Wren, then recently appointed Professor of Astronomy at Oxford, both proposed an Italianate city with wide streets punctuated by piazzas and quays along the river, but all such dreams proved vain. Wren, possibly England's greatest architect, replaced Old St Paul's with the masterpiece that now crowns Ludgate Hill, and designed 51 City churches, each one different; but, with the exception of King Street and Queen Street, which form a thoroughfare leading from the *Guildhall* to the river, the old medieval street plan reappeared almost without alteration. The greatest opportunity London has ever had was defeated by a multitude of individual interests and by the pressing need to rebuild as quickly as possible. None the less, all was not lost. Stringent new building regulations required houses to be of brick and stone with tiled roofs, and laid down rules about types of houses, from 'four-storey buildings' in 'high and principal' streets to much more modest dwellings in by-lanes and alleys.

The fire encouraged those who could to move westward, an exodus that was stimulated at the end of the century by William and Mary's preference for their palaces at Kensington and Hampton Court. Where the City grew piecemeal, with twisting courts and alleys running between the main thoroughfares, the West End was planned and developed with space and grandeur, as the view from the top of *Westminster Cathedral's* campanile makes very clear. Spectacular houses backed by a dignified square appeared on the Earl of St Alban's estate bounded by Piccadilly, Pall Mall and St James's, the provision for a church giving Wren an opportunity to design at least one building on a virgin site; Bloomsbury was developed by the Bedfords, streets and squares appeared on the Marylebone estate of the Duke and Duchess of Portland, and the notorious Nicholas Barbon – arrogant, persuasive, unscrupulous or charming as the occasion merited – built wherever he could. He succeeded in acquiring the Duke of Buckingham's house in the Strand for redevelopment, but only by agreeing to preserve the grandiose water-gate of 1626 which now looks over Embankment Gardens, and to use every word of the Duke's title in naming his new streets. George Street and Villiers Street are unexceptional enough, but at the bottom of the steps leading from the Strand to Buckingham Street is little Of Alley, renamed York Place by a faint-hearted authority.

Many of the original buildings have now disappeared, but delightful pockets of this period survive, among them the perfectly preserved, early eighteenth-century Queen Anne's Gate in Westminster, with carved porches and lamp brackets; the four brick houses of the 1730s in Pickering Place, approached by a narrow arched passageway off St James's; or the houses of 1722–32 in pedestrianized Meard Street, buried in the heart of Soho. Where all these buildings were of a deep red or brownish brick, some of the grander mansions were constructed in stone, among them the Italianate palace on the north side of Piccadilly devised by Colen Campbell for the 3rd Earl of Burlington, the patron and high priest of the mid eighteenth-century Palladian revival (see p. 125). Stone cladding also marked developments by the Adam brothers, active from the 1770s onwards. Sadly, only fragments remain of this Scottish trio's ambitious and speculative riverside development known as the Adelphi (from the Greek *Adelphoi*, brothers), with a long classical terrace supported by immense arches overlooking the Thames, but the east side of Fitzroy Square, just off the Marylebone Road, is still as they built it in the 1790s, the recesses and angles of the façade brought into high relief by an afternoon sun.

The climax of this controlled development came in the early nineteenth century, when the Prince Regent, the most aristocratic landlord of them all, asked his protégé John Nash, said to have been linked to his royal patron by ties much deeper than mere professional association, to build a grand new street linking his new palace of Carlton House towards the east end of Pall Mall with his Regent's Park estate to the north, which had just reverted to the Crown. Nash was to die in debt and with his reputation under a cloud for his mishandling of *Buckingham Palace*, but he is the only man to have ever produced and carried through a great plan for London, covering his buildings with revolutionary pale yellow stucco:

> Augustus at Rome was for building renowned
> And of marble he left what of brick he had found;
> But is not our Nash, too, a very great master?
> He finds us all brick and he leaves us all plaster.

Nash's brilliantly imaginative scheme drew the West End together, focusing the gently rambling squares on a strong north-south spine while also cutting off the more unsavoury streets of Soho from the refined inhabitants of Mayfair. This backbone was Regent Street, a

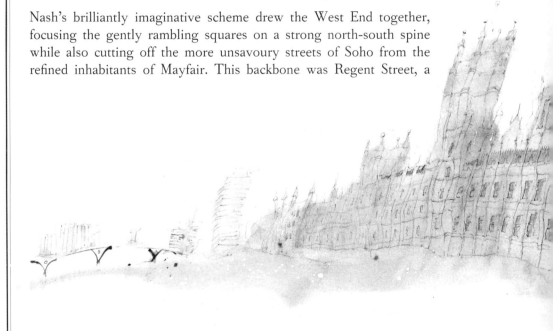

grand triumphal way sweeping north and west for over a mile. Where lesser men would have imposed a dead straight avenue like the Champs-Elysées, Nash made a virtue out of breaks and curves, building Piccadilly Circus where his route came to an abrupt halt at the end of Lower Regent Street, and then carrying it west round the graceful arc of The Quadrant. In another westerly swing further north, where the new road was joined to Robert and James Adam's Portland Place, the grandest street of eighteenth-century London, Nash filled the bend with the delightful church of All Souls, Langham Place, its rotund columned porch designed to lead the eye round the corner. Finally comes his master-stroke, the graceful colonnaded arms of Park Crescent, opening out towards grass and trees.

The park itself he saw as a kind of garden city, with classical villas dotted here and there among smooth lawns, clumps of trees and the curves of a two-armed lake. In the event, only a few of the projected villas were built (although more mansions are now being slotted in on the north-west side, near the Regent's Park mosque), but Nash's classical terraces framing the park are a delight, from the recreated pinnacled cupolas on Sussex Place to the statues adorning the magnificent central pediment of Cumberland Terrace, large enough to float mysteriously above the trees. Carlton House, the reason for all this drama, disappeared even before the scheme was completed, and the southern end of Regent Street now tumbles down a broad flight of steps into St James's Park, which Nash had transformed with new walks and trees and another graceful lake. This enterprising architect, now well over seventy, also devised Trafalgar Square on the site of the Old Royal Mews,

releasing James Gibbs's *St Martin-in-the-Fields* from its surrounding blanket of unattractive tenements. Here Charles I still rides towards his place of execution in Whitehall in a bronze statue of 1633, but the square is now dominated by Nelson's Column, a 145-foot fluted pillar of Dartmoor granite commemorating the Battle of Trafalgar, with a pigeon-besmirched likeness of England's greatest hero standing on top.

Gothic architecture reappeared under the Victorians, in G. E. Street's red and white Law Courts of 1868–82, in the pinnacled fantasy of George Gilbert Scott's St Pancras Station, one of London's greatest landmarks, and in Barry and Pugin's golden Houses of Parliament (see p. 19). The profits from the Great Exhibition of 1851, which brought visitors from all over the world to Joseph Paxton's Crystal Palace in Hyde Park, funded a string of museums and educational institutions in South Kensington and the massive circular Royal Albert Hall, an oval brick drum ringed with a frieze celebrating the triumph of the arts and sciences. After the building of a second bridge across the Thames at Westminster in 1750, links over the river multiplied, the most graceful being the Albert suspension bridge, of 1871–3, in pastel shades of pink, green and blue and with its original tollbooths still standing, the most impressive the pseudo-medieval drawbridge by the Tower, of 1886–94 (see p. 58). On its fringes London grew and grew, stuccoed streets and cheaper brick terraces creeping over the gentle hills rising away from the Thames, swallowing up villages that lay in their path. In 1700 no Londoner had been more than a mile from the river; by 1800 his journey could well have doubled; and today it would be possible to walk for hours and hours without reaching the Thames. Sadly, the city has turned its back on the river, hungrily reaching out along a web of motorways to the countryside which its inhabitants could once enjoy so easily.

2

POMP AND CIRCUMSTANCE

—— • ——

MEDIEVAL KINGS WERE constantly on the move, travelling with the royal train on ponderous progresses across the country, keeping the peace and quelling opposition by their presence, dispensing justice and collecting rents and taxes. Under the Tudors, government was strongly centralized on London, and here Henry VII and his son planned or refurbished a whole sequence of royal residences, moving from one to another along the highway of the Thames on lavishly appointed barges. The Conqueror had needed to support his authority with fortresses and displays of strength, but the early Tudors built simply to please themselves.

The acquisitive Henry VIII collected property as he did wives. Upstream of Westminster and the City, west along the fertile valley leading into the heart of England, he had residences at Chelsea, Kew, Richmond, Hampton Court and Windsor; he built St James's Palace on the site of a former leper hospital in what is now the heart of the West End; while downstream he revelled in his sea-palace at Greenwich, and when a young man was often at Eltham, where a Tudor great hall still sits on a moated site in the urban desert of south-east London. Late in life, at Cheam on what is now the southern outskirts of London, he built his last and most extraordinary creation, an extravaganza lavishly decorated with Italianate stucco, its skyline marked by onion-shaped cupolas and ornate weather-vanes. This palace of Nonsuch, Henry's building without compare, for which a whole village was cleared away, lasted less than two hundred years.

Others who came after had simpler tastes. George II's favourite residence was the now-vanished Richmond Lodge at Kew, while George III enjoyed the little Jacobean manor with Dutch gables which still sits in Kew Gardens about a mile away from the site of his grandfather's retreat (see p. 148). Like Nonsuch and the lodge, several royal buildings have now disappeared, only a gatehouse or a vaulted cellar indicating where they once stood; others are show places, open to the public, and some still house members of the royal family and their entourages. Once court and government were synonymous, but from the mid seventeenth century when Charles I went to the block for his belief in royal supremacy, effective power passed from the sovereign to his subjects' representatives in the Houses of Parliament.

The two greatest palaces London has seen – Westminster and Whitehall – lay side by side near the abbey which Edward the Confessor founded on an island in the Thames in the eleventh century. Westminster was originally Edward's palace, and this rambling place was to be the main residence of England's monarchs for 450 years, the comfortable apartments they enjoyed here much preferred to the more secure accommodation available in William the Conqueror's White Tower dominating the south-east corner of the City. The king who broke the pattern, as so much else, was Henry VIII. By the early sixteenth century Westminster was showing its age, and next door, almost, as it were, flaunted in the King's face, his arrogant and ambitious Cardinal, Thomas Wolsey, was transforming the residence he enjoyed as Archbishop of York, unwisely entertaining Henry and his court to lavish banquets, 'the like of which was never given by Cleopatra or Caligula'. On Wolsey's downfall, Henry took York Place for himself, renaming it Whitehall. This is where the porcine, psychopathic King married Anne Boleyn in 1533 and only three years later, having sent Anne to the block, was wedded to Jane Seymour; this is where he himself died in 1547 and the palace's thousand or so rooms were where Charles I displayed his magnificent collection of paintings, among them 28 Titians and nine Raphaels.

By the late seventeenth century the palace had become a warren of courtyards and gardens, halls and galleries which covered some 23 acres, stretching back from the Thames almost to St James's Park, with a tiltyard on the site of what is now Horse Guards Parade. Then, in 1698, a Dutch laundrywoman left linen drying too close to a fire and the brick and timber ranges burnt to the ground. All that survives is Inigo Jones's *Banqueting House*, a wine cellar, the remains of a Tudor tennis court behind Downing Street and part of a 280-foot riverside terrace which Christopher Wren constructed in 1691, its stonework and the steps down which William and Mary would have boarded the state barge now curiously exposed in Embankment Gardens.

Westminster, meanwhile, became the place from which the country was administered and, eventually, governed. When Henry moved out, Parliament and the highest court in the land remained behind, and they have been here ever since. For hundreds of years, the two houses – the Lords and the Commons – had to make do with makeshift accommodation, the Commons sometimes deliberating in

POMP AND CIRCUMSTANCE

Westminster Abbey's beautiful chapter house, and from 1550 meeting in the former chapel of St Stephen in the palace. The present Gothic building, one of London's best-known landmarks, with its purpose-built debating chambers, dates largely from the mid nineteenth century, when the old Palace of Westminster went up in flames. The government decided to hold a competition for the design of what had to be one of the most impressive buildings in the capital, stipulating that the style must be Gothic or Elizabethan. The winner, against 96 other entries, was the architectural genius Sir Charles Barry, who had enlisted the help of the equally brilliant but then very young Augustus Welby Pugin in the preparation of meticulously detailed drawings. The romantic façades with their rippling, endlessly repeated bays, pinnacles and golden vanes are Barry's, but the interior glows with Pugin's intricate ornamentation, from tiled floors and stained glass to inkwells and umbrella stands.

Begun in 1840, the New Palace of Westminster, as the Houses of Parliament are officially known, took twenty years to build instead of the projected six, every step of the way dogged with setbacks. Pugin died, out of his mind, in 1852, when only forty; Sir Charles Barry, disappointed and embittered, having been cheated out of his proper fee, in 1860, the year his unmistakable fretted silhouette could at last be seen in its entirety. His curiously pointed tower housing the clock known as Big Ben has become a national symbol, while at the other end of the building its height is balanced by the huge 336-foot Victoria Tower. This pseudo-medieval skyscraper is now used to house Parliamentary documents, the records kept here including a long petition from East Africa signed with thumb-prints. In among the Neo-Gothic are some genuine medieval remains, foremost among them the magnificent 240-foot hall begun in 1097, its hammerbeam roof of 1394–1401 the greatest in the world. When the Commons was hit by a bomb at the height of the Blitz in May 1941, Churchill instructed the firemen to 'save Westminster Hall at all costs'. This they did, but the Commons' Chamber burnt, and Sir Giles Gilbert Scott's reconstruction of 1945–50 sadly did not recreate Pugin's restless decoration. (Access to the Houses of Parliament is strictly controlled. Those who want to enjoy a debate when Parliament is in session can join the afternoon queues at St Stephen's entrance, but it is better to obtain tickets in advance from your MP (British residents), or embassy (non-British residents); guided tours can be arranged by application to your MP or, for non-British residents, by contacting House of Commons information, 071 219 4272, but this must be done well in advance.)

Government buildings now line the gently curving street running north from the Houses of Parliament across the site of the old Palace of Whitehall. On the western side, like a canyon between George Gilbert Scott's Home and Foreign Office (1868–73) and Sir Charles Barry's dignified façade to the old Treasury (1845), is the cleft of Downing Street, its entrance now blocked off by railings. This little cul-de-sac of late seventeenth-century terraced houses 'fit for persons of honour and quality' is the official residence of the Prime Minister and the Chancellor of the Exchequer, but the 'pleasant prospect into St James's Park' which the first occupants enjoyed is now partly screened by monumental architecture. Just to the north, reached through an archway guarded by mounted sentries on Whitehall, is the great sweep of Horse Guards Parade, with classical ranges designed by William Kent in c.1745–8 set round three sides of a courtyard. For most of the year, this vast gravelled space appears to be an exclusive car park, but in June, on the Queen's official birthday, it is the setting for the Trooping of the Colour, for which rehearsals take place for weeks beforehand, and in late May or early June for the similarly colourful Beating Retreat (see p. 179). Easily missed in the centre of

Whitehall, the streams of traffic dividing around it, is Sir Edwin Lutyens's Cenotaph, a plain, gently curving stele of Portland stone commemorating the dead of both world wars, while it was through a window in the Italianate façade of Inigo Jones's *Banqueting House* on the eastern side that Charles I stepped to his death in 1649.

Not surprisingly, after the Restoration, Charles's cynical and pleasure-loving son deserted Whitehall, the place of his father's execution, for the more congenial, rambling Tudor ranges of St James's. William and Mary preferred the apartments Wren created for them at *Kensington Palace* and *Hampton Court*, but Queen Anne, most of whose seventeen children were born here, and the Hanoverian monarchs also regarded St James's as their principal London residence. On 8 April 1795 the future George IV celebrated his disastrous marriage to Caroline of Brunswick in the palace, becoming so drunk on his wedding night that he lay supine in a fireplace. Not long afterwards, Nash began to build the Prince Regent a grandiose palace at the end of the Mall, and his niece Victoria moved in here almost immediately she became queen in 1837. *Buckingham Palace* has been the sovereign's town house ever since, but St James's, although no longer lived in by members of the royal family, is still the official centre of the court, foreign ambassadors being accredited here rather than to the more austere building down the road. Although only the turreted gateway facing up St James's Street is original, St James's Palace still looks Tudor, with battlemented and gabled façades in diapered red brick set around four courtyards. Every morning in summer crowds gather outside Inigo Jones's Queen's Chapel across the road from the palace to watch guardsmen lining up in Friary Court before setting off down the Mall for the changing of the guard at Buckingham Palace (see p. 179).

More original Tudor work survives at *Hampton Court*, way upstream, setting for some of the major scenes in Henry VIII's dramatic life, but the palace his father rebuilt at Richmond in 1501, and which Henry VII preferred to all other royal residences, has now largely disappeared. At its height this was a splendid place set around three courtyards, with Henry's private lodgings in the innermost quadrangle overlooking the river and gardens renowned for their exotic fruit. In contrast to Hampton Court and St James's, Richmond's grander ranges were built of stone, but the remnants that survive are in familiar mellow brick. On the south side of Richmond Green, leading towards the river, is a Tudor gatehouse, and beyond it, in Old Palace Yard, a surviving section of the outer court, casement windows now replaced by sashes but the outlines of a blocked-up ground-floor arcade clearly visible and faint diapering still discernible in the brickwork. Here Henry VII died in 1509 and here, almost a century later, his granddaughter Elizabeth I, Gloriana, slowly faded, propped up on a heap of cushions, her face greying beneath the white paint. Below the windows Sir Robert Carey waited for the ring with which he rode north to Scotland to give James I news of his succession.

Henry VIII was brought up here, but his favourite residence, until he wrested Hampton Court from Thomas Wolsey, was his birthplace, right the other side of London, on a bend of the Thames where the river broadens into an estuary and starts to smell of the sea. Here at Greenwich there had been a palace since 1427, when the learned Humphrey Duke of Gloucester, brother of Henry V, built his Bella Court on the banks of the Thames. (The collection of books and manuscripts which he amassed would form the nucleus of the Bodleian Library in Oxford.) On Humphrey's mysterious and sudden death in 1447, Bella Court was seized by his nephew Henry VI and the 17-year-old Queen Margaret of Anjou, who spent lavishly on their new acquisition, renaming it Pleasaunce and covering it with plaster daisies, the queen's emblem. Henry VII razed this palace to the ground, building in its place a familiar Tudor assemblage of brick and stone ranges round a sequence of courtyards, with a banqueting hall and a tiltyard as at Hampton Court.

Henry VIII was born in this new palace of Placentia in 1491; here he married Catherine of Aragon and into his life came Anne Boleyn. They all lived together, these three, while Henry's passion for Anne grew and the proceedings to rid himself of his no longer youthful wife started a chain of events from which there was no retreat. Did he, I wonder, remember any of the ardour which had prompted his love letters to Anne, written in his own hand, when he signed her death warrant at Greenwich in 1536? And what effect could these events have had on the two young girls who were born here, Catherine's daughter Mary and Anne's daughter Elizabeth? Greenwich was also the place where Henry both married and, within a matter of months, hastily unmarried Anne of Cleves, to the relief of both, and here his only son Edward VI was to die of tuberculosis in his sixteenth year.

Despite the domestic dramas, Henry loved Greenwich, staging splendid tournaments in the tiltyard and sallying forth in his gilded barge to visit the naval dockyards downstream at Woolwich and upstream at Deptford, where the Ravensbourne joined the Thames. Woolwich was where the *Henri Grâce à Dieu*, the greatest battleship of its age, was launched, and in these yards was established the naval supremacy which led to the defeat of the Armada in 1588. Henry also had his armoury at Greenwich, importing craftsmen from Germany to make the fine pieces now on display in the *Tower of London*. And this was the place where the young Walter Raleigh is supposed to have laid a cloak across a puddle for his queen and where he is said to have scratched on one of the windows, 'Fain would I climb, but that I fear to fall', Gloriana adding below, 'If thy heart fail thee, climb not at all.'

Approaching Greenwich from the river, it seems that there is still a great palace here, its pedimented, neo-classical ranges stretching back from the Thames to frame a vista to Inigo Jones's *Queen's House*. This is the grandest view in London, a magnificent set-piece of receding white stone with the slopes of Greenwich park rising up behind. But despite the studied dignity of these façades, this is no palace. Charles II, faced with dilapidated and decaying buildings at the Restoration, had resolved to revive the glories of Tudor Greenwich, but only one block of the grandiose scheme produced by John Webb, Inigo Jones's nephew, was completed before the king ran out of money. Some thirty years later, William and Mary decided to convert the project into a naval hospital and home for seamen, a charitable foundation to rival Charles II's Royal Hospital overlooking the river at Chelsea. Wren, who had designed the rather severe classical blocks upstream with an open colonnade where the infirm could sit and watch the world go by, was called upon again. At Greenwich, he excelled himself, incorporating Charles's building into the stunning composition seen today, with domed turrets framing the central vista through which Queen Mary could still enjoy the view of the river from the Queen's House. Wren died before his scheme could be completed, and it was finished off by Nicholas Hawksmoor and Sir John Vanbrugh.

The most impressive interior is Wren's Painted Hall, where every inch of the walls and ceiling is covered with paintings by James Thornhill. A mixture of mythology, allegory and symbolism exalting the monarchy and the triumph of peace and liberty over tyranny, Thornhill's complicated composition is a confusing array of cloud-born deities, superfluous cherubs and portraits of the royal family and other notables, among them Galileo with his telescope and the dark figure of Copernicus holding up a model of the solar system – allusions to the astronomical observatory which Charles II had founded up on the hill behind (see p. 93). Thornhill himself appears in the bottom right-hand corner of the end wall, his outstretched hand suggesting that he would have liked a more generous payment for his nineteen years' work, and one of the more energetic of the pensioners, still being punished for drunkenness and swearing at the age of 96, is said to have been the model for the figure of Winter. Across the central avenue is the chapel, rebuilt in 1779 after a fire, the rococo decoration in delicate pastel shades designed by James 'Athenian' Stuart providing a vivid contrast to the baroque interior over the way. The buildings are now occupied by the Royal Naval College and the hall is a dining-room, as was originally intended, with a lingering aroma of cabbage and Windsor soup. I wonder how many of the young officers who now crowd the long tables ever give a thought to Admiral Lord Nelson, who lay here in state after his death at Trafalgar in 1805. (Hall and chapel open Mon–Wed, Fri–Sun 14.30–17; admission free.)

THE BANQUETING HOUSE

Whitehall, SW1

——— • ———

underground Westminster, Charing Cross,
Embankment (Circle, District, Bakerloo, Northern
and Jubilee lines)

THIS CLASSICAL BUILDING halfway down Whitehall is now flanked by monumental interpretations of the same style, but when first built its stone façades divided by columns and pilasters must have stood out strangely among the Tudor brick and timber structures of the rambling palace of Whitehall which surrounded it. When fire destroyed most of the palace in 1698, only the Banqueting House and two gates survived.

Built for James I by Inigo Jones in 1619–22, the Banqueting House was as revolutionary as Jones's *Queen's House* at Greenwich, introducing architecture of a kind never seen before in Britain. Pediments crown the lower windows, a frieze of garlands runs below the roofline parapet, and a strong cornice divides what appear to be the two principal storeys. Faced in creamy Portland stone, it cost the princely sum of £15,618 14s and took nearly three years to complete.

Inside, above a service basement, the building is one great, empty room, 110 feet long and ringed by a balcony between the two rows of windows, supported on ornate brackets. This unfurnished interior was the setting for court masques and other entertainments, the first of which was staged by Inigo Jones in 1622. Three years later James I died, and it was his son Charles I who commissioned Rubens to execute the nine great paintings which fill the panels of the ceiling. Rubens had come to England in 1629 as a diplomat, charged with improving relations between England and Spain, and Charles had seized the opportunity to engage the greatest painter of his day. His allegorical canvases celebrating the wise and just rule of James I were all designed to be seen from particular points in the hall, as the diagram installed there explains. From below, there is a confusion of naked flesh and swirling drapery, the well-cushioned thighs and posteriors of an attendant crowd of plump cherubs much in evidence. This baroque extravaganza in a chaste classical interior is all the better for being 55 feet above the ground; it is also one of the few decorative schemes executed by Rubens to survive *in situ*.

The paintings were not installed until 1535, and only a few years later Charles left London to raise an army in the north, the beginning of four years of Civil War. He did not see the inside of the Banqueting House again until the bitterly cold morning of 30 January 1649, when he stepped through a window on to the scaffold which had been set up in Whitehall for his execution. Here, nothing was as he expected. A barrier draped in black hid him from the silent crowd watching in the street below and only those around him heard the speech which he had so carefully prepared, restating the beliefs which had lost him the throne. Even worse, the customary waist-high block had been mislaid, and the king was forced to lie, as if upon a bed, thrusting out his hands to signal to the executioner that he was prepared. In the great room he had just left, Rubens's canvases celebrated the principle of divinely-ordained kingship for which Charles was dying.

Open: Tues–Sat 10–17, Sun 14–17; admission
charge; audio guide

BUCKINGHAM PALACE

SW1

—— • ——

underground Green Park (Jubilee, Piccadilly and
Victoria lines), Hyde Park Corner (Piccadilly line)

S PALACES GO, the grandiose building facing down the Mall is neither old nor attractive, the grey stone of Sir Aston Webb's severe classical façade of 1913 only relieved by the gilded railings and ornate gates enclosing the forecourt and by the scarlet uniforms of the guard. Traffic swirls dangerously in front of it, racing round Webb and Thomas Brock's huge circular monument to Queen Victoria and narrowly avoiding the tourists who plunge recklessly across what is a multi-lane highway.

Behind Webb's frontage, which is all that the crowds who throng here can see, is the palace of warm Bath stone which Nash created from 1825. Ostensibly involved in repairing and remodelling the 1st Duke of Buckingham's red-brick mansion of 1702–5, which had been sold to the Crown in 1762, Nash overreached himself, overspending recklessly.

Nash was dismissed in disgrace in 1830, and when Queen Victoria came to the throne in 1837 the huge white elephant was scarcely habitable, with faulty drains,

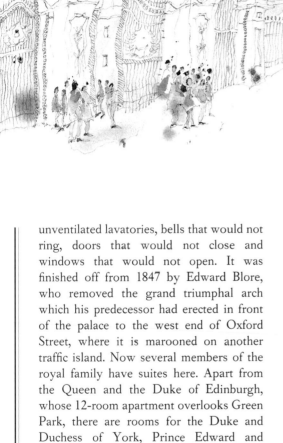

unventilated lavatories, bells that would not ring, doors that would not close and windows that would not open. It was finished off from 1847 by Edward Blore, who removed the grand triumphal arch which his predecessor had erected in front of the palace to the west end of Oxford Street, where it is marooned on another traffic island. Now several members of the royal family have suites here. Apart from the Queen and the Duke of Edinburgh, whose 12-room apartment overlooks Green Park, there are rooms for the Duke and Duchess of York, Prince Edward and Princess Anne. The royal standard flying over the building indicates that the Queen is in residence.

The palace's best façade, Nash's long garden front, can be enjoyed by those invited to one of Her Majesty's garden parties; the less exalted can see it, when the trees are bare, from the top of a double-decker bus heading down Gloucester Place. You can also get a glimpse of Nash's architecture by visiting the ROYAL MEWS in Buckingham Palace Road, entered through an imposing Doric arch which suddenly appears in the long curve of the palace wall. This spacious quadrangle with a classical archway piercing each side is a cheerfully informal place, with accommodation for grooms and their families on top of the coach-houses and stables. Here you can see an array of gleaming coaches, among them a baroque gold extravaganza carved with mermen, and the tack room. The royal horses are lined up for visitors in one large stable, the bays on one side, Her Majesty's greys, for the sovereign's use only, on the other. Just up the road an awning flags the QUEEN'S GALLERY, an artificially lit, galleried room with changing exhibitions of treasures from the Royal Collection. Not everything is old. As well as jewel-like miniatures by Nicholas Hilliard, paintings by Canaletto, Rubens, Van Dyck or Claude, illuminated manuscripts and the linen overshirt, threaded with gay blue and pink ribbons, which Charles I wore for his execution, you may see drawings of John Betjeman and Edith Sitwell by Felix Topolski, mouths feeble, eyes pouched, all humour gone in the sexless collapse of old age.

Open: ROYAL MEWS Wed, Thurs 14–16, admission charge, toilets; QUEEN'S GALLERY Tues–Sat 10.30–17, Sun 14–17, admission charge

HAMPTON COURT

Hampton, 12 miles west of central London

—— • ——

British Rail to Hampton Court (from Waterloo),
or by boat from Westminster Pier or Richmond
(see p. 181)

WHERE *Windsor Castle* reeks of the Middle Ages, Hampton Court is peopled by Tudor and Stuart ghosts, and by the stately ladies in sweeping skirts who paraded in William and Mary's formal garden. This great brick palace on the banks of the Thames was the setting for Henry VIII's matrimonial adventures; his queens, one after the other, were briefly happy here before the jealousy and paranoia of their lord, fed by rumours and intrigues, poisoned and destroyed their lives. Scarcely had stonework and tracery been carved with the initials of Anne Boleyn, for whom the infatuated Henry divorced Catherine of Aragon, than the king's passion turned to Jane Seymour, whom he married the day after Anne was beheaded. Poor Jane died here after giving birth to Edward VI, and here the king was persuaded to believe in the treachery of his fifth queen, the youthful Catherine Howard. Desperate to clear herself, Catherine ran screaming through the long passages and tapestry-hung galleries searching for Henry, but she never found him, and died on the block, like Anne, on Tower Green. Legend has it that her ghost runs still, appearing to visitors in the Haunted Gallery. Henry's elder daughter, the sad Mary Tudor, honeymooned here with her unpopular husband, Philip II of Spain, and then spent month after month watching vainly for signs of a child. Elizabeth I, red-haired and high-spirited, required her many suitors to travel across Europe to be flirted with and entertained here before she turned them down, as in her heart she always knew she would.

Approached from the west, Hampton Court is still Tudor, its long rambling outline a confusion of red-brick turrets and twisted chimneys, with the pinnacled silhouette of Henry's great hall visible over the lower outer ranges. Beyond the turreted gateway, spacious courtyards are set one behind the other, the first, a grassy square, now marred by the unsightly ticket office, the second, more intimate, all cobble and stone. These cloister-like spaces were part of the great house built from 1514 by Cardinal Thomas Wolsey, Henry's Lord Chancellor, whose new residence rapidly assumed the proportions of a palace, with a staff of nearly five hundred to serve the luxuriously furnished apartments and to create the entertainments which were reported across Europe. But this prince of the Catholic church, the son of an Ipswich butcher, overreached himself. Henry watched and waited, and when Wolsey failed to persuade the Pope to annul the King's marriage to Catherine of Aragon, the Cardinal's downfall was certain. The King took Hampton Court for himself; the disgraced Cardinal, stripped of his offices, died before he could be tried for treason.

Wolsey's building was conservative, its layout monastic, but high up on the red and purple brickwork of the two gatehouses are terracotta medallions of Roman emperors by Giovanni da Maiano, among the first examples of Italian Renaissance art in England. The inner gatehouse also carries the shining golden face of the astronomical clock made for Henry VIII in 1540. Dials set one within the other indicate not only the hours, the months and the phases of the moon, but also the time of high water at London Bridge, vital information for the boats which plied between Hampton Court and Westminster. As intriguing is the flaming sun circling the Earth, its path echoing the beliefs of a world which had not yet been overturned by Galileo and Copernicus. Renaissance motifs appear again on the painted and gilded ceiling – all blue and gold – which survives in the most intimate of the small panelled rooms which once made up Wolsey's private apartments, a glimpse of the lavish decorative schemes with which the Cardinal surrounded himself. Below it are sixteenth-century paint-

ings depicting scenes from the Passion of Christ, a dog gnawing a bone underneath the table at the Last Supper, a crowd already gathered on the hill to which Christ labours to carry his cross. But it was Henry who created the focal point of the medieval palace, the great hall, 97 feet long and 40 feet high, which dominates the inner court. Carved pendants like gilded stalactites hang from the ornate hammerbeam roof, playful painted faces peering down on the crowd below from the supporting beams. So anxious was the King to see the hall finished that he ordered his carpenters to work night and day, lighting the shadowy vaults with

hundreds of candles when dusk fell. Below the hall is a warren of stone-flagged Tudor kitchens and brick-floored cellars, service courts like little streets round about once housing the subsidiary larders, boiling houses and pastry houses from which the court was fed.

Approaching Hampton Court from the east, across the park, you see a quite different palace. Magnificent gardens on this front are overlooked by a long brick and stone baroque façade, 23 bays wide, with a roofline balustrade and a central pediment supported on Corinthian columns. What had been the Tudor state apartments were remodelled from 1689 for William and Mary by Sir Christopher Wren, who created parallel public and private suites for his two sovereigns round a charming colonnaded courtyard with a central fountain. Old and new are cleverly combined so as to give the illusion of a new palace. The formal apartments themselves, the Queen's to the north and the King's to the south, form a long procession of gaunt rooms like a colossal untenanted flat, with pompous allegorical paintings by Antonio Verrio, some grandiose decorative schemes by Vanbrugh, who carried out alterations for George I in 1716–18, and often sparse furnishings helping to conjure up a rather institutional atmosphere. But occasionally you will want to linger. In the lovely Queen's Gallery, with seven long windows looking on to the garden, ornate Delft tulip vases like slender china pyramids form splashes of blue and white beneath the eighteenth-century tapestries and monochrome cartoons by Carlo Cignani. The

private dining-room is similarly welcoming, its mellow panelling hung with insubstantial deities by Pelligrini. Sadly, the King's formal apartments, with carvings by Grinling Gibbons and a gallery hung with the seventeenth-century tapestries based on Raphael's cartoons in the *Victoria & Albert Museum*, were damaged in the fire of 1986, and are not scheduled to reopen until 1992.

Pictures from the royal collection hang throughout the palace, among them a gallery of curiously similar court beauties by Sir Godfrey Kneller, their mostly rather vacant faces prompting one visitor to exclaim, 'If these are beauties, god preserve us from the rest.' Elsewhere are D. Mytens's stylized portrait of Charles I and Henrietta Maria, who spent their honeymoon here, the young couple shown holding hands and with lap dogs gambolling round their feet; Sebastiano Ricci's *Adoration of the Magi*, in which the holy baby leans forward to grab a grizzled king by his hair; and Cristofano Allori's *Judith with the Head of Holofernes*, in which the artist is said to have modelled Judith on a former lover who had reduced him to misery, and to have painted a self-portrait on the bearded, severed head. The Allori currently adorns the suite designed by William Kent for the young Duke of Cumberland in 1732, an elegant Palladian apartment suggesting a town house rather than a palace. Restrained nudes hanging either side of the fireplace in the principal room, their eroticism suffused with respectability, were no doubt thought appropriate for what was the bedchamber of a fourteen-year-old boy. Some of the most important pictures in the palace are now assembled in the Renaissance Gallery, where changing displays of Flemish, German and Italian works may include a self-portrait by Raphael, compositions by Lorenzo Lotto, Correggio and Tintoretto, Holbein's *Noli me Tangere*, and *The Massacre of the Innocents* by Pieter Brueghel the elder. Alas, many works are not adequately labelled or are so placed that their attributions are difficult to read, and as the official guidebook makes only scant reference to paintings, it is not easy to appreciate what is here.

Whatever you may think of the interior of the palace, Hampton Court's extensive gardens wrapped round it on three sides are superb. Wren's baroque east front still looks over the Versailles-like layout created by Charles II, with three great avenues radiating from a wide gravel terrace in front of the house and disappearing into the park across a semi-circular canal bordering the formal gardens. Giant clipped yews framing the walks near the house – Virginia Woolf's 'black pyramids' – give way to mature limes beyond the garden, and the central vista becomes the Long Water, a ribbon-like canal which runs due east for over a mile. Nothing remains of William and Mary's swirling parterres of clipped box and yew, but one of the thirteen fountains which they created here still plays in the middle of the central avenue.

The site of the original sixteenth-century garden lies below the south front, between the palace and the Thames, where Tudor brick walls shelter two sunken formal gardens laid out around rectangular pools, and a re-creation of an Elizabethan knot garden with arabesques of lavender, box and gravel. A dense shrubbery framed by raised walks, one partly covered by a hornbeam tunnel, was once the privy garden where Elizabeth I used to take brisk exercise, slowing her pace if she thought she was being watched, its south end closed by the graceful curves of an exquisite wrought-iron screen commissioned from Jean Tijou by William III. Set right on the edge of the river is the little red-brick banqueting house with a castellated parapet built for the King by Wren's assistant William Talman, its main room decorated with scantily clothed deities by Verrio.

Filling a greenhouse nearby is the extra-ordinary great vine planted by Capability Brown in 1768, the canopy spreading from the gnarled and twisted stem capable of producing over two thousand pounds of grapes in a good year. The vinery adjoins a long orangery, but this rather austere, unwelcomingly chill building, far from being filled with fruit, is now used to display one of the greatest works in the Royal Collection, the *Triumphs of Julius Caesar* by Andrea Mantegna, painted in the late fifteenth century and acquired by Charles I from the Duke of Mantua. Unlike so many other priceless treasures which belonged to the King, these nine canvases depicting a procession of the spoils of war, with elephants and other exotic beasts in among the statues, armour and dejected prisoners, were not disposed of by Parliament after his execution.

North of the palace is the triangular maze planted for Queen Anne in 1713, the last echo of a large formal Wilderness devised by the court gardener Henry Wise. The maze, perhaps Hampton Court's most popular feature, has long since lost its charm, the earth paths now asphalted and the yew hedges contained by iron railings, but over-confident visitors can still lose their way, as Jerome K. Jerome's character Harris did in *Three Men in a Boat*. Around it paths meander through long grass planted with trees and flowering shrubs and with a show of daffodils in the spring; the only sign of the grand new approach which Wren planned here is his magnificent Lion Gate aligned with a mile-long chestnut avenue across Bushy Park. Henry VIII's tiltyards have disappeared, but one of his five brick viewing towers still survives, although now ignominiously converted into a tea-room. A Jacobean real tennis court, probably on the site where Henry VIII used to play, is still very much in use. Visitors can watch a game in progress, the players with their ricocheting balls caged behind thick nets like animals in a zoo.

Open: mid Mar to mid Oct 9.30–18, mid Oct to mid Mar 9.30–16.30; gardens all year 7–dusk (maze 10–16 in winter); admission charge to palace and maze; toilets; guided tours Mon–Sat in summer; banqueting house, tennis court and some apartments closed in winter

THE JEWEL TOWER

Abingdon Street, SW1

— • —

underground Westminster (Circle and District lines)

ACROSS THE ROAD from the Houses of Parliament (see p. 19) is a moated, three-storey, L-shaped tower of rough Kentish ragstone, one of the few survivals from the medieval Palace of Westminster. Built in 1365–6 by Henry de Yevele to house Edward III's personal jewellery, gold and silver, plate and furs, this fourteenth-century safe has massively thick walls and deep window embrasures, and in the apartment for the Keeper there is a fine stone vault with carved bosses. A spiral staircase in a projecting turret leads to the large bare room, with a closet off, which fills each floor. By the reign of Henry VIII the tower had become a kind of royal general store, housing not only the King's bed linen and soft furnishings but also personal items such as his chessmen and walking-sticks. The tower now displays pottery found in the moat, fragments of medieval carvings from buildings in Westminster, and a selection of alternative designs for the Houses of Parliament, one of them a Tudor pastiche with pepperpot turrets.

Open: Daily 10–18 (16 Oct–Easter); admission charge

KENSINGTON PALACE

Kensington Gardens, W8

— • —

underground High Street Kensington (Circle and
District lines), Queensway (Central line)

EARLY ON THE MORNING of 20 June 1837, the porter of this rambling brick mansion was roused by the furious knocking of the Archbishop of Canterbury and the Lord Chamberlain. Upstairs, in the large, rather fussily furnished bedroom now on show, slept the young Princess Victoria. The two men had driven all night from *Windsor* to tell her that her uncle William IV had died and that she was now queen. The eighteen-year-old girl received them alone in her sitting-room, wearing a white dressing-gown and with her hair loose about her shoulders. A few hours later she held her first privy council in the red saloon downstairs, where the black mourning dress she wore is on display. 'Five feet high, but she not only filled her chair but the room,' reported the Duke of Wellington.

Now overlooking the west side of one of London's most popular parks, this sprawl-ing conglomeration of apartments set around three courtyards has little of the grandeur usually associated with royal residences. When William III purchased the site in 1689 there was a Jacobean house here. Suffering from chronic asthma, the King needed to get away from the smoke and damp of Whitehall, and the then airy village of Kensington seemed the ideal choice for his London residence. As at *Hampton Court*, which William and Mary were transforming with great splendour, Wren was engaged to improve the house, but here contented himself with a neat con-version rather than any attempt at show. Even the long south front of 1695–6, prob-ably by Wren's able assistant Nicholas Hawksmoor, with four Portland stone vases crowning a brick attic storey over the central bay, is primarily domestic, designed to overlook formal Dutch gardens stretch-ing down to what is now Kensington Road.

William and Mary, who loved Kensington, both died at the palace: she of smallpox in 1694, at the early age of thirty-two; he after a fall from his horse at Hampton Court in 1702 (he had begged to be carried back to London). So too did Queen Anne, who collapsed with apoplexy in 1714 after overeating. This heavy-jowled, dour-looking woman, only one of whose seventeen children survived infancy, had also delighted in Wren's house, but it was not grand enough for George I, who added a suite of state

ments for the Queen, his 84-foot gallery preceding a series of small, intimate rooms, in one of which, a panelled closet, Queen Anne conducted the disastrous interview which ended her long friendship with the Duchess of Marlborough, the Duchess later complaining that she had been kept waiting 'like a Scotch lady with a petition'. Apart from some panelling, the elaborate cornices, and the gilt mirrors with carved surrounds by Grinling Gibbons in the gallery, few original features survive, and there is

rooms fit for a palace, with decorative schemes by William Kent. George II was the last reigning monarch to reside at Kensington, but several members of the royal family now have apartments here, notably the Prince and Princess of Wales and Princess Margaret.

The main entrance to the palace is on the west, but public access is from a path off the Broad Walk to the east, via what was Queen Mary's garden door of 1690–1. A plain oak staircase leads to Wren's apart-

little reason to linger here. Much more memorable are the King's Gallery and the state apartments in the south-east corner of the palace. The 96-foot gallery, much grander than the Queen's, runs most of the length of Hawksmoor's south front, and was intended to display the finest pictures in the royal collection. The walls are still hung with paintings, but these are mostly of the seventeenth century and not as fine as the works William III enjoyed. Apart from Van Dyck's beautiful *Cupid and*

Psyche, the room is dominated by two huge canvases: Rubens's characteristically fleshy *Jupiter and Antiope* of 1614, the two naked maidens sprawled under an awning obviously sleeping off a very good lunch, and Snyders's boar hunt of 1653. Intriguingly, Snyders was also responsible for the collection of dead game in the Rubens picture, although the two canvases are separated by some forty years. These overpowering pieces tend to deflect attention from the other paintings, among which are a serene seascape by Jan Porcellis (c.1584–1632), with a gentle mist coming off the water, and a rare self-portrait by Artemisia Gentileschi (born c.1597), a green dress setting off her dark hair, a look of fierce concentration on her face as she works at her canvas.

Painted panels by William Kent punctuate the gallery's coved ceilings, but his most original decorative schemes survive on the King's Staircase and in Colen Campbell's state rooms. Above Wren's staircase of 1692–3, with its steps of black Irish marble and wrought-iron scrollwork by Jean Tijou supporting the mahogany handrail, Kent painted the illusion of an Italianate gallery. Figures in late seventeenth-century dress jostle for position along the balustraded arcades like the crowds who would have thronged the staircase on court days. The red uniforms of a couple of beefeaters stand out on the left, two Turks can be seen on the far right, and a youth nonchalantly perches above the stairwell. Kent's illusionist dome on the ceiling is less successful, but the figures looking down on the staircase over another balustrade include portraits of Kent himself and of his mistress Elizabeth Butler. For the King's Presence Chamber he designed an innovative Adam-style ceiling with delicate arabesques and other classical motifs picked out in brilliant reds, blues and greens on a white ground, and the classically inspired decoration of the principal state room is again a flourish of illusionist work, with *trompe-l'oeil* fluting on the massive pilasters, and painted shadows suggesting urns balanced on the cornice and coffering on the lofty ceiling.

More seventeenth-century works can be seen in this suite, among them paintings from the Gonzaga Collection at Mantua purchased by Charles I. Also here is an extraordinary black and gold clock of c.1743, acquired by George III's mother, with a tiny face like that on a pocket watch embedded in a classical temple about three feet high, crowned by a figure of Atlas. The council chamber is filled with many similarly ornate and grotesque objects shown at the great international exhibitions which the Victorians loved, the centrepiece of the room being an intricately carved ivory throne and footstool which was presented to Queen Victoria by the Maharajah of Travancore in 1851, the year of the Crystal Palace exhibition. Rooms on the ground floor are now used to display the Court Dress Collection, which includes the Princess of Wales's wedding dress.

Nothing remains of William and Mary's formal gardens laid out by Henry Wise below the south front, but Queen Anne's long, red-brick orangery, built in 1704 to designs by Hawksmoor and Vanbrugh, still survives to the north, adjoining the brick gateposts topped by urns which marked the limit of the seventeenth-century gardens. The orangery, now a restaurant, is elegantly baroque, with arches flanked by statues in niches at either end of the grand panelled interior and a glimpse of huge sculpted vases in the circular rooms beyond. An Edwardian sunken garden, reached from here via an avenue of bay and holly, suggests something of the original compartmental layout, with terraces ornamented with bedding plants leading down to a central fountain pool and the whole embraced by a pleached lime walk. A quite different scheme to the east of the palace, begun under George I, was the basis for the present Kensington gardens. Principally the work of Charles Bridgeman, who joined Henry Wise as Royal Gardener in 1726 and succeeded him two years later, this was one of the earliest English landscape gardens, a composition in grass and trees stretching away from a grand walk – now the Broad Walk – fringing the palace. Bridgeman's octagonal basin is now the Round Pond, from which his three original avenues still radiate into the distance, the central one punctuated by Watts's statue of *Physical Energy*.

Open: Mon–Sat 9–17, Sun 13–17; admission charge; toilets; tours by arrangement with curator

THE QUEEN'S HOUSE

Romney Road, Greenwich SE10

— • —

British Rail to Greenwich or Maze Hill (from
Charing Cross), Docklands Light Railway to
Island Gardens (see p. 181), or by boat from
Westminster Pier (see p. 181)

APPROACHING GREENWICH from the Thames, the white, symmetrical façade of the Queen's House with its roofline balustrade and a delightful double staircase curving up to the central entrance neatly closes the long vista through the baroque buildings of the Royal Naval College (see p. 22). But when first commissioned in 1616, this chaste, Palladian building was attached to the rambling Tudor palace of Placentia (see p. 21), its gabled red-brick ranges along the river providing a striking contrast to the stone of Inigo Jones's classically inspired architecture.

Designed for James I's wife Anne of Denmark, and completed for Charles I's consort Henrietta Maria in 1635, the Queen's House is effectively a Renaissance version of a Tudor gatehouse, planned to bridge the muddy Woolwich to Deptford Road which divided the palace gardens from Greenwich Park. The original H-shaped building with linked ranges standing either side of the highway was filled in by Jones's pupil John Webb in 1661–2, and the road itself was moved further north in 1697, but the cobbles of the original route can still be seen in the two courtyards enclosed by the three bridging wings. Like

Jones's *Banqueting House* in Whitehall, which it predates by three years, the Queen's House was architecturally revolutionary, the first truly Renaissance building in England and the model for the White House in Washington.

Now part of the *National Maritime Museum* complex, the Queen's House has been newly restored as a royal palace, with the rooms furnished as they might have been in the 1660s when the widowed Queen Henrietta Maria took up residence again after the Civil War. Apart from the paintings and some pieces of furniture and decoration, such as the splendid coved ceiling in the Queen's Presence Chamber, a grotesque fantasy in chocolate brown, scarlet and olive green, everything seen in the house has had to be reproduced, as almost nothing survives from the royal houses of this time. The effect is bizarre: the unblemished damask hangings (in one room grey and purple, in another a rich pea green), newly-grained panelling and chimney-pieces freshly realized from Jones's designs look more like a theatrical set than the real thing – the authentic, the hypothetical and the re-created all mixed up together.

Provided you only glance at the ceiling, where Orazio and Artemisia Gentileschi's original paintings have been reproduced, and do not dwell too long on the plaster-white statuary, one of the most successful rooms is the great hall, a 40-foot cube with a first-floor balcony carried on carved and painted brackets and a splendid black and white geometric pavement by Nicholas Stone. Off the hall is the graceful tulip staircase, a tight spiral of stone cantilevered out from the wall which winds upward in snail-like curves, a repeated tulip motif in the blue wrought-iron handrail and reproduction silver sconces lighting the way. Also memorable is the Italianate first-floor loggia looking over the park, where Henrietta Maria and her ladies could have watched a deer hunt. There are treasures from the National Maritime Museum in the brick-vaulted basement supporting the platform on which the house sits, and paintings by Lely, both Van de Veldes, Hogarth and Storck, but there is nothing to equal the works by Rubens, Raphael and Van Dyck from the Royal Collection which Charles I once housed here.

Open: Mon–Sat 10–18 (17 in winter), Sun from 14; admission charge; toilets; audio tour

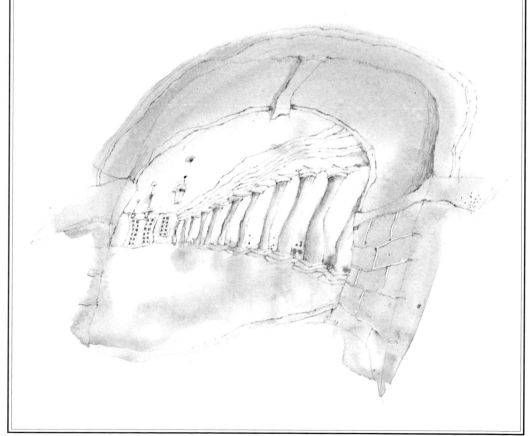

THE TOWER OF LONDON

EC3

— • —

underground Tower Hill (Circle and District lines)

THE TOWER SITS in the south-east corner of the City, just inside the line of the old Roman and medieval wall, guarding the river approaches to London. Whether you see it first from the river or on emerging from the underpass leading to the underground, it is a formidable sight, an unbroken line of battlemented walls and towers rising high above the deep grassy ditch of the drained moat. At its heart is the familiar turreted outline of the White Tower, William the Conqueror's three-storey keep, with its massive ragstone walls – 90 feet high and up to 15 feet thick – dressed with Caen stone from Normandy. Begun in 1078 as part of William's campaign to stamp his authority on his new country, and virtually completed by Edward I, who died in 1307, this fortress is a perfect example of early medieval military architecture, with two concentric walls wrapped around a central fastness.

Inside, the Tower is surprisingly domestic. Through the gateway to the inner ward is a secluded grassy square shaded by planes and limes, the chapel of St Peter ad Vincula which closes one end facing across the green to two ranges of gabled, half-timbered houses. This tranquil spot, where ravens hop about in the sun and crowds gather to watch the changing of the guard, also has some of the grimmest memories. A paved enclosure on the grass marks the spot where Anne Boleyn and Catherine Howard (Henry VIII's sec-

ond and fifth queens), Lady Jane Grey, and Elizabeth I's favourite, the Earl of Essex, were beheaded, their special status earning them the privilege of dying in comparative privacy, away from the crowds who thronged the public scaffold on Tower Hill. Lady Jane Grey, Queen of England for only nine days in the summer of 1553, had been the pawn of her scheming father-in-law the Duke of Northumberland, who persuaded the dying Edward VI to name her rather than his half-sister Mary Tudor as the next sovereign. Taken to the Tower to prepare for her coronation, Jane, not quite sixteen years old, soon found herself a prisoner. From the windows of the Queen's House overlooking the green, she saw her young husband, Lord Guildford Dudley, taken out for execution on Tower Hill and his headless body brought back in a cart, while below her men erected a scaffold for her own execution. Dudley's memorial is the heart-rending IANE inscribed by a window in the Beauchamp Tower where he was incarcerated, like a despairing cry in stone.

Many others were imprisoned here, their last hopes fading as they were brought by water to the low arch of Traitor's Gate. A deep tidal race used to fill the moat through this opening on to the Thames, but it is now reduced to a murky pool. Rooms in the Bloody Tower are displayed as they might have appeared during the thirteen-year confinement of Sir Walter Raleigh, with rush matting, carved Jacobean furniture, and a

copy of Raleigh's *History of the World*, which he wrote during his incarceration. Raleigh was also allowed to conduct scientific experiments, many of which were done in the company of the 9th Earl of Northumberland, the 'Wizard' earl, whom James I confined to the Tower for his supposed complicity in the Gunpowder Plot (see p. 150). What could their jailers have made of these two, bent for hours over their bubbling retorts, wreathed in the smoke of Raleigh's tobacco, as they attempted to distil salt water and manufacture medicinal cordials? Two Archbishops of Canterbury – Laud and Cranmer – were also lodged here, and this was where the young Edward V and his brother, the princes in the tower, were murdered.

The last person to be taken from the Tower for execution was the octogenarian Lord Lovat, beheaded in 1747 for his part in the Jacobite rebellion, his twisted, toad-like features captured in a portrait by Hogarth. The last prisoner here was Hitler's confused deputy Rudolf Hess, the 'maggot in the apple' as Churchill called him, who landed in Scotland on his improbable peace mission in May 1941 and was held in the Queen's House for four days. Some have even managed to escape, among them the dashing Jacobite Earl of Nithsdale, who slipped out of the Tower on the eve of his execution in 1716 dressed as his wife's maid and with rouge disguising traces of a beard. Others have died with enormous courage. Sir Thomas More, Henry VIII's Chancellor, who went to the block in 1535 for his refusal to support the split with the Pope, asked for help to mount the scaffold with the words 'I pray you, Mr Lieutenant, to see me safe up and for my coming down let me make shift for myself.' When told that he would just be beheaded, rather than also drawn and quartered, More commented, 'God forbid the king shall use any more such mercy on any of my friends.'

In its early days the Tower was a palace, not a prison, with sumptuously decorated apartments for the King and his family. What used to be Henry III's private chamber, an octagonal room on the first floor of the Wakefield tower, gives some idea of how these might have looked. Beneath the vaulted ceiling, like an elegant bell tent, are reconstructions of the great fireplace bearing the royal arms and the canopied king's chair, while an oratory in one of the deep window recesses, where the Lancastrian Henry VI was murdered in 1471 as he knelt in prayer, still has its original sedilia and piscina. The upper floors of the White Tower were once also lavishly fitted out, but all that remains of the King's suite here is the Norman chapel of golden Caen stone, with a simple Romanesque arcade forming an apse round the altar and a barrel-vaulted roof. Always quiet even at the height of the tourist season, this is the most atmospheric place in the Tower, and the serene architecture may perhaps have given strength to Lady Jane Grey as she prayed here on the night before she died. Here Henry VII's consort, Elizabeth of York, sister of the murdered princes, lay in state for three days

after her death in childbirth in 1503, her corpse surrounded by 800 candles.

After the calm other-worldliness of the chapel, it is startling to find yourself surrounded by the cases of weapons and armour which fill the rest of the White Tower, a collection which originated in the great arsenal which supplied medieval kings and their armies. Much of what is here will only excite the enthusiast, but anyone would respond to the massive German armour of c.1535–40 made for a man nearly seven feet tall, and to the suits made for Henry VIII at much the same time. More than any portrait, these made-to-measure metal carapaces vividly catalogue the physical degeneration of the King. The slim youth of 1520 who engaged in foot combat with Francis I at the Field of Cloth of Gold has twenty years later become a bloated and ungainly figure, with a 52-inch girth. His armour looks as if it were made for a gorilla, not a man.

The Oriental Armoury is housed in the Waterloo barracks, a battlemented and turreted building, erected by Anthony Salvin in 1845, which is also used to display the

Crown Jewels. As part of the security measures, visitors are required to keep moving, forming a long procession which winds past case after case of gold maces and flagons, wine coolers and state trumpets. The most valuable pieces are shown in a theatrically  lit, subterranean strongroom, where those who enjoy glitter and sparkle can feast their eyes on jewel-encrusted crowns, the sceptre which incorporates the largest cut diamond in the world, and an extraordinary gold fountain and perfume burner. Others might consider the plush velvet, ostentatious gems and showy plate rather vulgar. And almost nothing here is very old. Exquisite pieces representing six centuries of medieval craftsmanship were sold off or melted down by Oliver Cromwell after the execution of Charles I, only a twelfth-century anointing spoon surviving complete from before the Commonwealth. A band of watchful custodians now guards these treasures, but security was not always so rigorous. In 1671, when the jewels were in the Martin Tower, a certain Colonel Thomas Blood gained the confidence of the Keeper by disguising himself as a clergy-man and he and his accomplices succeeded in grabbing the sceptre, orb and crown. When caught, Blood insisted on speaking to the King, whom he is said to have charmed into pardoning him. Certainly, Charles II pensioned him off, but whether this was a reward for impudence or for some more sinister service no one seems very sure.

The Yeoman Warders, distinctive in their red and blue uniforms, are part of the Tower's appeal. As familiar are the grotesque ravens, the last survivors of the royal menagerie which used to be kept here. Its heyday seems to have been in the thirteenth century, when Henry III enjoyed three leopards, a white bear which fished in the Thames, a present from the King of Norway, and an elephant, the first to cross the Channel since the Roman emperor Claudius brought some with him in AD 43 to celebrate victory over the British. A large pavilion was built for the elephant, which lived on for three years.

The Tower suffers from its popularity, the sheer weight of numbers often diffusing the impact of steep spiral staircases, stone vaults, and walls carved with graffiti centuries ago. When the tourists have gone, however, this great medieval monument becomes itself again, as anyone who has attended the magical Ceremony of the Keys, when the Tower is locked up for the night, will know. The chief warder with his armed escort goes from gate to gate, lantern in hand, and all you hear is the sound of marching feet and the occasional shouted command. The ceremony ends beside Tower Green, where the full guard is dismissed for the night as the clock strikes ten and a trumpeter sounds the Last Post.

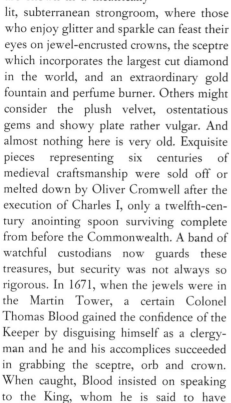

Open: Mar–Oct 9.30–17, Nov–Feb 9.30–16; admission charge; toilets; Yeoman Warder tours except in bad weather; to attend the Ceremony of the Keys, write for tickets (no charge; seven maximum) two months in advance to The Resident Governor, Queen's House, HM Tower of London, EC3, giving alternative dates and enclosing a stamped addressed envelope

WINDSOR AND ETON

Berkshire, 21 miles from central London

—— • ——

British Rail from Paddington to Windsor Central,
or from Waterloo to Windsor Riverside, journey
approx. 1 hour; by car via M4

THE VILLAGE OF ETON, with its world-famous public school, and the ancient town of Windsor, clustered around the largest inhabited castle in the world, face each other across the Thames to the west of London. Both are easily explored in a day's excursion, and those seeking a taste of the country could walk for hours in the 4,800 acres of Windsor Great Park, reached by a three-mile avenue stretching away from the fortress.

Windsor Castle is an Arthurian fantasy, a long sprawl of towers, turrets and battlements like a medieval walled city, set on a chalk ridge high above the river. The silhouette of this fortress is one of the most arresting sights in Britain, as magical for those who hurtle past on the M4, or who catch a glimpse from an aeroplane coming into Heathrow, as for those who see it across the green expanse of the park. This is the oldest of the royal residences, its history inextricably connected with that of the Crown and its very name, Windsor, shared with the present ruling dynasty.

Originating in a motte-and-bailey castle built by William the Conqueror in c.1070 as one of a ring of nine fortresses designed to protect the approaches to London, Windsor is now a palace as well as a stronghold and also shelters an ecclesiastical precinct within its long curtain wall. Entered by the forbidding twin-towered gateway built by Henry VIII, with its cavities for pouring burning liquids on to undesirable visitors, the castle stretches steeply uphill, its long thin wards following the outlines of the chalk outcrop beneath. About halfway up the slope is the massive bulk of the Round Tower, its grassy mound marking the site of the Norman motte, the dry ditch which surrounds it now laid out as a garden, with shady lawns and formal

borders. Below the tower is the more public lower ward, with St George's Chapel and the quarters for clerics, choristers and guards; above lie the sovereign's private apartments set round the grassy quadrangle at the peak of the ridge, fashioned out of medieval ranges in the 1820s for George IV by Jeffry Wyatville. Here too are the grandiose state rooms, a procession of formal interiors that are still used for banquets and receptions and for entertaining heads of state.

The state rooms are what visitors can see. Also largely created by Wyatville, many of these interiors reflect the deliberately medieval style which both the king and his architect thought appropriate for a castle: the gargoyles and carved and painted beams in the Waterloo Chamber and the timber roof studded with heraldic emblems in St George's Hall are as consciously archaic as the Gothic windows and the elaborate machicolations and turrets with which Wyatville crowned the exterior, the finishing touches in the castle's fairy-tale skyline. In contrast, the long reception room designed to display a set of eighteenth-century Gobelin tapestries is a grand French interior, with a riot of gilded plasterwork and ornate pier glasses, the deep bay of the window setting off a huge green malachite vase given to Queen Victoria by Tsar Nicholas I. Wyatville's restoration involved sweeping away splendid baroque interiors created for Charles II in 1675–83, but three of these, with characteristically fluid carvings of fruit and foliage by Grinling Gibbons and pompous allegorical paintings by Antonio Verrio, still remain among the more intimate suites for the king and queen. Verrio's *Banquet of the Gods* on the coved ceiling of the King's Dining Room would be enough to put most people off their food. While the deities in the central panel appear to be sitting round a completely empty table, the harrowing frieze on the coving is a collection of dead fish and game, all realistically spattered with blood.

Paintings from the Royal Collection hang throughout the apartments. In the Waterloo Chamber, the Duke of Wellington with upraised sword dominates Sir Thomas Lawrence's gallery of those involved in the defeat of Napoleon, the heroic poses of sovereigns, statesmen and generals contrasting with the crumpled figures of Pope Pius VII and Cardinal Consalvi, both of whom look ill at ease. But none of these compares with the collection of Old Masters in the King's and Queen's suites. Here is Rembrandt's portrait of an old lady, a web of fine lines etching her face, her black veil lined with gold. There are canvases by Dürer, Holbein and Gainsborough, Hogarth and Canaletto, and a series of haunting portraits by Van Dyck, among them the triptych of Charles I sent to Bernini in Italy so that the sculptor could produce a bust of the King without ever

having seen him, and a group portrait of Charles's five eldest children, showing the baby Princess Anne, who was to die when only four, struggling in the arms of the future James II. Van Dyck himself appears in a canvas by Rubens, his magnificent moustaches echoed in Rubens's own self-portrait, commissioned by Charles I, with penetrating eyes beneath a jauntily tilted fedora.

Artistic skill of a different kind is exhibited in the dolls' house presented to Queen Mary in 1923, its dignified classical façades by Sir Edwin Lutyens enclosing a series of exquisitely furnished interiors in which every object is one-twelfth of normal size. Seen in a darkened room, the house is lit by its own chandeliers and lamps, which reveal a grand dining-room set for dinner, not a knife or a glass out of place, and a library stocked with leather-bound books, each one specially written by contemporary figures such as Rudyard Kipling, Thomas Hardy, Arthur Conan Doyle or G. K. Chesterton (though who, I should like to know, has ever read them). Hot and cold water can be produced from the taps in the

green marble bathroom, the linen cupboards are stacked with towels and sheets, and someone in the kitchen is about to eat two boiled eggs in a blue eggcup. Equally impressive are the gleaming pre-war cars in the garage and the well-stocked cellars, with their shelves of jams and preserves, bins of wine bottles – some red, some white – and barrels of beer. Here the only inhabitant is a cat, watchful beside a mousetrap.

The chapel down the hill, its golden, gaily pinnacled outline contrasting with the grey stone of the castle's defences, dates back to 1475, when Edward IV determined to outshine the prominent but unfinished chapel of Eton College in the valley below and to provide a fitting setting for the ceremonies of the Order of the Garter founded by Edward III. Completed by 1528, the chapel's light and airy interior is one of the finest examples of English Perpendicular architecture, with delicate cluster columns supporting the elegant fan vaulting of nave and chancel, and walls which are more glass than stone. The great west window still boasts 66 of the original 75 figures of popes, kings, princes and saints which were inserted between 1503 and 1509, and there are delightful Tudor paintings. These include a strip cartoon of the martyrdom of St Stephen, with expressions of glee on the faces of those hurling flint-like rocks at the dying man, and four panels of kings in the south aisle, the young Edward V, who was murdered in the *Tower of London*, shown with his crown suspended above his head. There are many other treasures here too, among them Edward III's sword, over six feet long, and the swirling thirteenth-century ironwork on the startling scarlet doors behind the altar.

The richest part of the chapel lies beyond the eighteenth-century stone screen, where the banners of the Knights of the Garter hang above the ornately carved stalls of 1478–95. The fantastic wooden canopies above the seats are crowned with the

knights' brightly coloured crests, some dignified crowns or coronets, others faintly ridiculous, like the resplendent cock and the jaunty black and white cow. Every available space is filled with carved figures, and heraldic plates of enamelled copper and brass gleam on the backs of the stalls. An ornate oriel window high on the wall to the left of the altar was installed by Henry VIII for his first queen, Catherine of Aragon, so that she could watch the services in private.

Like Westminster Abbey, St George's is the burial place of kings. Henry VI, founder of Eton College and of King's College, Cambridge, lies to the right of the altar, just a few feet from Edward VII and his consort Alexandra. A slab by the altar steps marks the entrance to a royal vault, and just a few feet west another floor tablet records the remains of Henry VIII, who lies with his third queen, Jane Seymour, the mother of his only son. Also here is Charles I, buried in secrecy and silence during a heavy snowfall after his execution in Whitehall. His coffin was discovered by chance in the early nineteenth century, and for a few seconds the face painted by Van Dyck, the red hair flecked with grey, stared up at those who opened it – before crumbling into dust. The tablet records Charles's year of death as 1648, not 1649, as the new year was then reckoned as beginning in March. But the most extraordinary tomb is the white marble monument by Matthew Cotes Wyatt, Jeffry Wyatville's cousin, to Princess Charlotte, only daughter of George IV, who died in childbirth on 6 November 1817. Charlotte is shown rising heavenward as if leaping for a ball, her baby in the arms of an attendant angel, while at her feet hooded figures weep over the shrouded corpse her spirit has left.

Around the chapel are some of the most delightful buildings in the castle: a row of honey-coloured lodgings that could have been lifted from a Cotswold village; the half-timbered, red-brick horseshoe court of 1478–81; the dean's cloister dating from

1352–4, with arcading and a fragment of fresco from the chapel built by Henry III in the thirteenth century; and the intimate canon's cloister, with climbers smothering timber colonnades and shrubs set out in tubs. Nearby is the library terrace, with a panoramic view extending far over Eton and the wooded Thames valley to the Chilterns, and a steep drop to Thames Street, which curls round the foot of the curtain wall far below.

Close to the castle, behind the pedestrianized cobbled alleys stretching away from King Henry's gate, is the Royal Mews, with an exhibition of carriages and gifts received by the Queen. An alternative royal show is set in the Victorian central railway station, where the Royal Waiting Room of golden Bath stone, newly cleaned, is now the focus of a series of imaginative waxwork tableaux celebrating Queen Victoria's Diamond Jubilee in 1897, for which her extended family gathered at Windsor. A red carpet links the waiting room to a replica of the gleaming train which brought visitors from London, the carriages fitted out with polished sycamore panelling and silk upholstery. The station is gay with bunting and flags, while appropriate sound effects, from rousing martial music to

cheering crowds and shouted orders, help to inject an illusion of life into the carefully arranged figures and the phalanx of guardsmen presenting arms. This is a station I would happily use, every corner swept and garnished and the well-stocked refreshment trolley selling iced buns at 1d each.

Eton is only a twenty-minute walk away, across the bridge at the bottom of Thames Street. The long, gently curving High Street, many of its old houses now art galleries, antique shops or tea rooms, is almost self-consciously well preserved, with a touch of the film set about the Victorian letter-box and the tiny post office. The principal buildings of the school, laid out around two courtyards like a monastery or a university college, are at the far end, where an archway in the long brick façade of Upper School leads into School Yard, an expanse of roughly-laid flint and cobbles crossed by paths of Purbeck stone. Red-brick ranges ornamented with purple diaper work and crowned with twisted barley-sugar chimneys date back to Henry VI's foundation of the college in the 1440s, and

directly opposite the entrance is the turreted and battlemented Lupton's Tower, a soaring brick gateway of 1520 with a projecting double oriel window. Beyond is another court, smaller and more intimate, with a central fountain and brick cloisters, while Henry VI's inspired chapel towers over everything, the cupolas and pinnacles of its skyline as instantly recognizable as the silhouette of Windsor Castle. Like St George's, this is an exercise in Perpendicular Gothic, with huge windows and fan vaulting, but, unlike the chapel high on the hill above, not much of what you see here is original. The medieval wooden roof was replaced by the current coarse stone vaulting in 1959, and most of the chapel glass was destroyed by a bomb in 1940. Only the extraordinary murals of 1479–87 survive unaltered, the curiously monochrome compositions having been preserved for almost three hundred years under a coat of whitewash. The completed building is in fact only the eastern section of the grandiose pilgrimage church that Henry originally planned; the extent of his projected nave is now marked by a prominent cross on a house on the Maidenhead road opposite the main gate. Many of the houses round about are also part of the school, which now takes about 1,250 boys. The seventy scholars that Henry VI provided for had a hard time of it, rising at 5 a.m.,

invariably faced with mutton for dinner, their one solid meal, and condemned to a monotonous diet of Latin and Greek.

Those who are car-borne could combine an excursion to Windsor and Eton with a visit to Runnymede, the Thames-side meadow three miles south-east where King John signed Magna Carta in 1215, surrounded by his rebellious barons. Although now crossed by the busy A308, this is still an atmospheric spot, with a wooded hillside rising steeply behind the temple-like memorial. Only yards away, reached by a cobbled path through the trees, is a plain slab commemorating the American president John F. Kennedy, while the slope above is crowned by the Commonwealth Air Forces memorial to all those lost without trace in the Second World War.

Open: CASTLE precincts 10-dusk; state apartments, provided the sovereign is not in residence, generally weekdays 10.30–17, Sun 1.30–17, but days and times vary; St George's Chapel Mon–Sat 10–16, Sun 14–16, but closed before major ceremonies; presents and carriages Mar–Oct, Mon–Sat 10.30–17 (15 Sun), Nov–Feb, daily 10.30–15; admission charge except for precincts; toilets; guided tours of chapel; ROYALTY AND EMPIRE daily 9.30–17.30 (16.30 Nov–March, closed for two weeks in Jan); admission charge; toilets; ETON COLLEGE Apr–Oct 14–16.30 in term, 10.30–16.30 in school holidays, but closed early June; admission charge; toilets; afternoon guided tours

3

THE CITY

— • —

Unreal City
Under the brown fog of a winter dawn,
A crowd flowed over London Bridge, so many,
I had not thought death had undone so many.
Sighs, short and infrequent, were exhaled,
And each man fixed his eyes before his feet.
Flowed up the hill and down King William Street,
To where Saint Mary Woolnoth kept the hours
With a dead sound on the final stroke of nine.

T. S. Eliot: *The Waste Land*

ONCE EVERYONE LIVED in the City. Now, apart from those who inhabit the fortress-like tower blocks of the arid Barbican development beyond London Wall, almost nobody does. Every weekday, thousands pour across London Bridge – not all of them, one hopes, as disillusioned as T. S. Eliot's clerks – or emerge like moles from the catacombs of the Underground, or from the maw of Cannon Street Station, flooding back again in the evening to leave their offices and banks to a skeleton staff of caretakers and custodians.

The City has always been the commercial centre of London, and its financial clout was early translated into political power and influence, and used to gain its merchants special privileges. When medieval kings came begging for money and support, funds would be granted – but only at a price. Thus, Henry I, drained by an almost continual war in Normandy, empowered the citizens in 1132 to elect their own sheriff, although in theory he was a representative of the Crown; control of the Thames from the mouth of the Medway to Staines was handed over to the City Corporation in 1197 by Richard I, who had just returned from the Crusades and was desperately short of money; and in 1215, a few weeks before he signed the more famous Magna Carta, King John was forced to confirm the City's right to elect a mayor, the first of whom, Henry Fitzailwyn, had been appointed in 1192.

This special status is still very apparent. Within the huge conurbation that London has now become, the City is a separate entity, with its own police force and its own ruling body: the Mayor and Corporation. Within the City, the Lord Mayor ranks before everybody except

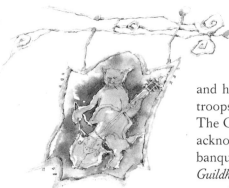

the Sovereign, and he has the right to seek an audience with the monarch. He is Admiral of the Port of London, Chancellor of the City University, and has the password to the *Tower of London*. No troops can enter the City without his permission. The City's influence on the government is publicly acknowledged at the annual Lord Mayor's banquet, when the Prime Minister comes to the *Guildhall*, the Corporation's parliament and palace, to make a major speech on government policy and the country's international position. A few days before the banquet, the newly-elected Mayor will have driven through the City in a glistening gold coach (displayed for the rest of the year in the *Museum of London*) to take his oath of office, the pomp and pageant of the procession – known as the Lord Mayor's Show (see p. 180) – more than equal to the splendour of royal occasions. Sadly, Lord Mayors no longer process up the Thames in a barge with silver oars, as Sir John Norman did in 1452; and ever since 1711, when an incumbent was knocked off his horse by a drunken flower girl, no mayor has ridden in the procession.

Behind this august official are the mysterious City guilds or livery companies, whose members alone have the power to elect the Mayor and his Sheriffs. These influential private organizations, membership of which, like being educated at Eton or Harrow, admits you to a powerful contact network, originated in medieval fraternities set up to maintain standards and regulate conditions in a particular craft or trade. Typically, a guild would control prices and wages, could decide who might practise the craft, and had powers to punish those guilty of poor workmanship. Their distinctive uniforms led to members being known as livery men, and thus to the guilds being called livery companies. There are now nearly a hundred of them, dominated by twelve Great Companies which are ranked in a strict order of precedence reflecting their medieval status. Top of the list is the Mercers' Company, whose members once controlled the vitally important textile trade, exporting wool and woollen cloth and importing fine linen, velvet and silk. Close behind come the Grocers', Drapers', Fishmongers', Goldsmiths', Skinners' and Merchant Taylors'. Most unusual is the Cordwainers' company, whose members made harnesses, shoes and bottles from goatskin imported from southern Spain. Surprisingly, some livery companies have only been established very recently, among them the Air Pilots' and Air Navigators' Guild; the Launderers' Company, granted their livery in 1977; and the very twentieth-century Actuaries' and Arbitrators' companies.

Where the last two are very much professional associations, many of the medieval foundations are now only linked with the industries from which they sprang through their charitable and educational activities. But there are exceptions. All fish sold in the City must still be inspected by officials of the Fishmongers' Company, and most of the Clockmakers' are still connected with the trade. Some still exercise archaic customs or have very special privileges. Only the Dyers' and Vintners', for example, share the Sovereign's right to keep swans on the Thames; and once a year the Vintners' still process to church with nosegays held to their nostrils. A porter in a white smock and top hat goes before them, sweeping the road with the kind of broom usually associated with witches and black cats.

Sadly, the Great Fire which devastated the City in 1666 (see p. 13) destroyed 44

THE CITY

of the guild's medieval halls, decorated with carved woodwork and filled with valuable plate, and many of those that were rebuilt were again razed during the Second World War, when the area laid waste by bombs was roughly equal to that burnt out in the seventeenth century. About thirty companies still possess halls in the City, but most are neither very old nor accessible. For the curious, the halls of the Dyers', Tallow Chandlers' and Skinners' companies form an attractive group on Dowgate Hill, the hall of the Tallow Chandlers', dating from 1672, overlooking a secluded arcaded courtyard.

The Mayor and Corporation govern an area of some 677 acres, or just over a square mile, stretching from the *Tower of London* on the east to the sites of Temple and Holborn bars on the west, and from the Thames to Smithfield and Moorfields on the north. The positions of the two former westerly bars, or gates, are now marked by griffins, one a bronze monster perched high up in the middle of Fleet Street outside the Temple, the others grinning, silver creatures set on obelisks either side of Holborn beneath the Elizabethan façade of Staple Inn. The heart of the City is the hub-like *place* about Bank underground station, from which eight streets radiate out like the spokes in a wheel. On the north side is the massive, dependable bulk of the *Bank of England*, to the east the imposing portico of the *Royal Exchange*, and to the south the even more grandiose classical façade of the Mansion House, the official residence of the Lord Mayor, with six Corinthian columns supporting a sculpted pediment. Built by George Dance the Elder from 1739, with alterations by his son, the Mansion House is palace, court and prison: a theatrical Egyptian Hall is the climax to a sequence of imposing state rooms, but down in the basement there are eleven cells, one of which once held the suffragette Emmeline Pankhurst.

A Manhattan-like collection of office blocks and skyscrapers is clustered just to the east of the Bank intersection. Here is the austere 330-foot Stock Exchange tower, where the trading floor which once seethed with excitement has been largely deserted since Big Bang in 1986, when a computerized price information system was introduced (the public gallery overlooking the floor is now closed); Richard Seifert's 52-storey column housing the National Westminster Bank, a 600-foot human anthill designed to sway gently in the wind; and the futuristic *Lloyd's* building, half industrial plant, half Victorian conservatory. Every street seems to hold the offices of an international financial institution, an oil company, or an insurance corporation. It is incredible to think that P. G. Wodehouse, creator of Jeeves and Bertie Wooster, once made his living in this self-important world, although his career at the Hongkong and Shanghai Bank came to an abrupt end on the day he dashed off a short story on the first page of a new ledger.

In among the concrete, glass and steel, or only yards from the formidable windy corridor of Upper Thames Street, which now severs much of the City from the Thames, are mazes of little courts and alleys, often concealing a church or an old pub, or opening out into sudden patches of greenery. The ruined walls of St Dunstan in the East, gutted in the Second World War, are now the setting for a secluded and beautifully tended garden, with smooth lawns, a fountain, and climbing plants

creeping through the glassless windows, while at the west end Wren's tower still soars triumphant. On 23 April 1668, Pepys, accompanied only by a link boy, just avoided being mugged here: 'Walking towards home, just at my entrance into the ruines at St Dunstan's, I was met by two rogues with clubs . . . so I went back and walked home quite round by the Wall.' Pepys's own church, with a rather touching bust of his wife set high up to the left of the altar, is St Olave's in Hart Street, a short distance north-east, entered through a grisly gateway of 1658, ornamented with clusters of hollow-eyed skulls.

Just occasionally you see buildings which suggest how the City must have looked when rebuilt after the Fire. Most imposing is the College of Arms on Queen Victoria Street, a handsome brick building of the 1670s, wrapped round three sides of a courtyard, with brick pilasters topped with stone capitals, a roofline parapet, and a splendid gilded wrought-iron screen on to the street which was brought here from Goodrich Court in Herefordshire after the Second World War (the original gates and railings went to help the war effort). This seventeenth-century building is the home of the royal heralds, an extraordinary anachronism who have been part of the sovereign's household since the thirteenth century, if not before. Nowhere else will you find a collection of people with more archaic and evocative titles, conjuring up visions of banners and chain mail, roaring fires and roasting venison: Garter, Clarenceux, and Norray and Ulster King of Arms; Portcullis, Rouge Dragon, Rouge Croix and Bluemantle Pursuivants; and the heralds, York, Richmond, Windsor, Somerset, Lancaster and Chester. Should you wish to pursue your family's coat of arms, someone here would help you – for a fee. But to meet one of these officers would undoubtedly be a mistake. Instead of a shining figure in golden armour, you would probably be faced by a portly gentleman in late middle age, traces of the egg he had for breakfast on his three-piece suit.

Quieter and less obvious than the College of Arms is Frederick's Place off Old Jewry, a cobbled eighteenth-century backwater of yellow brick with torch extinguishers and classical doorways. For three years from 1821 the young Benjamin Disraeli worked at No 6, where he was articled to a solicitor. And one of the most extensive concentrations of early Georgian buildings lies in Spitalfields, just east of the City, where Huguenot refugees from France built the fine brick houses with prominent, well-lit attic storeys where silk-weavers sat at their looms.

What the city has now almost lost is the noise and bustle of open-air markets and any feeling that this was once a great port. Only Bread Street, Wood Street, Milk Street and other tributaries remind us that Cheapside once hosted a big medieval street market. Booksellers and publishers congregated around *St Paul's Cathedral* to the west; the precincts which once buzzed with their activity are now an arid modern waste, but by the mid 1990s the soulless sixties blocks should have been replaced by an Italianate piazza with classical façades in brick and stone. At Smithfield, London's largest meat market still operates from Sir Horace Jones's confident blue and cream wrought-iron arcades of 1851–66, with octagonal domed turrets at each corner and dragons breathing fire over the entrances, but fish are no longer sold at Jones's more sedate Billingsgate market, where dolphins entwined on the pedimented façade look down on Lower Thames Street, and the fruit and vegetable traders have gone from Spitalfields.

As to the port, the classical Customs House of 1812–25 still stares expectantly out over the river beside Billingsgate, but the great system of docks below *Tower Bridge* which once connected Britain with her empire is being ambitiously redeveloped, old warehouses turned into stylish apartments and secluded basins into yacht marinas. One such is St Katherine's Dock, just downstream of Tower Bridge, now a prettified tourist attraction with planted troughs overhanging the quays and with the remnants of a collection of old ships, including some authentic Thames barges, in among the luxury craft. Rising triumphantly over this Docklands area, as part of the Canary Wharf project, is an 800-foot tower, a massive new landmark visible from far into Kent and Sussex.

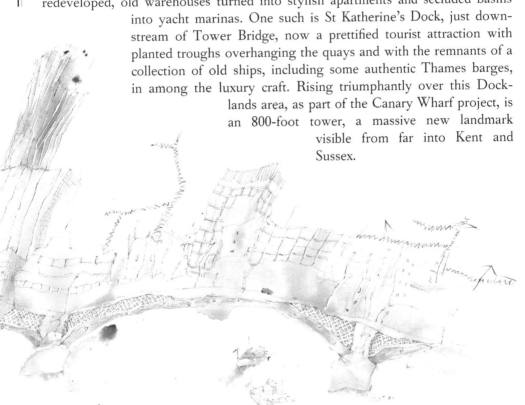

BANK OF ENGLAND

Threadneedle Street, EC2

———— • ————

underground Bank (Central and Northern lines)

T HE GREAT MASS OF the Bank of England sits at the heart of the City, overlooking a starfish-like intersection. Known affectionately as 'the Old Lady of Threadneedle Street', the Bank is no frail and timorous great-aunt, but a plumply domineering grandmother, quietly confident of everything she surveys.

It was not always so. Founded only in 1694 by a government desperate for cash to finance yet another struggle with France, the Bank's funds were initially raised from 633 subscribers, who were promised 8 per cent on their money. Until 1708, the Bank had to make its way against competition from other financial institutions (no bad thing, some might say), in 1715 it weathered a Jacobite plot to burn the premises down and in 1780, at the height of the Gordon riots, a mob advanced on the building, those who defended it apparently using melted-down inkwells for their bullets.

No such excitements disturb what is now the hub of financial life in the City, and the central bank of the United Kingdom, executing monetary policy on behalf of the government, issuing bank notes, and supervising the operation of the money markets. The present grandiose premises, filling an island-like block with roads on every side, date largely from 1924, when the Bank was rebuilt to plans by Sir Herbert Baker. The style is massy and monumental, an echo of the imperial government buildings which Baker and Sir Edwin Lutyens composed for New Delhi. Those who

trudge wearily round it, though, see only the elegant curtain wall, designed for maximum security, with which the eccentric and individual Sir John Soane (see p. 100) surrounded his earlier rebuild of 1788–1833, decorating his windowless surfaces with fluted columns and pilasters. Although said to have had no sympathy with Soane's work, Baker must have liked something about it as he removed two sculpted capitals to his garden in Kent, where they form an elegant bird-bath.

There is no access to the interior of the Bank, but visitors to the small museum that traces its history can see a reconstruction of one of Soane's toplit banking halls, its rounded arches and shallow dome suggesting a newly-converted Byzantine basilica. In this dignified, church-like interior, model clerks in period dress are seen working at oak ledger rests on mahogany counters. Most of the exhibits in the museum seem worthy rather than exciting at first glance, but in among the displays of early bank notes and cheques, and of the Bank's silver plate, are some more evocative items, such as the forged notes produced by the inmates of Sachsenhausen concentration camp during the Second World War, and the caricatures of bank staff by Robert Browning, father of the poet, who was a clerk here from 1803 to 1853; the faces he drew straight out of Dickens. Alternative specimen signatures by Nelson – one with his right arm, the other with his left – are a little difficult to make out, but there is no mistaking the names on the thankyou letter which George V's children wrote to Kenneth Grahame, author of *The Wind in the Willows*, who was secretary of the Bank from 1898 to 1908.

Museum open: Mon–Fri 10–17; admission free; toilets; entrance in Bartholomew Lane

THE GUILDHALL

Aldermanbury, EC2

— • —

underground Bank (Central and Northern lines),
Moorgate (Circle, Northern and Metropolitan
lines), St Paul's (Central line)

THE SEAT OF CITY government since the twelfth century, the place where Lord Mayors are elected and the administrative council meets, the Guildhall is the symbol of the City's political influence and power. Although severely damaged in the Great Fire of 1666, when it is said to have glowed like a palace of gold, and again during the Second World War, the gaily pinnacled building tucked away behind Wren's St Lawrence Jewry still inhabits a fifteenth-century shell and sits on the most extensive medieval crypt in London, with cluster columns of Purbeck marble supporting a massive stone vault. The façade overlooking Guildhall Yard is a charming mixture of Gothic, classical and oriental, with a playfully pinnacled projecting frontage and a slender wooden spire rising from the centre of the steeply-pitched roof. The porch, often hidden behind a red-and-white striped awning, is original, early fifteenth-century work, but the golden-tiled roof was added in the 1950s and the pinnacles and Indian-style windows were conjured up by George Dance the Younger, who refronted the hall in 1788–9.

Inside, the huge, 152-foot hall with its bare stone walls and modern hammerbeam

roof dates from 1411, when it was the second largest in England, only the King's Hall at Westminster surpassing it. Now ringed by grandiose monuments, one of them a determined likeness of Winston Churchill, and the setting for splendid banquets, this church-like place was once used as a courtroom. Those who were tried here include the 25-year-old Anne Askew, one of the Protestant martyrs of Mary Tudor's reign, who was so weakened by torture that she had to be carried on a chair to Smithfield to be burnt; Lady Jane Grey and her husband Lord Guildford Dudley, committed to the Tower in 1553 (see p. 36); and Archbishop Cranmer, who was sentenced to death in the same year but then pardoned, only to be burnt at the stake in Oxford in 1556. Rather discouragingly, when Sir Nicholas Throckmorton was found not guilty of treason in 1554, the verdict was considered unsatisfactory and the jury was thrown into prison.

A modern interpretation of a cloister links this medieval survival to a loud new building housing the Guildhall library and the oldest clock museum in the world, the collection of the Worshipful Company of Clockmakers. Beautifully decorated long-case clocks tick gently against the walls, and cases of watches include the wrist-watch worn by Sir Edmund Hillary when he made the first ascent of Everest in 1953.

GUILDHALL open, unless closed for a function, Mon–Fri 10–17, Sat 10–16; admission free; CLOCK MUSEUM open Mon–Fri 9.30–16.45; admission free

LLOYD'S

Lime Street, EC3

——— • ———

underground Bank (Central and Northern lines)

LLOYD'S IS ONE of the City's great institutions, the international insurance business conducted here bringing in over £24 million in premiums every working day. What is now a huge association of members arranged in four hundred syndicates began in the 1690s, when Edward Lloyd's coffee-house close by the *Tower of London* became known as a place where shipowners and merchants could insure craft and cargo. By 1771, the informal network of underwriters had crystallized into a society with fixed rules. Once only concerned with marine risks, Lloyd's will now insure almost anything, from nuclear power stations and communication satellites to a dancer's legs. The Channel Tunnel project is insured with Lloyd's, and the 1990 Van Gogh exhibition in Amsterdam was covered for £3 billion. Lloyd's also prides itself on prompt payouts, even after major disasters such as the San Francisco earthquake of 1905 or the sinking of the *Titanic* in 1912. Unlike a limited company, members are personally liable, and thus are required, if necessary, to meet insurance obligations with their private

wealth. But the 'names' are no longer involved in the business, which is conducted on their behalf by professional underwriters.

Since 1986 Lloyd's has been housed in the most innovative building in London, a futuristic structure of glass, steel and concrete designed by the Richard Rogers partnership. Ducts and pipes are exposed, glass-sided lifts whizz up and down on the outside, and little blue cranes speckle the structure, but in the middle rises a huge and beautiful glass atrium, like a Victorian conservatory, the curve of its barrel roof 200 feet above Lloyd's Room on the ground floor. From the visitors' gallery five floors up you can look down on the Room, from where subtly lit, glass-sided escalators like moving sculptures carry brokers to the underwriters in the galleries above. A classical rostrum topped by a clock houses the bell of *HMS Lutine*, which sank with all hands in 1799. The bell is still rung to herald important announcements, but it no longer sounds for every loss at sea.

Viewing gallery open: Mon-Fri 10–14.30; admission free

THE MONUMENT

Monument Street, EC2

— • —

underground Monument (Circle and District lines)

THE GREAT FIRE, which destroyed four-fifths of the City in three days (see p. 13), is commemorated by Sir Christopher Wren's Monument, a Doric column of Portland stone 202 feet high which was erected between 1671 and 1677. In almost any other capital this massive symbol would be the focus of a vista, or mark the intersection of major thoroughfares, but here it is hidden away in a little square. Neither its position nor its height is incidental. Just east of here, at a distance of 202 feet, is the cobbled alley of Pudding Lane, with a plaque on the corner marking the site of the baker's shop where the fire started. The Monument is crowned by a flaming gilded urn, while a bas-relief at its foot shows the City as a ravaged lady, her hair dishevelled, smoke and flames billowing out of the building behind her. The bearded figure of Time is lifting her up and Charles II in Roman dress urges on the task of rebuilding.

Those with strong leg muscles can climb the spiral staircase which winds upwards for 311 steps to a balcony just below the urn. In Dickens's *Martin Chuzzlewit*, the gatekeeper sends a couple on their way up the staircase and returns to his chair laughing: ' "They don't know what a-many steps there is!" he said. "It's worth twice the money to stop here. Oh, my eye!" ' The doorkeeper was wrong. It is a tough ascent, but well worth it. The dome of *St Paul's Cathedral* dominates the view west, while downriver is the Gothic outline of *Tower Bridge*, with the *Tower of London* beside it. Far upstream round a great bend in the Thames, is the shadowy outline of the Houses of Parliament (see p. 19), curiously intermixed with the chimneys of Battersea Power Station.

Open: Mar–Sept, Mon–Fri 9–18; Sat, Sun 14–18; Oct–March, Mon–Sat 9–16; admission charge

ROYAL EXCHANGE

EC3

———— • ————

underground Bank (Central and Northern lines)

SIR EDWARD TITE's imposing classical building of 1841–4, with sculpture by Richard Westmacott the Younger on the pediment above the porticoed entrance, stands on the site of the exchange opened by Sir Thomas Gresham in 1570. Since 1982 this dignified edifice has been the home of the London International Financial Futures Exchange (LIFFE), a very recent money market spawned by the risks and opportunities inherent in inflation and volatile interest and exchange rates. It is now the leading futures exchange in Europe, handling over 160,000 transactions a day. A visitor's gallery overlooks the long trading hall, packed with traders, runners and LIFFE officials and the scene of furious, frenetic activity.

The noise is tremendous, and every so often cheers, roars and shouts erupt from the crowd of dealers congregated in the middle of the room. Messages are thrown across the hall, many of them adding to the sea of paper underfoot, and traders can be seen communicating with their back-up staff by means of elaborate hand signals. And this is no sombre, grey-suited gathering. Colourful jackets in bright mustard yellow, orange and green stripes, or vivid sky-blue are worn by almost everyone in the room, a distinctive identification system which adds to the feeling that you are witnessing a piece of live theatre.

Open: Mon–Fri 11.30–13.45; admission free

TOWER BRIDGE

SE1

———— • ————

underground Tower Hill (Circle and District lines)

ONE OF LONDON'S best-known landmarks, Tower Bridge stretches 2,980 feet across the river just below the *Tower of London*. With its gothic towers ornamented with gargoyles and statue niches, the bridge is perfectly in tune with the great medieval fortress, as it was decreed it should be. Designed as a double drawbridge sandwiched between two suspension bridges, so that tall ships could still have access to the Pool of London, it was built between 1886 and 1894 and opened with great ceremony by the Prince of Wales. Once the drawbridges of the 200-foot central span would be raised up to fifty times a day, but the decline in shipping coming into London means that the bridge is now opened no more than five or six times a week.

Now worked by electricity, the bridge was originally operated by the gleaming, steam-fired green and red pumping engines which can be seen in the museum, their cogs and valves still adjusted with huge spanners from the rack mounted on the wall. Visitors are also taken up to the high-level walkways almost 140 feet above the river, with views over the City to the west and the Docklands redevelopment to the east. Upstream you can see several other bridges; as yet nothing spans the Thames between here and its mouth but plans are afoot for a huge concrete arch to form a new link a few miles downstream.

Open: Daily 10–18.30 (16.45 Nov–March); admission charge; toilets

4

GALLERIES AND MUSEUMS

— • —

THERE IS AN ENORMOUS NUMBER of galleries and museums in London, ranging from small collections on local history to the internationally-known *British Museum* and *Tate Gallery*. It would take a couple of months to visit every one, and a book much bigger than this would be needed to describe them all. All the major museums and galleries are included here and there is also a strong coverage of other places of general interest which are easily accessible and regularly open. There are a few minority-interest museums at the end of this section, on p. 114, but some excellent collections which have a very specialist appeal or which require a journey to an otherwise rather unappealing part of the city have been omitted. Among them are the William Morris Gallery in the Victorian craftsman and poet's childhood home in Walthamstow (Forest Road, E17), and the excellent Horniman Museum in south London (London Road, Forest Hill, SE23), where the imaginative and lively displays on the beliefs, crafts and customs of primitive peoples round the world easily surpass what is on offer at the *Museum of Mankind* in Piccadilly.

Some places have been omitted because it is questionable whether anyone should be encouraged to go there, in particular the London Dungeon (28/34 Tooley Street, SE1), a celebration of torture and cruelty through the ages. The fledgling Museum of Garden History in a converted church next to the Tudor gatehouse of Lambeth Palace (Lambeth Palace Road, SE1) will one day, I am sure, be as fascinating as its name suggests, but as yet its displays are in an embryonic stage. Also not included are several galleries which host temporary exhibitions, foremost among them the Barbican Art Gallery in the City (Level 8, Barbican Centre, Silk Street, EC2), the gallery of the Institute of Contemporary Arts (The Mall, SW1), the Hayward Gallery on the South Bank (Belvedere Road, SE1), the Serpentine Gallery in Hyde Park, the Whitechapel Gallery in the East End (80 Whitechapel High Street, E1) and the excellent Photographer's Gallery at the western edge of Covent Garden (5–8 Great Newport Street, WC2). Rotating displays – and very limited opening hours – are also a feature of the Saatchi Collection of Modern Art, hung in a converted warehouse in St John's Wood (98a Boundary Road, NW8).

Some of the best shows, including the *British Museum*, the *National Gallery*, *National Portrait Gallery* and *Tate Gallery*, are free, and some other institutions, such as the *Imperial War Museum* and the *Science Museum*, offer free days or periods. At the height of the tourist season, major venues in central London tend to get more and more crowded as the day progresses, and it is best to see them, if you can, in the morning. But a day or more is needed to cover the largest collections.

HMS Belfast

Symons Wharf, Vine Lane, SE1

— • —

underground Tower Hill (Circle and District lines),
London Bridge (Northern line); boats to ship from
Tower Pier

JUST UPSTREAM FROM *Tower Bridge*, moored well out in the river, is the dark grey shape of this Second World War battle cruiser, its superstructure bristling with guns. Inside it is vast, a warren of decks set one below the other and connected by steep, ladder-like companion ways. This floating town, over 600 feet long, was home to some 800 officers and men, with a bakery, an operating theatre and many other essential services to cater for the crew.

Launched on 17 March 1938 from the Harland and Wolff yard in Belfast, *HMS Belfast* played a key role during the war. Terse, almost laconic entries in a copy of the ship's log for 'D Day' – 6 June 1944 – give few clues that she led the bombardment of the Normandy beaches to support landings by the Allied troops:

15.30 Enemy fighter chased off by two Spitfires.

18.56 Large fires and clouds of smoke all along beaches.

22.15 Gunner Mayo died on board.

23.20 Flak all round.

07.25 Commencing landing troops.

Only numerous references to the bombs raining down into the sea suggest something of the tension there must have been on board. Similarly, carefully plotted diagrams which look like an elaborate game illustrate how *HMS Belfast* and five other British ships gradually cornered the German battle cruiser *Scharnhorst* in the Barents Sea on 26 December 1943, eventually sinking her with shells and torpedoes. The captain of the *Scharnhorst* refused to surrender, his final defiant message to Berlin proclaiming, 'We will fight to the last shell.' Out of a crew numbering nearly two thousand, only 36 survived, none of them officers.

Visitors to the ship are given an extensive tour, from the Admiral's Bridge with its row of telephones to the boiler room, a forest of lagged pipes, instrument gauges and narrow walkways. The mess deck and officers' cabins show how the men lived in 1939, the lower ranks sleeping in hammocks. Displays cover the history of *Belfast*, the role of the Navy's cruisers in both world wars, the development of the battleship, the Navy today and, for the technically minded, the calculations involved in firing the guns which are such an obvious feature of this war machine.

Open: 20 March–31 Oct, daily 10–17.30; 1 Nov–19 March, daily 10–16; admission charge; toilets

BETHNAL GREEN MUSEUM OF CHILDHOOD

Cambridge Heath Road, E2 9PA

——— • ———

underground Bethnal Green (Central line)

A
N OUTPOST of the *Victoria and Albert Museum* housed in an unusual iron-framed building in the heart of the East End, the Bethnal Green Museum is stuffed with toys of every kind, dating from the seventeenth century to the present day. There are shadow puppets, model trains, rocking horses, regiments of toy soldiers and any number of dolls. Games include an Alice in Wonderland chess set and Victorian inventions designed to improve the mind, and there are streets full of doll's houses, from grand classical mansions to suburban villas. Look out for Miss Miles's house of the 1890s, with its billiard room and a shower bath behind a screen; for the Whiteladies House of 1936 with its swimming pool, tennis court and gay young things sipping cocktails on

the balcony; and for the carved Bavarian furniture in the beautifully-detailed Nuremberg house of 1673, the earliest in the museum. In the first-floor gallery are displays of children's clothes and furniture, including a mahogany kneehole desk of c.1870 which would be just right for a five-year-old learning to write.

In term time, Bethnal Green is full of the murmur of school parties, but much that is here, such as the 1950s children's outfits, will particularly appeal to adults. Moreover, the building itself is an architectyural curiosity, a very early example of the iron-framed glass-houses pioneered by Sir Joseph Paxton in the Crystal Palace. Sadly, though, it lacks the colonnaded cloister planned to front the street.

Open: Mon–Thurs, Sat 10–18, Sun 14.30–18; admission free; toilets

THE BRITISH MUSEUM

Great Russell Street, WC1

———— • ————

underground Holborn (Central and Piccadilly lines),
Tottenham Court Road (Central and Northern
lines)

T HERE IS A FEELING of something momentous going on at the British Museum. This is partly because the place looks so solemn: the vast pedimented portico with its fluted columns could be the entrance to some awe-inspiring temple, the spacious forecourt across which visitors stream like ants perhaps the setting for terrible ritual ceremonies. There is even the suggestion of an inner sanctum in the great domed reading room, where only those with passes may gain admittance. Somehow, this central powerhouse, where papers and books are researched and the tools of academic debate sharpened – even, one

assumes, by those who slumber gently through the afternoons – seems to invest the rest of the place with a sense of purpose. Or perhaps it is the ghosts of those who have been here before, urging us on to higher things. Karl Marx laboured for years, writing his three-volume *Das Kapital*, while his family starved in Soho; George Bernard Shaw wrote five novels here, the young Charles Dickens devoured book after book, and the poet A. E. Housman used to seek solace in the library when he had finished his day's work at the Patent Office in Chancery Lane. The vast circular room looks eternal, but even here changes creep in. W. B. Yeats, who 'shrank from

lifting the heavy volumes of the catalogue', would be much happier with the microfiche listings of recently-published works. Now the whole library, with its miles of subterranean stacks, is due to move to a monolithic building by St Pancras Station. The British Museum will never be the same again.

The collections on display here are far too big to cover in a few hours, or even in a day. The excellent souvenir guide by John Julius Norwich directs you to selected highlights, but even this tour is by no means short and would tax most people's powers of concentration. Lord Norwich optimistically suggests it would take you $2\frac{1}{2}$–3 hours altogether. Do not be deceived. You would do well to complete it in a single visit. The only way to tackle the British Museum is to be selective.

The museum is renowned above all for its collection of antiquities, with a substantial sequence of galleries displaying sculptures, reliefs, vases and paintings from the great civilizations which blossomed on the shores of the Mediterranean and along the rivers watering the deserts of the Middle East: ancient Egypt, Assyria, Greece and Rome. Best known are the Greek marbles of 447–438 BC, brought to London by the Earl of Elgin in the early nineteenth century. Now shown in a rather antiseptic, purpose-built gallery, these monumental friezes which once adorned the Parthenon in Athens show the celebrations for the birthday of Athena, the city's patron saint. A procession of horsemen, chariots and sacrificial sheep and cattle – one beast with its head raised, bellowing at the sky – marches down either side of the room, to converge towards the gods seated at one end.

But, despite the flying hooves and tossing manes, there are other reliefs as good as these. In the rooms devoted to the Assyrian empire of the seventh century BC are set-pieces which once adorned the great palaces of Nineveh one a strip-cartoon battle with desperate hand-to-hand fighting and retreating soldiers fleeing on camels, another an extended lion hunt, the cornered beasts writhing on the ground in realistic death agonies, a third showing a servant with locust kebabs. And for studies of the human

form, seek out the darkened cupboard-like room which displays the frieze of c.400 BC from the temple of Apollo discovered on a lonely mountain spur in the Peloponnese. A continuous relief of energetic bodies, some clad in flowing drapery, circles the gallery.

The general arrangement is both geographical and chronological, moving from Egypt through Assyria to Greece and Rome, but it is difficult to believe some of the pieces are separated by over a thousand years. There is as much intelligence and sophistication in the sandstone head of the Egyptian King Mentuhotpe II (2060–2010 BC), or in the painting of c.1400 BC of a nobleman hunting in the marshes from a reed boat, butterflies darting over the water and birds scattering in alarm as his tabby cat leaps towards them, as in the terracotta ladies who chat confidentially on a bench in an ornament of c.100 BC, or in the Greek figure vases. Some pieces are huge, like the granite figure of Amenophis III, each finger of his clenched fist the width of an arm, or the human-headed winged bulls which once stood at the gates of a city, their five legs arranged so that they appear stationary when seen from the front, but walking forward when seen from the side. Others seem designed for a mantelpiece or a coffee table, among them the delightful blue hippo only a couple of inches long of c.1900 BC, his back covered in stylized plants as if he has been wallowing in a pool. A black basalt slab covered in white hieroglyphs and ancient Greek is the Rosetta Stone, discovered in 1799 in the Nile delta by some of Napoleon's soldiers. What it says is unremarkable enough; its importance lies in the fact the text is written in three scripts

and two languages, thus providing the key to the inscriptions of ancient Egypt. And no one should miss the Portland vase, dating from about the time of Christ, its translucent outline only ten inches high decorated with white figures which stand out in relief against the blue glass ground. Smashed into more than two hundred pieces by a drunken visitor in 1845, it has been painstakingly restored.

Moving from these galleries into those devoted to early Britain and western Europe is a sobering experience. Suddenly the world has become a darker, more primitive place. And there is no hint of a Mediterranean sun in the raised pathway constructed over a Somerset marsh nearly six thousand years ago, or in the crumpled figure of Lindow man, the victim of a ritual killing, whose leathery corpse was preserved in a peat bog for hundreds of years. There are, to be sure, Iron Age wine flagons inlaid with coral, decorated bronze shields and collars of twisted gold such as Queen Boudicca must have worn, but there is an underlying savagery which suggests life was hard.

A Roman mosaic pavement discovered in Dorset in 1963 has some of the serenity of the south, and Roman civilization surfaces again in the Thetford treasure, probably buried towards the end of the fourth century, when the empire was disintegrating. Who could resist the silver spoons with their handles fashioned as duck's heads, long coiled necks ending in prominent beaks? The Romans also left us the Vindolanda tablets, found among the ruins of a fort near Hadrian's Wall. What appear to be unpromising slivers of whitish wood are in fact letters and military documents, one a record of food and drink consumed at the fort during a few days in summer, a list which includes barley, wine and fish sauce, another a personal missive which mentions a gift of fifty oysters. Some really exceptional pieces date from the twilight centuries which followed the Romans, among them a casket carved out of a whale bone; a marble sarcophagus from about AD 300, decorated with the story of Jonah; and the Lycurgus cup, a dull sludge-green object until it is illuminated, when it is suddenly transformed into a translucent ruby red. Glistening silver bowls, gold buckles, and jewellery encrusted with garnets came from the Sutton Hoo ship burial, discovered on a blasted sandy heath in Suffolk in 1939.

The medieval collection is not as good as that in the *Victoria & Albert Museum*, but there are several outstanding objects in the room devoted to the Waddesdon bequest, the gift of Baron Ferdinand de Rothschild. Seek out the reliquary of c.1400 made for the Duc de Berry, with a spine from the Crown of Thorns seen through a window of rock crystal, while golden angels below sound the last trump as the dead rise naked from their graves. An exquisite is the early sixteenth-century miniature boxwood altarpiece with a high relief carving of the crucifixion, a tiny soldier in the crowd massed at the foot of the cross reaching up to offer our Lord a sponge carried on the end of an impossibly slender spear. Next door is a room filled with clocks and watches, and elsewhere you can see galleries devoted to the superb Oriental collections, with outstanding displays of south Asian sculpture, Islamic art and sixteenth-century Turkish pottery.

Amid all these treasures, it is easy to overlook the rooms devoted to the British Library collections, partly a changing exhibition of prints and drawings, partly a permanent display of outstanding manuscripts and documents. Here you can see the seventh-century illuminated manuscript known as the Lindisfarne gospels, one of Leonardo da Vinci's notebooks, Shakespeare's first folio of 1623, and the death warrant of Elizabeth I's favourite, the Earl of Essex, signed by the Queen's characteristically bold hand. There is a drawing by an eyewitness of the execution of Mary Queen of Scots, the manuscript of *Jane Eyre*, a working draft of Joyce's *Finnegan's Wake*, scoured through with deletions, additions and changes, and Captain Scott's last diary, the entry for 17 March 1912, when Oates made his heroic sacrifice, reading, 'I know that poor Oates was walking to his death.' There are even some scrawled lyrics by the Beatles, which look as if they have been hastily composed on the backs of menus at the end of a good meal.

This outstanding museum, one of the greatest in the world, was founded posthumously in 1753 by the rich physician Sir Hans Sloane, who suggested in his will that Parliament might like to purchase the collections he had spent a lifetime assembling for the sum of £20,000, about a quarter what they were worth. A state lottery not only raised the necessary money but also enough funds to purchase the manuscripts of Robert Harley, the 1st Earl of Oxford, and Montagu House in Bloomsbury as well. The collections grew so rapidly as a result of continuing gifts and purchases that Montagu House was soon too small, and the present grandiose building was begun by Robert Smirke in 1823. The central courtyard Smirke originally designed was subsequently filled in to create the beautiful reading room, roofed by one of the largest copper domes in the world.

Open: Mon–Sat 10–17, Sun 14.30–18; admission free; toilets; guided tours (charge); Reading Room shown hourly, Mon–Fri, 11–16

Cabinet War Rooms

Clive Steps, King Charles Street, SW1

———— • ————

underground Westminster (Circle and District lines), Charing Cross (Bakerloo, Jubilee and Northern lines)

THESE CRAMPED, windowless, sub-terranean rooms in a basement just off Whitehall were converted to act as the nerve centre of Britain's war effort against Nazi Germany, protected from bombs by a three-foot thick reinforced concrete slab. Here Churchill and his cabinet met when the raids on London were at their height, here Churchill could occasionally be persuaded to sleep, and from here he made several historic broadcasts.

At one end of the long corridor is the Cabinet Room, set out as it was for a five o'clock meeting on 15 October 1940. Churchill's wooden chair, with a fire bucket beside it for his cigar ends, faces a hollow square of baize-covered tables. The walls are a functional yellow brick and the ceiling is criss-crossed with red girders and pipes giving reinforcement and ventilation. Down the corridor is the Map Room, manned day and night throughout the war and the heart of Churchill's operations. An array of coloured telephones, the 'beauty chorus', informed those on duty of events at the front. Everything was meticulously recorded on the maps lining the walls, zig-zags of coloured wool marking the German advance into Russia and the Soviet forces' subsequent progress across eastern Europe. Here too the fate of every convoy was anxiously monitored, a thick stream of pin-pricks crossing the North Atlantic providing a vivid visual record of Britain's reliance on America. Across the corridor is the cell-like broom cupboard fitted with a transatlantic telephone link to enable Churchill to speak directly to President Roosevelt, with a clock showing both London and Washington time.

The sound of intermittent air-raid sirens, the rumble of exploding bombs, ringing phones, and recordings of speeches and broadcasts add a further touch of realism to this atmospheric place. It is a sobering thought that, had the fortunes of war been reversed, the defeat of Britain would in all probability have been concluded with hand to hand fighting in these stuffy under-ground rooms, just as the Third Reich ended in a bunker in Berlin.

Open: Daily 10–18; admission charge; toilets; audioguides

COURTAULD INSTITUTE GALLERIES

Somerset House, Strand, WC2

— • —

underground Covent Garden (Piccadilly line),
Temple (Circle and District lines)

THIS IS ONE OF London's most digestible art collections, now re-housed in the elegant rooms of Somerset House. Even a cursory glance at the new catalogue produced to mark the Courtauld's recent move reveals that the building is no convenient backdrop for the paintings, but of great interest in its own right. The site once held the rambling palace built in 1547–50 for the Duke of Somerset, Protector of the boy-king Edward VI, who went to the block in 1552 on trumped-up charges of treason. Elizabeth I lived here as a princess, riding out to greet her half-sister Mary when she became queen; James I lay here in state for a month after his death; and Inigo Jones made additions to the palace for Charles I's Queen, Henrietta Maria. At the end of the eighteenth century, however, the picturesque conglomeration of Tudor and Jacobean buildings was swept away and replaced by William Chambers's imposing Palladian edifice of 1776–1801.

While some consider Somerset House to be a masterpiece of Georgian classical architecture, others find it conservative and over-studied. Designed to accommodate a number of government departments, such as the burgeoning Navy Office, it is built round a large interior courtyard, and has an immense frontage on the Thames. Although now partly screened by the Victoria Embankment, this waterfront façade, with later extensions by Sir James Pennethorne and Robert Smirke, is still one of the most impressive on the river, an 800-foot sweep punctuated by pedimented porticoes and with a shallow central dome. Originally, the huge rusticated arches on which the building sits gave onto the Thames, and boats slid in through two water-gates to unload beneath the vaults. The Strand wing, which was finished first, is much shorter, with a heightened central bay adorned with statues marking the three-arched entrance leading into the courtyard. This range was reserved from the start for three learned societies, the *Royal Academy*, the Royal Society and the Society of Antiquaries, and it is the Fine Rooms which they occupied which now hold the Courtauld's collections. It is worth walking into the courtyard to get the feel of the place, and to see John Bacon's statue of George III with the River Thames at his feet.

The galleries are on two floors on the west side of the entrance range, reached by a toplit stone spiral staircase with an elegant balustrade. None of the rooms is very large and the paintings, hung mostly at eye level, are sometimes crowded too closely together, or hidden inconveniently behind doors, or so placed that you have to dance around to find a spot where you can see them without the glare of reflected light. Elegant plaster ceilings are picked out in pink, lavender and other pastel shades and the walls reflect Chambers's original colour schemes, a fierce green in what was the Royal Society's Meeting Room unfortunately forming the backdrop to much of the superb collection of Impressionists and

Post-Impressionists. Here is Manet's *A bar at the Folies-Bergère*, his blonde barmaid with a deep fringe and a low-cut black dress staring over the crowded room we can see in the mirror behind her, oblivious of the still life Manet has contrived on the marble-topped bar: oranges in a cut-glass dish, roses in a champagne glass, and an assembly of bottles, one of them carrying his signature on its label. Monet's *Vase of Flowers* over one of the fireplaces looks carefully drawn from across the room, but dissolves at close quarters into a confusion of pink, green and blue. There are paintings by Degas, Renoir, Pissarro and Sisley, a Van Gogh self-portrait, Cézanne's blue *Le Lac d'Annecy*, and Tahitian women by Gauguin. Toulouse-Lautrec's decadent *Tête-à-Tête Supper* shows the wreck of a once-striking face.

These canvases, almost all of them from the bequest of the textile industrialist Samuel Courtauld (1876–1947), the principal benefactor of the galleries, form the nucleus of a collection which has been swelled by several subsequent gifts and now encompasses over five hundred paintings, the earliest dating from the fourteenth century. Polyptychs and panels from Italy and the Low Countries glisten with gold-leaf, among them a coronation of the Virgin in which one of the four attendant angels is looking inquiringly at us, not at Jesus's mother. Rubens is well represented, his luminous *Landscape by Moonlight*, with stars sparkling in the trees like fairy lights,

contrasting with an intimate portrait of Jan Brueghel the Elder and his family, the painter's little girl shown staring up into her mother's face. There are also portraits by Van Dyck, Lely and Gainsborough, including Gainsborough's affectionate painting of his ageing wife, soft faced and grey haired.

In the middle of the top floor is the Great Room, where the *Royal Academy* used to hang its Summer Exhibitions from 1780 until 1836. Almost square and rising 32 feet to a lantern in the roof, this is distinguished by the RA line, a moulding about seven feet above the floor. Prominent works were hung either on or below the line; those thought less worthy, or submitted by the less influential, were ruthlessly consigned to the wall above, whatever their size. Over four hundred paintings used to be crammed in here for the annual exhibitions, but the room is now used for thematic displays. Flanking it are small galleries devoted to twentieth-century artists such as Roger Fry, Walter Sickert, Oskar Kokoschka and Ben Nicholson, with painted furniture decorated by Duncan Grant from Fry's Omega workshops.

Part of the charm of the Courtauld lies in the way the paintings have been acquired. This eclectic collection reflects the tastes and preferences of a group of benevolent individuals, not the decisions of committees.

Open: Mon–Sat 10–18, Sun 14–18; admission charge; toilets

CUTTY SARK

King William Walk, Greenwich, SE10

———— • ————

British Rail to Greenwich (from Charing Cross);
Docklands Light Railway to Island Gardens (see
p. 181); or by boat from Westminster Pier (see
p. 181)

WHEREAS THE *Kathleen & May* just up the Thames is one of the last two survivors of Britain's once sizeable coastal sailing fleet, the *Cutty Sark* is the only remaining example of the elegant ocean-going clippers which once crowded London's docks. The clipper was the classic sailing ship of the nineteenth century, a great white bird skimming across the water under a huge spread of sail, its graceful lines designed for beauty as well as speed. This queen of sailing ships evolved first in the United States, where its immediate ancestor was a fast coastal packet known as the Baltimore clipper, but the revolutionary

design was soon being copied and improved in British yards.

Launched at Dumbarton on the Clyde on 22 November 1869, the *Cutty Sark* is built of teak on an iron frame, with spars of Oregon pine and masts of iron. The last word in speed, she is 212½ feet long but only 36 feet wide, and her tapered razor-sharp bow was designed to cut through the water under some 30,000 square feet of canvas. Intended to win the tea race from China, she never succeeded in being first in London with the new season's crop, and made her fastest times at the end of her career on voyages to Australia under Captain Richard Woodget. On one legendary occasion, in 1889, she did the outward passage in 78 days, actually overtaking the new P & O steamer *Britannia* on the way, and she once ran 363 miles in a day. She carried a crew of twenty-eight, and in calm weather the pigs and other livestock they took with them were allowed to roam around the deck when the boat was under way.

The *Cutty Sark's* three masts and spiderweb of rigging is the first sight to greet visitors arriving at Greenwich by boat. Now trapped in a permanent dry dock, with a quay between her and the river, this elegant vessel seems like a whale stranded on dry land, a creature divorced from its natural environment. On board, ropes are neatly coiled, brasswork gleams and the wood of the decks is bleached almost white, while the accommodation includes a saloon panelled in teak and bird's eye maple, for the use of the captain and his officers. Here, in what is perhaps the most atmospheric part of the ship, you can imagine the log being written up every night by the open fire, while the oil lamp swung overhead, or the captain bending low over the chart table nearby. The original crew's quarters are much less palatial, with oilskins hanging up beside narrow, coffin-like bunks built into the sides of the ship.

Below decks, impressions of tea chests and wool bales suggest the cargoes she once carried, but most of the hold is given over to a collection of figureheads from merchant ships, one of them a representation of the young Florence Nightingale. Sadly, the knell of the *Cutty Sark* and her kind had been sounded even before she was launched. The opening of the Suez Canal earlier in the same month had provided a short-cut for steamers sailing to China which the clippers could not follow.

Open: Mon–Sat 10–18, Sun 12–18; admission charge

DULWICH PICTURE GALLERY

College Road, SE21

——— • ———

British Rail from Victoria to West Dulwich, or
from London Bridge to North Dulwich (a 10–15
minute walk from either station: down Gallery
Road from West Dulwich, through the village
from North Dulwich)

THIS SMALL, LITTLE-VISITED gallery in a rural setting four miles south of Trafalgar Square houses one of London's most enjoyable picture collections, particularly strong in seventeenth- and eighteenth-century art. Twelve airy, top-lit rooms hold an impressive collection of Old Masters, among them works by Rembrandt, Van Dyck, Rubens, Murillo, Tiepolo, Watteau, Canaletto and Claude. Dulwich is also strong on English portraiture of the period, with several characteristic Gainsboroughs, and canvases by Romney, Reynolds and Lawrence. To come here requires a special expedition from central London, but it is well worth it. Unlike the *National Gallery* and the *Tate*, Dulwich is very rarely crowded, and the pictures are some of the finest in England. The old village itself is a collection of Georgian houses and rustic cottages, some unexpectedly weather-boarded, and there is an attractive park just across the road from the gallery.

The arrangement of the rooms highlights the strengths of the collection. Three Rembrandt portraits, including one of a red-haired young man who may be his son, and another of a rosy-cheeked girl leaning on a pedestal, her left hand playing with the gold chain which draws attention to her plunging neckline, are surrounded by the works of his pupils and rivals. Among them is a typically detailed interior by Gerrit Dou (1613–75), a richly coloured hanging in green, red, blue and gold looped back to reveal a woman at a clavichord, a glass of wine at her elbow, a vase of flowers half seen at the casement window. Something of the same intimacy pervades the seventeenth-century Dutch landscapes, the elegiac dewy Cuyps bathed in a soft evening light suggesting the warm glow of Italy rather than the uncertain weather of northern Europe. Meindert Hobbema's *Wooded Landscape with a Watermill* has a similarly dream-like quality, the golden mill-pond as viscous as treacle, but Jacob van Ruisdael's windmills could only be in Holland, their dark, scumbled shapes looming menacingly against a stormy sky. A lovely still life by Jan van Huysum (1682–1749) combines poppies, flax, larkspur, tulips, forget-me-nots, convolvulus and roses in one of those compositions which he completed over several months, adding blooms as they came into flower.

The Dutch landscapes can be compared with Italian scenes produced by contemporary artists who worked in Rome. Dominant among them is a serene late canvas by Claude, a dream-like, blue-green panorama with a round-towered castle crowning a densely-wooded hillside and white sails dotting the distant sea. Murillo, who spent his whole career in Seville, only knew the harshness of southern Spain. He is thought to have posed his own sons for the well-fed urchins who play amidst classical ruins, their rags tattered but picturesque, only their feet noticeably dirty, and his daughter may have been the model for the gypsy-like, Andalusian flower-girl, with a white rose in her dark hair. Also here is one of his devotional works, in which a round-faced peasant madonna holds a realistic little boy who plays with his mother's rosary.

The English portraits form a class of their own, the sitters mostly cool and detached. The beautiful and gifted Linley sisters gaze out of Gainsborough's canvas, the elder, besieged by suitors, soon to elope with the playwright Sheridan while en route to a Continental convent, both girls to die in their prime of tuberculosis. Sarah Siddons, the greatest tragic actress of her age, is

dramatically portrayed by Reynolds, the now crazed surface of his experimental paint in no way detracting from the composition. More memorable than these is Van Dyck's deathbed portrait of Lady Venetia Digby, one of the greatest beauties of her day, who died suddenly in 1633 at the age of 33. She lies as if asleep, her curls beneath a cap, the scattered petals of a rose upon her sheet. Her husband, the adventurer Sir Kenelm Digby, was inconsolable, ever afterwards keeping the portrait close beside him.

Opened in 1817, seven years before the *National Gallery*, Dulwich has the distinction of being Britain's first public gallery. The collection dates back to 1626, when the actor-manager Edward Alleyn bequeathed some 39 pictures to Dulwich College, a combined school and almshouses he had founded some years before. The College, now a leading public school, is today largely housed in a red-brick Italianate building up the road, but the original ranges clustered round a courtyard still stand beside the gallery. Since the seventeenth century, the collection has grown to over 650 paintings, a substantial number of which should have formed the basis of a Polish national gallery. In 1790, Stanislaus Augustus, King of Poland, had commissioned the dealer Noel Desenfans to acquire paintings for a collection to be assembled in Warsaw, and in the uncertainties and troubles of late eighteenth-century Europe the dealer was able to purchase many out-

standing canvases. Sadly for Stanislaus Augustus, his kingdom ceased to exist in 1795 and Desenfans was left holding the paintings. Undeterred, he decided he would create his own gallery, used his wife's fortune to carry on buying, and lined his house with his acquisitions. In 1811, four years after Desenfans's death, his life-long friend, the painter Francis Bourgeois, who had helped him with his purchases, bequeathed the collection to Dulwich.

The gallery, a long, low building in yellow brick, was purpose-built by Sir John Soane. His finely proportioned rooms at the heart of the present gallery are a pleasure to wander in. His severe exterior, ornamented only with recesses, still survives on the west, where the almshouses he incorporated in the design, their windows bricked-up, now form additional hanging space. Projecting from this range, with its roofline suitably ornamented with funeral urns and sarcophagi, is Soane's mausoleum for the bodies of the founders: Desenfans, his wife and Francis Bourgeois. Inside, you come upon this classical tomb unexpectedly, its two chambers bathed in a lurid glow from amber glass. It is almost as if the trio were determined to keep an eye on the custodians of their collection.

Open: Tues–Fri 10–17, Sat 11–17, Sun 14–17 (closed 13–14); admission charge; toilets; guided tours Sat, Sun at 15 and for parties by arrangement

GIPSY MOTH IV

King William Walk, Greenwich, SE10

———— • ————

British Rail to Greenwich (from Charing Cross);
Docklands Light Railway to Island Gardens (see
p. 181); or by boat from Westminster Pier (see
p. 181)

JUST A FEW YARDS away from the *Cutty Sark* lies another concrete-bound sailing boat, the craft in which Francis Chichester became the first man to sail round the globe single-handed. Greenwich is where he landed in July 1967, and it was here that the Queen knighted him, using the same sword with which Elizabeth I knighted Drake after his circumnavigation in 1581. Not content with simply completing the voyage, Sir Francis had set out to equal the average speed of the *Cutty Sark* on its Australian run, racing his boat on every one of the 226 days he was at sea. Even more remarkable, he undertook this voyage at the age of 65, when he was already suffering from cancer. *Gipsy Moth IV* is dwarfed by its neighbour, but seems surprisingly roomy inside, with berths for a crew of five. The interior is shown as Sir Francis had it, with a row of instruments above his bunk, cartons of sprouting cress, and the bottle of champagne that was broached to celebrate his 65th birthday while he was at sea.

Open: Apr–Sept, Mon–Sat 10–18, Sun 12–18 (Oct to 17); admission charge

GIPSY MOTH IV.

THE IMPERIAL WAR MUSEUM

Lambeth Road, SE1

— • —

underground Lambeth North (Bakerloo line)

HE IMPOSING BUILDINGS of what used to be the Bethlem Royal Hospital are the setting for one of London's most imaginative museums, largely devoted to the First and Second World Wars, its style established immediately by the two huge naval guns mounted in front of the porticoed entrance. Directly inside, filling the huge central hall are the most important weapons and vehicles in the collection. These range from a V2 rocket and a heavily armoured Jagdpanzer – a massive German tank destroyer – to a tiny one-man German submarine; the cockpit of one of the Japanese fighter aircraft flown by kamikaze pilots in suicide attacks; and the 14-foot *Tamzine*, a tiny open boat which ferried men from the beaches during the desperate evacuation from Dunkirk. Aeroplanes loom overhead, viewing galleries round the hall bringing visitors face to face with a First World War Sopwith Camel and a Battle of Britain Spitfire. The cockpit of a Halifax bomber relays the crew's conversation as they shoot down their attacker, and there is also the rear fuselage and engine from the Messerschmitt flown by Rudolf Hess when he made his futile 'peace' journey to Scotland in May 1941. Soaring above them all is a German mast periscope, through which the dome of St Paul's looks as if it were just across the road instead of two miles away.

But the horror of it all emerges only in the galleries on the floor below, where exhibits, letters, documentary film and recorded personal reminiscences bring alive the reality of war. An account of the landing at Gallipoli in 1915, the narrator's voice as drained of emotion as if he were reading the weather forecast, describes barges piled high with mutilated bodies, a pier of dead men forming a bridge to the shore and the sea red with blood. The poet John Masefield writes from the trenches on the Western Front in October 1916, graphically conveying the devastated landscape of the once fertile valley of the Somme: 'Imagine ... no single tree left intact ... and that no man can tell where villages were. To say that the ground is "ploughed up" with shells is to talk like a child. The ground ... is gouged and blasted and bedevilled with pox of war, and every step you are on the wreck of war ... with defilement and corpses and hands and feet ... all flung about and dug in and dug out again.' Ordinary, everyday objects take on a quite different significance here. There is a pair of butterfly water-wings used by an escaped prisoner who swam the River Ems, an oil-stained camisole from a survivor of the *Lusitania*, the liner sunk by a German submarine on 7 May 1915 with the loss of 1,195 lives, and a nurse's cap worn by Edith Cavell, the rector's daughter shot by the Germans for helping Allied soldiers escape from Belgium. There is also one of the extraordinary pigeon parachutes, like something out of Monty Python, which were dropped behind enemy lines with messages for the civilian French. The Arab revolt in the Middle East is captured on film, with camel-mounted troops riding into Damascus, while a sand-coloured centipede several inches long and a bloated sun spider convey something of what those fighting in the desert had to face.

The Second World War displays are similarly evocative. Here are the caravans Field-Marshal Montgomery used on his north African campaigns, one of them fitted up with a luxurious bath. A section of the notorious Burma–Siam railway recalls the sixteen thousand prisoners of war who died

in its construction, and there are vivid reminders of the concentration camps: messages written on cigarette paper and smuggled out of Auschwitz, a letter describing Belsen after liberation, and one of the yellow stars of David that all Jews in German-occupied territory had to wear. Here too are examples of wartime propaganda posters and briefings, including a German film showing invading tanks advancing across the lush countryside of Belgium and France and an English leaflet giving instructions on how to deal with US servicemen: 'Be a little more friendly than you normally would.' An egg, a scatter of tea and small lumps of cheese and butter graphically illustrate the reality of food rationing, and a diner at London's Café de Paris describes the night the dancing stopped and she looked up from the bomb-blasted wreckage to see people still sitting on the balcony that ran round the dance floor – but without their heads. As vivid are the changing exhibitions of paintings by war artists, including Stanley Spencer, Paul Nash, Sir John Lavery, Edward Bawden, Edward Ardizzone and Graham Sutherland. Some of the works, such as Paul Nash's evocation of blasted trees and shell-scoured ground, show the horrors of war; others are pastoral and domestic, such as Elsie Hewland's scene in the cloakroom of a nursery school for the children of war workers.

Throughout the museum, the aim is to involve visitors rather than to treat them as observers. The 'Blitz experience', in which visitors are crowded into a realistic brick-lined shelter, demonstrates what it must have been like to endure a heavy air raid, with the ground periodically shaken by falling bombs, the smell of smoke, flashes lighting up the sky and scenes of devastation. In a re-creation of the Flanders trenches, a frantic officer gives orders over a field telephone while a party prepares to go over the top, explosions briefly revealing the shattered landscape ahead of them; and in 'Operation Jericho' you can experience what it was like to be in a bombing raid over France: the simulated cockpit in which you sit judders and lurches realistically as a contemporary film unfolds the view from the pilot's seat, from take-off in England to the location of the target and safe return.

Open: Daily 10–18; admission charge, except Fridays; toilets

KATHLEEN & MAY

St Mary Overy Dock, Cathedral Street, Southwark, SE1

——— • ———

underground London Bridge
(Northern line); or British Rail
to London Bridge (from
Waterloo East)

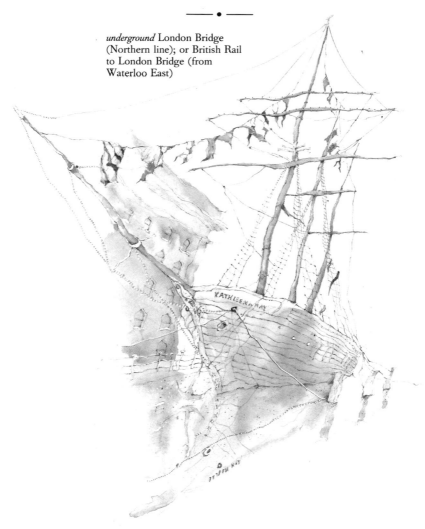

JUST WEST OF Southwark Cathedral, a group of redeveloped warehouses towers over the narrow inlet of St Mary Overy Dock. In this slot of dark water rides the *Kathleen & May*, ropes to the quay suggesting she might take off down river at any moment. Launched in 1900 from a port in North Wales, this three-masted wooden trading schooner is one of the last two survivors of the sailing fleet which worked the waters of Great Britain and Ireland, carrying cargoes of coal, salt, iron, gunpowder, stone, grain and other bulky goods, and putting into small rural ports. Her last cargo under sail alone was carried in 1931, and her working life finally ended in 1960. Her capacious cargo hold is now used for an exhibition on the coastal trade, but on deck and in the quarters for the crew there is a flavour of a vanished way of life. Four seamen lived and slept in the cramped fo'c'sle, with its built-in bunks, and meals were prepared on the coal-burning stove in the galley. Aft is a tiny panelled saloon, warmed by an open fire, for the master and mate. Unlike the *Cutty Sark*, the *Kathleen & May* still has the smell of a boat, an indefinable aroma linking it to the sea.

Open: Mid Feb–end Nov, daily 10–17; end Nov–mid Feb, daily 11–16; admission charge

LONDON TRANSPORT MUSEUM

Covent Garden, WC2

—— • ——

underground Covent Garden (Piccadilly line)

COVENT GARDEN'S FORMER flower market of 1871–2, with its graceful cast-iron columns and glazed roof, now looks like a rather unusual transport depot, with buses, trams and underground rolling stock marshalled in neat rows. Until 1800, when no part of the city was more than half an hour's walk from the river, London's main traffic artery was the Thames, but as its population increased in the nineteenth century, so did the demand for land-based public transport. Using an imaginatively wide range of material, from recordings of personal accounts to early posters, tickets and documentary films, this museum covers the development of the present sophisticated interlinked system over almost two hundred years.

A green and yellow 'knifeboard' horse-drawn bus of c.1875, on which passengers on the upper deck sat back to back, is complete with top-hatted driver, a blanket over his knees to keep out the cold. Another gaily painted vehicle is a replica of the first omnibus to operate in London, introduced by George Shillibeer from Paris in the 1820s, its interior furnished with long padded seats and ruched curtains. But the predominant colour is London Transport red, used for the Edwardian electric trams, 1930s trolleybuses and today's very familiar

double-deckers. The first underground railway in the world opened in London on 10 January 1863, the carriages pulled by steam locomotives like the gleaming example on display, specially adapted to reduce the build-up of steam and smoke in tunnels. Here too is one of the original 'padded cell' carriages, well upholstered but effectively windowless.

Working models illustrate many aspects of transport technology, and realistic simulations include a journey in a tube-driver's cab, during which ghostly lights rushing towards you transform themselves into stations and appropriate sound effects suggest passengers getting on and off. Some of the most fascinating material relates to London in the Blitz, when underground platforms became air-raid shelters and temporary canteens were served by a food train which stopped for just twenty seconds at every station. A Second World War poster exhorts: 'To speed up service, please provide your own cups.' All shelterers had to obtain a ticket, either a period reservation or for one night only. Most sophisticated of all is the diagrammatic underground map designed by the ingenious Harry Beck in 1933, a composition in straight lines and diagonals which replaced spaghetti-like confusion.

Open: Daily, 10–18; admission charge; toilets

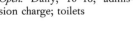
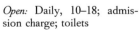

THE MUSEUM OF LONDON

London Wall, EC2

———— • ————

underground Barbican (Circle and Metropolitan lines), Moorgate (Circle, Northern and Metropolitan lines) and St Paul's (Central line)

HOUSED IN A 1970's building in the south-west corner of the Barbican complex, the Museum of London is reached along some of the high-level concrete walkways which criss-cross one of the City's most controversial post-war developments. It is most easily approached up the flight of steps from Aldersgate, where a streak of colour like the thread which led Theseus out of the Minotaur's labyrinth guides visitors to the museum entrance on a covered concourse above street level. Unlikely as it may seem, this stark triangular piazza marks the place where, in 1738, John Wesley, the founder of Methodism, had the profound religious experience which changed his life, an event now commemorated by the huge metal flame which stands here.

The impressive museum, its purpose-built galleries arranged around a central court, presents a picture of London from prehistoric to modern times. Detailed models, reconstructions of historic interiors, paintings, costumes and a huge range of artefacts, from primitive stone axes to a fourteenth-century trumpet and a chess board with elegant ivory pieces which once belonged to Samuel Pepys, combine to build up a vivid picture of London life through the centuries and of the high standards of craftsmanship which have characterized the city. Many of the earlier exhibits were recovered from the Thames, or unearthed during redevelopment.

Necklaces, carved reliefs and gleaming red tableware from Roman times indicate a thriving, cosmopolitan city, importing amber from the Baltic, marble from Turkey, Italy and Greece, glass from Germany and pottery from Spain and France. Reconstructions of comfortable Roman interiors from the heyday of the Empire are set either side of an intricate, geometric mosaic pavement, while the uncertainties of the fourth century (see p. 10) are illustrated by a hoard of deliberately buried sculpture, including an exquisitely carved head with not a curl out of place representing Serapis, the Egyptian god of the underworld. Then, as now, shirkers were not popular. A few lines roughly scratched on a clay tablet record that 'for the last fortnight Australis has been wandering off on his own every day'. A group of battle-axes recovered from the north end of London Bridge were probably lost in the desperate attempt to stop the advance of later invaders, the ruthless Viking army which put Canute on the English throne.

In the medieval section, a large window looks out on to a surviving section of the old city wall, complete with two projecting, semicircular bastions, almost as if you could step, like Alice, into another world. A delightful weigh-beam of 1572 ornamented with dragons and a lizard may have been provided for merchants using Thomas Gresham's new *Royal Exchange*, and a set of beechwood mats once carried the sticky desserts the Tudors delighted in – quince cheese, marchpane and crystallized fruit. Brilliantly coloured, tin-glazed earthenware and exquisite glass, such as the bulbous Parr Pot or the elegant Scudamore cider glass, show the increasing skill of home-based industry. There is another hoard in this section, too, a collection of Elizabethan jewellery found by workmen under the floor of a cellar in Cheapside during redevelopment in 1912. The treasure was acquired for the then infant London Museum by their scout, George Lawrence, who went round the pubs where the labourers drank and persuaded them, with

small financial inducements, to part with their finds. When the news broke, the museum was accused of acquiring treasure trove by sharp practice, and it was forced to give up part of the hoard to the *Victoria and Albert*, and another third to the Guildhall Museum. Happily, as the latter amalgamated with the London Museum to form the basis of the present collection, two-thirds of the hoard are now reunited. In among the stones and cameos are fossil fish teeth, or toadstones, which the Elizabethans believed protected them from illness.

Not far away is a highly realistic re-creation of the Great Fire of 1666 (see p. 13), in which scudding clouds indicate the strong wind fanning a distant glow and the growing conflagration gradually lights up the Gothic silhouette of old St Paul's Cathedral and a panorama of half-timbered houses. Pepys's diary provides the commentary, and sound-effects suggest collapsing timbers and crackling flames.

The range of the exhibits is enormous. There are the duelling pistols used by Colonel Lennox and Frederick, Duke of York, on Wimbledon Common in 1789, a recipe book of 1767, with a section devoted to 'little family suppers of four things', an ornate piano made for the Great Exhibition of 1851, a reconstruction of a Victorian pub, with a game of dominoes in progress, and a recreated nineteenth-century barbershop with luxurious marble fittings and personal mugs for regular customers. There are even the brown and black Art Deco lifts which graced Selfridges department store in the 1920s.

Of all the displays, the most magnificent is the Lord Mayor's coach, its ornate golden body set on huge red wheels and decorated with painted panels reflected in a glassy pool which keeps the woodwork moist. Built in 1757, this rococo fantasy is still wheeled out every year to form the centre-piece of the Lord Mayor's Show (see p. 180).

Open: Tue–Sat 10–18, Sun 14–18; admission free; toilets

MUSEUM OF MANKIND

6 Burlington Gardens, W1

———•———

underground Green Park (Jubilee, Piccadilly and
Victoria lines), Piccadilly Circus (Bakerloo and
Piccadilly lines)

THERE IS A deeply sonorous ring to this offshoot of the *British Museum*, as if its curators are prepared for some cataclysmic disaster that will overtake us all. Sadly, the lofty rooms already feel as if all human life has left the Earth, but if you can overcome the lethargy that washes over you when you step through the doors, it is worth persevering. The museum has space to show only a fraction of its huge ethnographic collections, which are rotated in changing thematic displays, but a couple of galleries hold permanent exhibitions which illustrate the range of what is held here and the greatest treasures. All natural materials, from fish scales and porcupine quills to bark and bamboo, seem to have been pressed into service. A glittering necklace from Melanesia has been created out of beetle legs; and a silvery, fragile fedora from Botswana is made of spider's web stretched over a cane frame, like a hat for a tree man. There are mocassins from North America, boots of leather, felt and cotton from Tibet, and a charming bamboo and vegetable fibre basket from the Philippines, used to catch grasshoppers. More sinister are the shrunken heads from Ecuador, or the menacing head-taker's basket from the Naga people of Assam, its exterior decorated with a row of miniature skulls.

The treasures, too, inspire mixed feelings. Some, such as a cascade of coral beads from Benin, beautiful filigree pendants studded with turquoise and agate from Turkestan, or a silvery pearl shell necklace from Kiribati, are purely ornamental pieces. Others strike a chill. A human skull decorated with a mosaic of turquoise, lignite, shell and iron pyrite stares out of a display of Aztec pieces from Mexico, and beside it is the ornamental knife used to pluck the hearts from living victims in sacrifices to the sun.

Open: Mon–Sat 10–17, Sun 14.30–18; admission free; toilets

MUSEUM OF THE MOVING IMAGE

South Bank, Waterloo, SE1

———— • ————

underground Waterloo (Bakerloo and Northern lines)

A VERY RECENT ADDITION to the South Bank Arts Centre on the south side of Waterloo Bridge, this museum, known as MOMI for short, is a totally absorbing exploration of the history of the moving image, offering an enormous range of imaginatively presented material and numerous opportunities for visitor participation.

The arrangement is chronological, leading visitors from early optical amusements such as Chinese shadow puppets, the camera obscura and the zoetrope, which produces the illusion of motion, to the most sophisticated film and television productions. Sometimes the focus is on the technology, sometimes on the larger-than-life characters who seem always to have been associated with this industry, and sometimes on film and its forerunners as art forms, or as instruments of propaganda. Appropriate settings add to the fun, extracts from the documentary films sparked off by the Russian Revolution, for example, being presented in a replica of a contemporary railway carriage, the interior fitted out with hard wooden benches and the projectionist dressed as a Revolutionary. Similarly, First World War propaganda footage is seen in a re-creation of a sandbagged dug-out. With over ninety video screens, there are literally hundreds of film extracts to be seen, and a full-scale Odeon cinema complete with gleaming chromium doors offers a non-stop series of classics, the silent films authentically accompanied by live piano music.

Extracts from Chaplin's first films, made in 1914–17, are part of a corner devoted to this comic genius. The memorabilia displayed here include not only his familiar cane and hat but also reminders of his poverty-stricken childhood: records from the Hanwell Poor Law School for 1896, when Chaplin would have been seven, list a very rare, two-hour visit from his mother. Charlie's parents separated when he was a year old and his mother, who was unable to support him, was forced to put both him and his half-brother Sydney into an orphanage.

Another corner of the museum illustrates the Hollywood star system, and the restrictions covering conduct both on and off the screen which were to become enshrined in the notorious Hays Code of 1930. Gable's 'Frankly, my dear, I don't give a damn' in *Gone with the Wind* (1939) cost producer David O. Selznick a $5,000 fine, and stars were forced to sign contracts guaranteeing good behaviour. One such document, binding John Gilbert to Metro pictures in 1924, declares: 'The artist agrees to conduct himself with due regard to public conventions and morals . . .'. It also required Gilbert to provide his own wardrobe.

The star-struck can sit in a make-up booth or be interviewed by Barry Norman, but any illusions will be destroyed in the special effects department. Here, you can see how easy it is to soar effortlessly over the Thames on film, and the fearsome King Kong is revealed as an 18-inch high model, with rubber muscles and a coat of rabbit fur.

One word of warning. There is a great deal to see at MOMI, and it is very easy to get bogged down in the earlier exhibits and not to allow yourself enough time to enjoy what comes later. Pacing a visit is essential, and recurring wall charts which show you how far you have got have been designed to help you do precisely that.

Open: Tue–Sat 10–20, Sun and Bank Hols 10–20 Jun–Sep (10–18 Oct–May); admission charge; toilets

THE NATIONAL GALLERY

Trafalgar Square, WC2

———— • ————

underground Charing Cross (Bakerloo, Jubilee and
Northern lines), Leicester Square (Piccadilly and
Northern lines)

THIS IS ONE OF THE world's greatest galleries, with a wide-ranging collection that illustrates the history of western painting from c.1300 to the end of the nineteenth century, from icon-like altarpieces by Duccio and Giovanni di Paolo to the pointillist techniques of Seurat and a *Jugendstil* portrait by Gustav Klimt. Here you can see Uccello and Botticelli, Jan van Eyck, Brueghel and Holbein, Leonardo, Michelangelo and Raphael, Titian, Tintoretto and Veronese, over twenty Rembrandts, works by Rubens and Van Dyck, El Greco and Velázquez, Claude and Poussin, Venetian scenes by Canaletto and Guardi and landscapes by Constable and Turner. There is also a representative cross-section of French Impressionists, although what is here does

not compare with the breadth of coverage in the *Courtauld*, and in January 1991 the range was temporarily extended by a five-year loan of paintings, sketches, drawings and sculptures by Cézanne, Seurat, Van Gogh, Picasso, Braque and Miró from the Berggruen collection of modern art. There are forty works by Picasso alone, illustrating most of the important phases in the artist's career.

The particular strength of the gallery is that it shows the great figures in European art at their best. Moreover, except where works have been removed for cleaning and conservation, the entire collection of over two thousand pictures is permanently on display, with no masterpieces stacked in inaccessible basements or only viewable by special arrangement. In general, if you

know a painting is in the National Gallery, you can expect to be able to see it.

Until recently, regular visitors could also thread their way unerringly through the maze of rooms to the place where they knew their target was hanging. But the National Gallery is now in the throes of a revolution. In conjunction with the opening of the new Sainsbury wing, the traditional nineteenth-century hang by which paintings were grouped by nationality is being replaced by a chronological arrangement. The rethink is both pointing up national traits, as in the sequence of assured 18th-century British portraits, or the small rooms full of Dutch interiors and scenes from daily life, and hinting at the existence of a general European language, particularly evident in the group of haughty court portraits by painters such as Velázquez, Van Dyck and del Mazo.

The Sainsbury wing itself is hung with the earliest works in the collection, dating from 1260 to the first years of the Italian Renaissance. Walking through the cool, grey-walled, top-lit galleries is like visiting a rather well-endowed Roman basilica, with carefully contrived vistas framed by round-headed arches focused on glowing altarpieces and the glimpses of crucifixions, baptisms, annunciations and other suitably devotional subjects on every side. Among the stylised icon-like images, glinting with gold leaf, and the exercises in perspective, such as Crivelli's *Annunciation*, with its sharply receding walls, are the earliest naturalistic works, such as Cima da Conegliano's *Christ Crowned with Thorns*, the red-rimmed eyes intense with suffering.

The galleries are at the top of the new wing, reached from the street by way of a vast processional granite staircase walled in glass which fills the whole east side of the building. On the floor below is the ultimate adult toy, a computer system offering a visual encyclopedia of the whole collection. Here, using easily-operated terminals, visitors can explore the gallery's holdings, pursuing a favourite artist or works of a particular period, or looking at the National's collection of still-lifes. The system will even print out a plan to show you where the paintings you want to see are located.

For those who are less certain of their interests, the National Gallery produces a useful guide, suggesting a few great paintings which should not be missed. This will point you to such treasures as the Wilton Diptych of c.1395, with Richard II in a gorgeous red and gold robe kneeling to the Virgin Mary, the wings of her attendant angels like a row of banners behind her, or Jan van Eyck's *Arnolfini Marriage*, in which the absorbed couple, she in a pea-green dress, he sinister in a vast black hat, make their vows in a comfortable merchant's house in Bruges, a glimpse of a garden through the window beyond them. Also highlighted are the Leonardo *Cartoon* of c.1506–8, executed in black and white chalk on eight sheets of paper; a late self-portrait by Rembrandt, painted in the year he died; Holbein's *The Ambassadors*, his two wealthy young men standing on a section of the mosaic pavement which can still be seen in *Westminster Abbey*, their assured figures surrounded by objects alluding to death and the relentless march of time; and the languorous *Rokeby Venus*, the only one of Velázquez's four nudes to survive, the long sensuous back showing no signs of the damage inflicted by a suffragette in 1914. And you will take in a Vermeer, a Seurat, a Constable and Van Dyck's vast equestrian portrait of Charles I, this king who was the greatest art patron of all English monarchs now appropriately placed in the midst of a collection which he would have delighted in.

But only the most determined could hurry through without pausing on the way. Here is Raphael's portrait of the aged Pope Julius II, the man who commissioned the ceiling of the Sistine Chapel from Michelangelo, the white beard he grew to mourn the loss of Bologna as part of the papal dominions dating the canvas very exactly to 1511–12. There is also an unfinished *Entombment* by his protégé, in which the tensions in the grouped figures straining to support Christ's body suggest that Michelangelo might almost have had a sculpture in mind, and there is Bronzino's arresting *Allegory* of the 1540s, with its naked figures of Venus and Cupid. Too powerful for overwrought sensibilities in Victorian times, these marble-like nudes were discreetly touched up with drapery and strategically placed foliage.

What would these men have made of Cézanne's lumpish bathers, his distorted figures in a landscape inspired by Renaissance themes showing none of their skill in painting the human form, or of Monet's *Water Lilies*, a wash of colour with crimson splashes in a shimmering formless pool? A much earlier work, painted when Monet fled to London to escape the Prussian war of 1870, is his shadowy *The Thames below Westminster*, with the Houses of Parliament seen through the misty greyness of an early morning.

The Dutch and Flemish masters are crowned by a series of Rembrandt portraits, those of his young wife Saskia, and of Hendrickje Stoffels, with whom Rembrandt lived after Saskia's early death, contrasting with several disturbing canvases of the very old, their eyes assessing, even judgmental. Similarly individual is a row of late Turners, a series of atmospheric, indeterminate images dominated by *The Fighting Téméraire*, painted when the 98-gun warship which had seen service at Trafalgar was being towed to Rotherhithe to be broken up. The great ship looms ghostlike above the glassy water, the only reality the hard black shape of the tug against her bows. A couple of earlier works are juxtaposed with canvases by Claude, whom Turner admired tremendously, an arrangement which allows direct comparison of the two artists' use of light and perspective, Claude's sense of enormous distance being conveyed by ever tinier buildings and trees.

Britain's national collection dates only from 1824, when the connoisseur Sir George Beaumont cunningly offered to bequeath his own collection to the nation provided the government acquired the 38 masterpieces that had belonged to the banker John Julius Angerstein. The canvases, including two Rembrandts, four Claudes, and works by Canaletto, Raphael, Rubens and Van Dyck, were housed in Angerstein's house in Pall Mall until

William Wilkins's purpose-built gallery, with a long classical frontage on Trafalgar Square, opened in 1838. Since then, both the collection and the building have expanded enormously, the former benefiting particularly from the inspired directorship of Sir Charles Eastlake, who spent a decade scouring Italy for masterpieces until his death at Pisa in 1865. Unlike the Louvre or the Prado, the National Gallery has not had an expropriated royal collection to build on, but many of the paintings which came its way in the early years were the fruits of European revolutions, taken from the palaces of dispossessed French and Italian aristocrats.

Open: Mon–Sat 10–18, Sun 14–18; admission free; toilets; guided tours Mon–Sat

The National Maritime Museum

Romney Road, Greenwich, SE10

— • —

British Rail to Greenwich or Maze Hill (from
Charing Cross); Docklands Light Railway to
Island Gardens (see p. 181); or by boat from
Westminster Pier (see p. 181)

OF ALL THE GREAT engagements which have proved to be crucial in the history of Great Britain, the victories of Trafalgar and Waterloo live on most strongly in the public imagination, their heroes transported from history into legend. While the ghost of the Duke of Wellington still hovers over *Apsley House*, his mansion at the west end of Piccadilly, Horatio Nelson is the presiding spirit at the Maritime Museum. It is impossible to define the magic which irresistibly attracts people to the displays which honour England's most famous admiral, a short man who had lost an eye and an arm, suffered terribly from seasickness, and who fell passionately in love with a lady with a somewhat shady reputation. One of Romney's many paintings of Emma Hamilton stands out in a row of admirals' portraits, her lovely face set off by a broad-brimmed hat. Nearby is the uniform Nelson was wearing when he was fatally wounded at Trafalgar in 1805, felled by a musket shot from a sniper on the French ship *Redoubtable*. The bullet hole in the shoulder of his coat is clearly visible and there are bloodstains on his breeches. A lock of hair cut off by the faithful Captain Hardy and delivered to Emma is one of many other relics and mementoes, among them the only known letter in which Nelson refers to his wounds: 'Eye in Corsica, Belly off Cape St Vincent, Arm at Tenerife, Head in Egypt – I ought to be thankful that I am what I am.'

Turner's huge canvas of Trafalgar, commissioned by George IV in 1824, shows the *Victory* in a confusion of billowing sails, the pale shadows of other ships behind her receding into the distance like a fleet of ghosts. This atmospheric painting is part of the world's largest collection of marine pictures, which includes oils and drawings by the Van de Veldes, father and son, who recorded engagements with the Dutch in the seventeenth century; portraits by Sir Peter Lely, Gainsborough and Reynolds; and battle scenes from the American War of Independence by Nicholas Pocock. One of the greatest naval engagements in history is commemorated in a richly-coloured canvas of the Battle of Lepanto, 1571, when the combined navies of Spain, Venice and the Papacy smashed the Turkish fleet; this was the last major battle to be fought with oared galleys, and the boats with their banks of red oars look like brilliantly-coloured beetles skating over the water. Here too is the work of artists who took part in exploratory expeditions, among them William Hodges' dream-like paintings of Tahiti, executed on Captain Cook's second voyage of 1772–5.

These paintings and the Nelson exhibits are shown in the galleries which chart voyages of discovery and Britain's rise as a great commercial and naval nation. Here too are cases of exquisite model ships, many of them produced for the Admiralty to show the design of a new man-of-war. Most were made at the same time as the boats they represent, from the wooden *St Michael* of 1669, with its intricately decorated poop, to the *SS Great Britain* of 1843, the first major vessel to be built of iron, designed by Isambard Kingdom Brunel. Full-sized boats are housed in the Neptune Hall, a barrel-roofed area dominated by the 106-foot steam paddle-tug *Reliant*, built in 1907, its huge red paddle-wheels now turning in air. Visitors can walk through the boat and inspect the huge multi-tubular boilers and the spartan crew accommodation, a far cry from the re-creation of a first-class cabin on the *Empress of Canada* in 1960.

In the theatrically lit Barge House next door is the most memorable of the museum's exhibits, the glittering gold and red barge produced in 1732 for George II's eldest son Prince Frederick, whose wife Augusta started the botanic garden at Kew (see p. 147). Designed by William Kent, this barge would look more at home on the Grand Canal in Venice than on the Thames. A golden dolphin stretches forward from the prow; the gilded cabin, like a state coach with its wheels removed, undulates with dolphins and seashells, and even the keel has a dolphin painted on it, presumably to entertain the fishes. Only 6½ feet in width, the barge is 63 feet long, with 24 red oars laid out in a neat row for the twelve oarsmen. This exotic fantasy was last used in 1849, when Prince Albert was taken by water to open the Coal Exchange in the City.

The buildings of the National Maritime Museum lie either side of Inigo Jones's *Queen's House*, part of an architectural complex which also includes the *Old Royal Observatory* and the Royal Naval College (see p. 22). Designed in the nineteenth century to accommodate a school for naval children, long classical wings by Daniel Alexander set off Inigo Jones's masterpiece, to which they are connected by colonnades built in 1807 to commemorate Trafalgar. The school moved to Suffolk in 1933 and the museum was established a year later, largely through the generosity of the millionaire Sir James Caird. The permanent exhibitions are now housed in the larger, west wing, with its additions of 1862 by Philip Hardwick, and the east wing is devoted to temporary displays and the education centre. The museum is large, and some of the galleries will only absorb those who have a major interest in what they show. The Nelson relics, Barge House and Neptune Hall are particularly enjoyable, and the museum hands out a plan which shows the location of outstanding items in other galleries.

Open: Mon–Sat, 10–18, Sun 14–18; admission charge; toilets

NATIONAL PORTRAIT GALLERY

St Martin's Place, WC2

———— • ————

underground Charing Cross (Bakerloo, Jubilee and
Northern lines)

GREAT ART IS NOT important here. While there are portraits by masters such as Holbein, Hilliard, Rubens, Reynolds and Lawrence, the primary aim of the gallery is to record outstanding figures in the life of the nation. The focus is on the sitter, rather than on the hand wielding the paintbrush. Six hundred years of British history are seen in the faces of those who made it, some of them lined and anxious, like the hunchbacked Richard III, murderer of the Princes in the Tower, who nervously fingers his rings; some tired old men, like Queen Victoria's favourite, Disraeli; some, like Winston Churchill in Walter Sickert's sketch of 1927, looking out at the world with supreme confidence. The gallery is above all about human personality, the set of a mouth or the tilt of a head as illuminating as pages of biography. Oil paintings predominate, but there are also drawings, miniatures, busts, photographs and caricatures, some of the latter, such as Pellegrini's sensual vision of Oscar Wilde, particularly revealing.

Displayed on three floors in an L-shaped building wrapped round the back of the *National Gallery* – 'like the bustle of a woman's dress,' as Henry James remarked – the portraits are arranged in a chronological sequence, with rooms devised to illustrate specific periods and themes, such as the early Stuarts and the Civil War, the arts in the eighteenth century, the struggle for America, or the early Victorians. The spread of those included becomes wider through the centuries. The earliest canvases, dating from the fourteenth and fifteenth centuries, are almost exclusively of royalty and aristocracy, but gradually other faces begin to creep in, and by the nineteenth century all areas of life are represented.

The medieval monarchs are stylized and formal, their portraits strongly reminiscent of poses in religious art. The earliest painting from the life is Michel Sittow's portrait of Henry VII of 1505, the king like an avaricious money-lender, his long fingers clutching the frame. The founder of the Tudor dynasty appears again in Holbein's preparatory drawing for a painting in Whitehall Palace (see p. 18), his thin willowy figure half masked by the bull-like form of his son Henry VIII, massively broad-shouldered, his eyes mere slits in his fleshy face. And I wonder how the ageing Elizabeth I, 44 years on the throne, her withered skin plastered with white paint and only her jewel-encrusted dresses still glorious, regarded the coronation portrait executed when she was in her mid twenties, luxuriant red-gold hair cascading down her back, the face that of a girl who has not yet turned into a queen. These regal Tudors would never have been portrayed in the relaxed pose of Charles II, lolling in a chair, his half-turned face pouchy from the pursuit of pleasure. Beside him hang likenesses of

both Nell Gwyn and Catherine of Braganza, Nell in a plunging shift, his wife sweet-faced above a high lace collar.

Royal figures always seem familiar, their images half remembered. Those who are representative of their age are often more arresting – a well-known name suddenly brought to life. Here is the only portrait of Shakespeare which can claim to be a likeness, a golden ring glistening in his ear. The diarist Samuel Pepys frowns out at us, perhaps because, as he himself records, 'I sit to have it [the portrait] full of shadows and do almost break my neck looking over my shoulders to make the posture ...' Here too is the aged philosopher Thomas Hobbes, painted c.1669–70 when he was

82, his hair snow white, his blue eyes still alert and shrewd, and a pugnacious self-portrait of William Hogarth, his short frame concentrated on the canvas he is working on, a cap perched on the back of his head. Emma, Lady Hamilton, in one of Romney's many portraits, incongruously appears in the 'Britain at War' room so that she can hang next to Lord Nelson. Other telling conjunctions include Boswell and Johnson in portraits by Reynolds, but far more revealing is James Barry's rough sketch of the lexicographer, his vulnerability and melancholia clear in his face. Boswell looks self-satisfied, as well he might; had he not attached himself to Johnson, he would never have been as well known as he is. Reynolds himself appears in a self-portrait of 1772–3, painted shortly after his return from Rome, and he was also responsible for a devilish likeness of Laurence Sterne, author of *Tristram Shandy*, who looks as if he is cooking up another novel to shock his contemporaries. William Blake, on the other hand, has been caught by Thomas Phillips as if receiving a vision, the rapt expression on his face apparently achieved by persuading him to talk about the Archangel Gabriel.

Towards the end of the eighteenth century, men of science and industry become increasingly prominent. Handsome Michael Faraday, discoverer of electricity, leans casually on one arm, Stephenson broods over a drawing of a beam engine, and Charles Darwin appears as a God-like figure with a long white beard. Best of all is a photograph of 1857 showing Isambard Kingdom Brunel standing jauntily in front of the huge launching chains of his steamship *Great Eastern*, the links like a bizarre sculpture behind him, his crumpled top-hatted figure smoking a cigar like a bookie at the races. Exploration and empire are also represented: a drawing by Augustus John captures T. E. Lawrence in Arab dress; a photograph of Scott shows him at base camp before he set out on his tragic journey to the South Pole; and a portrait of the explorer Sir Richard Burton by Frederic Leighton reveals the long scar on his right cheek, the legacy of an undignified skirmish in Africa.

Some pieces, crude in themselves, are among the gallery's most treasured possessions. A tiny drawing of Jane Austen by her sister Cassandra, the alert face with curls escaping from beneath a cap set on a shadowy body, is the only authentic portrait of one of Britain's greatest novelists. And a rough, cracked oil painting showing three girls with distant eyes is Patrick Branwell Brontë's portrait of his talented sisters Charlotte, Emily and Anne, a picture which lay forgotten, folded up on top of a cupboard. The arts and literature in the nineteenth century spawned many other interesting works, among them G. F. Watts's charming study of his seventeen-year-old wife Ellen Terry, framed by red camellias, and John Singer Sargent's watchful *Henry James*. J. E. Blanche's *Aubrey*

Beardsley wears a grey suit set off by a pink carnation, a cane in his gloved hand; Robert Louis Stevenson looks unkempt, long hair over his collar; Keats sits in the garden room at what is now *Keats House* in Hampstead, his nose buried in a book. Whistler, whose sublime *nocturnes* are a highlight of the *Tate Gallery*, is portrayed by Walter Greaves as a debauched rake with top hat and eye glass.

Significantly, the optimism and enterprise of the nineteenth century spawned the National Portrait Gallery itself, which was seen as a source of inspiration and as an example for future generations. Founded in 1856 as a result of the initiative of the 5th Earl of Stanhope, for many years it had no satisfactory home, opening in the present imposing Italianate palazzo only in 1896. In its earlier days, apart from the ruling sovereign and his or her consort, no living person could be represented, but this rule has now been modified. As a result, the section devoted to twentieth-century personalities blurs the distinction between past and present, and the reputations of some of the figures portrayed here are perhaps destined to die with them. These rooms are also the most 'showy', with many photographs and drawings seen on revolving displays. Some portraits, such as an egg tempera of Dirk Bogarde or a chalk drawing of Kathleen Ferrier, are conventional in style, others wildly individual. Maggi Hambling's painting of the chemist and crystallographer Dorothy Hodgkin, for example, shows a figure with four arms, frenetic activity in every inch of the canvas. Most controversial are the recent portraits of the royal family, Annigoni's stern and formally posed monarch of 1969, the Queen's body formless beneath an enveloping scarlet cloak, contrasting with Bryan Organ's relaxed images of the Prince and Princess of Wales, he in his polo clothes, she in casual trousers and an open-necked shirt, or with Alison Watt's view of the Queen Mother, teacup at her elbow.

Open: Mon–Fri 10–17, Sat 10–18, Sun 14–18; admission free; toilets

THE NATURAL HISTORY MUSEUM

Cromwell Road, SW7

———— • ————

underground South Kensington (Circle, District and
Piccadilly lines)

THE NATURAL HISTORY MUSEUM shows us for what we are, just one species in a world of enormous diversity and complexity. And one where once successful creatures can disappear, leaving nothing but the odd pile of bones and an occasional fossilized footprint. Dominating the cathedral-like entrance hall is the 85-foot skeleton of the dinosaur *Diplodocus*, one of the largest land animals that ever lived, his tiny head on its giraffe neck peering at visitors over the ticket desk. Like the even more fearsome *Tyrannosaurus rex*, whose savage eyes and flesh-ripping teeth seem to have been designed for science fiction, these creatures who once stalked the Earth in their thousands vanished 60 million years ago.

The museum has come a long way since it opened on this site on 18 April 1881. Although some galleries are conventionally arranged, with labelled specimens in glass cases, no one coming here now could leave with 'nothing but sore feet, a bad headache and a general idea that the animal kingdom is a mighty maze'. The aim is always to put creatures in context, showing how they have evolved and how they interact with each other and their environment. The museum is fun, its new displays designed to entertain as well as inform. It is also a visual treat with some exhibits of extraordinary beauty, such as the tiny humming-birds and brilliantly plumaged birds of paradise, and others involving mind-bending leaps of scale.

A life-size model of a blue whale hangs over one of the mammal galleries like a vast barrage balloon. This extraordinary animal, with eyes so far apart on either side of its enormous carcase that it must surely have double vision, is now desperately rare: a population of 200,000 in 1900 has been reduced to a few thousand in Antarctic waters. Other creatures are clustered round it as if seeking the protection of its bulk, some, such as the rhino, also threatened. A video show of a hippo moving underwater, graceful and at home; another dolphins at play; and there are haunting recordings of whale calls – eerie, unmistakable cries which can carry for distances of up to 160 miles.

The bird galleries are more conventional, with perfect specimens mounted in decorative groups. An albino robin and blackbird look as if they have taken on winter plumage; an ostrich reclines in a puff of feathers; the flightless dodo and the American carrier pigeon gaze sadly at visitors, as if they know they are extinct. British birds cluster in a pavilion at one end, and recordings of their songs enliven realistic re-creations of habitats such as a sea-cliff, a corner of deciduous woodland, or a stretch of river bank. Nearby, jewel-like tropical moths and butterflies form colourful abstract paintings, the mounted specimens enriched by displays on natural camouflage and migration. Frail creatures which come vast distances to Britain include the Camberwell Beauty, originating in Scandinavia, and the Clouded Yellow butterfly from the southern Mediterranean. Much more popular is the new Creepy Crawlies exhibition, an imaginative and absorbing glimpse into the world of insects and other arthropods. Life-cycle videos show a chrysalis transformed into a Swallowtail butterfly, its wings gradually unfolding in a graceful ballet, and the curious metamorphosis of a ladybird. A replica kitchen is teaming with the creatures which share our homes, and a huge termite mound with a nest deep underground illustrates insect communities. Upstairs, a statue of Darwin presides over a

gallery devoted to evolution and the theory of natural selection. Here too are cases of rocks and minerals, a link with the Geological Museum that is now part of the same complex.

Where the Natural History Museum is concerned with life on Earth, the Geological Museum covers the Earth itself, how it was formed and the treasures it contains. Behind a replica of a cliff-like rockface in Scotland, video displays in a darkened gallery introduce the wonders of the universe and the birth of the Solar System. Here are pieces of the oldest rocks on earth, formed 3,800 million years ago, and a transparent pyramid encasing a fragment of Moon rock, its white, crystalline interior covered by a jet black crust. A volcano erupts dramatically on film, ejecting firework-like fountains of lava and red and yellow rivers

which swallow all in their path. Visitors can even experience a simulated earthquake. To the accompaniment of a growing roar, which gradually drowns the sound of children's voices, the earth moves – but only slightly.

Nearby are cases of gemstones, a jeweller's delight of opals, jade, rubies and emeralds and other decorative materials, the stones unreal in their richness and profusion. Prized objects include a large veined vase of the now exhausted Derbyshire Blue John, and the Murchison snuff box which was given to Tsar Alexander II in 1867, the royal portrait on its lid framed with diamonds. More immediate is the exhibition devoted to oil and gas in the North Sea, appropriately housed in a mock-up of an oil platform, and the displays showing how different minerals are used in the home.

With so much to see, few visitors pause by the mineral curiosities that once belonged to Sir Hans Sloane, part of the wide-ranging collection which this learned physician bequeathed to the nation in 1753 and which became the basis of the *British Museum*. His 10,000 or so animal specimens, and 334 volumes of pressed plants, were soon swollen by material brought back by explorers, such as the meticulously-detailed drawings of plants and animals by Sydney Parkinson, who had sailed round the world with Captain Cook in 1768. The natural history exhibits remained with the rest in Bloomsbury for over a hundred years, but in the nineteenth century it became increasingly clear that they needed a home of their own. Alfred Waterhouse's building, begun in 1873 and first opened in 1881, is a triumph: its Romanesque arches, the vast cathedral-like central hall with an arched barrel roof and the ornate decoration all seem entirely appropriate as a setting for the works of the creator. The massive 675-foot frontage on the Cromwell Road is a wall of buff and blue-grey terracotta, part medieval monastery, part French château, with 192-foot spired towers flanking the deeply recessed arch of the central doorway. The façade is studded with terracotta animals, those on the left species which still exist, those on the right creatures which are extinct; sadly, one or two should now be creeping slowly across the building. Inside, the detail is just as fine, with golden fruit glinting on the stylized panels of foliage on the ceiling of the hall, and a tribe of little monkeys clambering up the terracotta pillars encasing the steel frame. A grand staircase leads visitors to the upper galleries, and another is carried over the hall on a Venetian bridge. Man, 'the greatest beast of all', once adorned the central gable of the building, but he has been removed.

Open: Mon–Sat 10–18, Sun 13–18; admission charge, but free 16.30–18 (17–18 Sat, Sun and Bank Hols); toilets

The Old Royal Observatory

Greenwich Park, SE10

———— • ————

British Rail to Greenwich or Maze Hill (from
Charing Cross); Docklands Light Railway to
Island Gardens (see p. 181); or by boat to
Greenwich from Westminster Pier (see p. 181)

HIGH ON THE hill above the
National Maritime Museum at
Greenwich is a curious, top-heavy,
red-brick building. Built by Sir
Christopher Wren in 1675 for the
first Astronomer Royal, John Flamsteed, with a large observatory room
perched on top of domestic quarters, this is
Britain's oldest scientific institution, spon-
sored by Charles II in order to solve one of
the most pressing navigational problems of
the day: the calculation of longitude.

Small panelled rooms looking out over
the Thames are shown as the first Astronomer Royal might have had them, while
the lofty Octagon on the floor above has
been furnished as it appeared in a contemporary engraving, with a wooden telescope tube supported on a ladder. Rooms
at the back of the house are filled with
instruments concerned with astronomy,
timekeeping – Greenwich time became the
world standard in 1884 – and navigation.

Among them are models of the heavens
made when it was believed the Sun went
round the Earth, the orbits of the planets
forming a complicated mesh of interweav-
ing rings. Some imagination is needed to
add flesh to these displays; more appealing
for most visitors is the metal strip marking
0° longitude, where you can stand with a
foot in each hemisphere, or the large red
time ball on Flamsteed House which drops
daily at 1 p.m.

Flamsteed's serious observing was done
in a building at the bottom of the garden,
where you can see instruments used by the
observatory's two most famous Astro-
nomers Royal: Edmond Halley, who, in
1705, predicted the return of the comet
named after him, and Sir William Herschel,
who discovered Uranus in 1781. But none
of Flamsteed's equipment remains. Charles
II required him to provide his own instruments and, not surprisingly, his widow
removed them all at his death.

Sadly, there is no longer a working
observatory here. Driven out of London in
1948 by murky skies and bright lights, the
Royal Observatory was re-established at
Herstmonceux Castle in Sussex, but now
this too has closed.

Open: Mon–Sat 10–18,
Sun 14–18; admission
charge; toilets

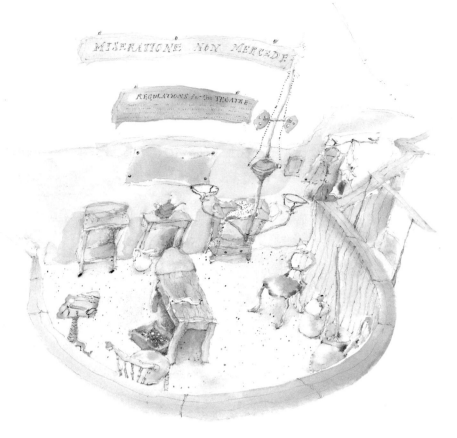

OLD ST THOMAS'S OPERATING THEATRE

Old St Thomas's Church, St Thomas's Street, SE1

——— • ———

underground London Bridge (Northern line); or
British Rail to London Bridge (from Waterloo
East)

JUST OFF Borough High Street, a door in a red-brick tower opens onto a steep spiral staircase which leads to what was the attic of St Thomas's Church. In a cramped, top-lit space under the roof is the only remaining example of an early nineteenth-century operating theatre, formed in 1821 out of what was then a herb garret on the south side of St Thomas's Hospital. The patients treated here were all women, from adjoining female wards. When the hospital moved in 1862, the theatre lay forgotten for a century.

Tightly packed standings for student spectators rise steeply from a rough wooden operating table. Beneath it is a box of sawdust to absorb blood dripping from the table, and a mop and a bucket stand ready nearby. Sawdust was also packed between the floorboards, to ensure no bloodstains appeared on the ceiling of the church. There is no heating, no plumbing and no ventilation. The operations performed here were carried out without anaesthetic and without any regard to infection. The jug and bowl on a stand were for the surgeon to wash his hands after rather than before the operation, and the purple frock coat hanging on a peg was typical dress for the occasion. Not surprisingly, many patients regarded death as preferable to surgery.

A small museum in an adjoining attic illustrates surgical knowledge of the period, with displays of fearsome instruments and a bizarre collection of 'specimens' There is also a section devoted to the nursing pioneer Florence Nightingale and to the activities of the apothecary and herbalist.

Open: Mon, Wed, Fri 12.30–16; admission charge; introductory talk for booked groups

ROCK CIRCUS

The London Pavilion, Piccadilly Circus, W1

——— • ———

underground Piccadilly Circus (Bakerloo and
Piccadilly lines)

THIS OFFSHOOT of *Madame Tussaud's*, with waxworks of leading rock and pop performers from Lonnie Donnegan, Buddy Holly and Elvis to the androgynous Marc Bolan, Madonna, Sting and Michael Jackson, uses up-to-the-minute technology to create the illusion that you are watching your heroes perform. Headphones triggered by infra-red signals play a snippet of each artist's greatest hit as you stand in front of them, and the final half-hour 'concert', staged in a revolving auditorium, is compèred by an animated Tim Rice and staged by robots which almost move their lips in time to the music. Most convincing are Bob Dylan, who thrashes his guitar with realistic gusto, and a heavily drugged Janis Joplin, who rises dopily from a garden seat to sing her number. Costumes and effects, from Mick Jagger's purple jump suit to the flashing car which accompanies Chuck Berry, have been lovingly recreated, but sadly the waxworks themselves are very variable – early portraits of the Beatles and of the perennially boyish Cliff Richard being particularly unconvincing – and the animation is just not quite good enough. Nevertheless, you can spend an enjoyable hour or two here.

Open: Daily 11–21; admission charge; toilets

THE ROYAL ACADEMY

Burlington House, Piccadilly, W1

———— • ————

underground Green Park (Jubilee, Piccadilly and
Victoria lines), Piccadilly Circus (Bakerloo and
Piccadilly lines)

AN ITALIANATE TRIUMPHAL arch on Piccadilly leads into the courtyard of the grandiose building housing the Royal Academy, the only survivor of the great mansions which once lined the north side of Piccadilly. Founded in 1768 with the support of George III, and with Sir Joshua Reynolds, whose statue rises out of a sea of parked cars in the courtyard, as its first president, the Academy was set up to foster the fine arts in Britain, providing free tuition for 77 students and an effective market-place for the output of the mature and distinguished. Forty Academicians were elected from among those who contributed to the exhibitions, and those thus honoured were required to give the Academy a painting or other example of their skill. Such patronage was sorely needed: there were no galleries where contemporary artists could display and sell their work, and art education as such scarcely existed.

Today there are fifty RAs, among them the sculptor Elisabeth Frink, whose bronze horse straddled by a naked man stands just

a few yards away at the end of Dover Street. Since the opening of the new Sackler Galleries on the top floor in 1991, a selection of the important works contributed by academicians since the eighteenth century, including canvases by Turner, Constable, Fuseli, Reynolds and Gainsborough, are now, for the first time, permanently on display and visitors can also expect to see Michelangelo's marble relief of the Madonna and Child, one of very few sculptures by this genius outside Italy. This work of 1504–5 now stands at the head of the uncompromisingly 20th-century staircase, largely built of glass, which leads to the new rooms. The galleries are used for important loan exhibitions for much of the year, and for the annual Summer Exhibition from mid June to mid August. Held without a break since 1769, this hotch-potch of some 1,400 works selected from those submitted by amateurs and professionals from all over the country is hung with little regard for seeing pictures at their best: frames jostle shoulder to shoulder, and subtle effects are lost in a general blur of colour. Artists used to be able to retouch their paintings on designated Varnishing Days, which Turner, who often sent in unfinished works, would use to complete his canvases. Submissions by Academicians were always accepted, although a Constable landscape which once got mixed up with the 'outsiders' was turned down by the selection committee, and the offended artist refused to let it go forward once the mistake was discovered.

The exterior of Burlington House is a Victorian palace, its heavy Renaissance-style façades of 1868–73 associated with converting the existing building into a permanent home for the Academy. Sadly, the

elegant eighteenth-century colonnade by James Gibbs which curled round the forecourt was destroyed, but inside there are still traces of the Palladian mansion which Colen Campbell created in 1717–20 for that cultivated patron of the arts, the 3rd Earl of Burlington (see p. 125), including a first-floor saloon with a ceiling by William Kent, and decorations by Sebastiano Ricci on the main staircase. Ceiling paintings by Angelica Kauffmann and Benjamin West in the entrance hall were brought here from Somerset House (see p. 67), the Royal Academy's home from 1771 to 1836.

Open: Daily 10–18; admission charge; toilets; audio tours for some big exhibitions

THE SCIENCE MUSEUM

Exhibition Road, SW7

———— • ————

underground South Kensington (Circle, District and
Piccadilly lines)

THIS HUGE MUSEUM, with escalators and lifts linking seven floors of exhibits, was one of the important institutions which grew out of the Great Exhibition of 1851 (see p. 16). Appropriately, it was founded at the height of the Industrial Revolution, and the latest processes and discoveries of industry and science swell the collections every year. From the visitor's point of view, the exhibits vary greatly in general appeal: seventeenth-century telescopes covered in coloured vellum, an abacus, or fragile glasses with twisted stems are beautiful as well as functional, but there is little aesthetic appeal in the often highly complex apparatus and processes of late twentieth-century technology, and their impact depends on understanding them. Hidden away in the maze of displays are a number of fascinating and involving exhibits, such as those on the nature of light, with a simulated rainbow and rows of holograms, but the visitor has to find them for himself. There is no interpretation of the cryptic labels announcing 'Gas', 'Land Transport', 'Optics' or 'Electricity and Magnetism' on the museum plan, or any guidance on how to tackle the bemusingly vast galleries.

Not surprisingly, a large area on the ground floor is now devoted to space exploration and its spin-offs, centred on the Apollo 10 spacecraft that carried three astronauts round the Moon in May 1969 in a rehearsal for the first lunar landing a few weeks later. Inside the silvery capsule, like a giant top, models of the astronauts are packed closely together, permanently upside down. There are film sequences taken on board the Space Shuttle and from the latest probes to Jupiter, Saturn and Uranus, and demonstrations of satellite communications and of rocket technology.

These displays are part of a sequence on power and transport, sandwiched between early industrial machinery, such as one of the huge steam engines developed for use in the mines of Cornwall and Derbyshire in the late eighteenth century, their nodding beams supported on massive piles of masonry, and vehicles of every kind. The *Puffing Billy* of 1813, the earliest surviving locomotive, and the *Sanspareil* and *Rocket* of 1829 are dwarfed by a huge diesel engine of the mid 1950s. On the other side of this lumbering giant is an array of historic cars, among them a Benz three-wheeler of 1888, like a horseless carriage, with a top speed of 15 m.p.h., a canary-yellow Rolls Royce of 1910 and a delicious bottle-green Morgan of 1913, its tiny cab just big enough for two. A gallery two floors above is filled with fragile early aeroplanes, including the insect-like Cody biplane of 1908, straight out of a Leonardo notebook.

There are many working demonstrations, among them a continuously operating seismograph rooted in the foundations of the museum building, which records shock waves from earthquakes across the world. Similarly, there is a constant record of air pollution day by day, the exposed filter papers stained frighteningly black by smoke and dirt. A re-creation of a drilling floor on an offshore oil rig, complete with throbbing mud pumps and a team of roustabouts, and a full-size model of open-hearth steel making are among a number of realistic reconstructions, and there are also demonstrations of facts we all take for granted but can never experience directly, such as the gently swinging pendulum used to show the rotation of the earth. Displays aimed particularly at children, where they can discover many scientific principles and applications for

themselves, are concentrated in the Children's Gallery in the basement and the newly-opened Launch Pad on the first floor.

Galleries at the top of the building are devoted to the history of medicine. An extensive collection of historical exhibits includes Captain Scott's medicine chest, clearly labelled British Antarctic Exhibition 1910, revolting artificial eyes, George Washington's ivory dentures of c.1795, and displays illustrating medical knowledge in the past. Dioramas recreate a Roman field station, a church-like hospital in sixteenth-century Spain, with the sick in rows of four-posters, and an amputation in c.1800, when the wretched patient would be given only a wad of leather to bite on as his leg was removed. There is material for several wet afternoons here.

Open: Mon–Sat 10–18, Sun 11–18; admission charge, but free 16.30–18; toilets

SIR JOHN SOANE'S MUSEUM

13 Lincoln's Inn Fields, WC2

———— • ————

underground Holborn (Central and Piccadilly lines)

DISPLAYED IN WHAT was Soane's own house, rebuilt by him in 1812, the collection accumulated by this highly individual neo-classical architect and preserved for the nation by Act of Parliament is the most extraordinary in London. Behind furnished eighteenth-century rooms looking out on to the leafy garden of the Fields is a warren of chambers and courts, apparently filled with the contents of a rather exclusive mason's yard. There are fragments of capitals and other ornaments from ancient Rome, pieces from buildings that Soane demolished or remodelled, such as the large capital from Inigo Jones's *Banqueting House*, which the architect refaced in 1829, and patterns for details on his own works. In among them are marbles, bronzes, busts, vases and other sculptures, including models by Soane's contemporary John Flaxman, who was a fellow Professor at the *Royal Academy*, and a cast of the Apollo Belvedere, said to have been made for Lord Burlington's villa at Chiswick (see p. 125).

Nothing is in any particular order or arrangement: pieces perch precariously on ledges and balustrades and cover every available inch of wall. The effect is both eccentric and charming, and the appeal of the place is greatly enhanced by Soane's highly original design, with sudden vistas down column-lined corridors, shafts giving glimpses of rooms yet unseen and lighting apparently subterranean cells, and a lofty central space rising to a dome. His living rooms seem almost ordinary by comparison, although all bear the stamp of his individuality: in the use of mirrors in the library, for example, or in the enclosed loggia which he created off the first-floor drawing-room.

The son of a bricklayer, Soane had the good fortune to marry an heiress, and it was his wife's money which financed his purchases. The centrepiece of the museum is the huge boat-like sarcophagus of Seti I, the translucent pinkish limestone of which it is made completely covered in stylized figures and hieroglyphics, and the shadowy outline of the goddess Nut traced on the bottom. Discovered in Egypt in 1817, this treasure dating from c.1370 BC was snapped up by Soane when the *British Museum* declined to purchase it for £2,000. As intriguing is his picture room, a box-like chamber, lit from above, with paintings hung three deep on hinged panels which open out to display more pictures behind. Architectural etchings and drawings, including many works by Piranesi, are overshadowed by Hogarth's *Rake's Progress* and *Election* series. The eight paintings cataloguing the downfall of the rake and his final incarceration in a madhouse were bought by Mrs Soane for £570 in a sale of the contents of William Beckford's Fonthill.

When the panels are open, you can look out from this room into the Monk's Yard, dominated by a grandiose tomb to Mrs Soane's pet dog Fanny and including a cloister composed of thirteenth-century material from the old House of Lords (see p. 19). In the Monk's Parlour behind, objects are half seen in a perpetual gloom, discreet lighting picking out vaguely Gothic details or the corner of a triptych. Elsewhere are Venetian views by Canaletto, one of the Alpine panoramas Turner executed during a brief respite in the Napoleonic Wars, a portrait of Soane by Sir Thomas Lawrence, paintings by Reynolds and Daniell, and 54 volumes of drawings by Robert and James Adam.

Sadly, Soane's Bank of England, his finest work, was considerably altered in the

1920s (see p. 50), but the picture gallery he built at Dulwich (see p. 71) survives largely unchanged. Drawings on display at the museum show designs for buildings London might have had, including the Whitehall scheme proposed in 1822, with a triumphal arch leading into Downing Street, and Soane's vision of 1794 for the Houses of Parliament, a vast classical build-ing with three porticoes overlooking the Thames and a statue-studded roofline parapet. Best of all is the ornate dog kennel designed for the Bishop of Derry, with three wings projecting from a central dome.

Open: Tue–Sat 10–17; first Tuesday of each month 10–17 and 18–21; admission free; toilets; guided tour Sat 14.30

THE TATE GALLERY

Millbank, SW1

—— • ——

underground Pimlico (Victoria line)

STANDING BESIDE THE THAMES on the site of an early nineteenth-century prison, the Tate is known by the name of its principal benefactor, the sugar magnate Sir Henry Tate, who financed the original purpose-built gallery designed by Sidney R. J. Smith and donated his collection of paintings, most of them works by fellow Victorians. Originally a satellite of the *National Gallery* devoted to modern British art, the Tate only achieved the independent status Sir Henry had envisaged in 1955. The gallery has been much enlarged since it first opened its doors in 1897 and now houses one of the world's most important art collections, with paintings attractively hung in a series of light and airy rooms either side of a lofty central corridor devoted to sculpture. Often seen as being associated particularly with modern art, the Tate's displays in fact cover an enormous stylistic and historical range, with works from the sixteenth to the twentieth century. Very recently re-thought, the paintings are now in a largely chronological sequence, with rooms arranged around carefully devised themes which are clearly explained. The rooms devoted to British and foreign art since 1874 are perhaps the only place in Britain where it is possible to appreciate the bewildering succession of movements since Impressionism and the cross-currents between them. What you cannot count on, though, especially where the modern collection is concerned, is finding a particular canvas on view. Although the Tate is a large gallery, the works on show are only a small proportion of the total number housed here. While the general coverage remains the same, rooms are periodically changed, so that works can be rotated and artists and themes presented in depth.

Sir Henry's dream of a national collection of British painting is realized in the initial sequence of galleries, which traces the evolution of native art from Tudor times to the mid nineteenth century. Stylized early portraits include the memorable painting of the Elizabethan Cholmondeley sisters, 'born the same day, married the same day, and brought to bed the same day'. They sit side by side in a double bed, fully dressed, their heads framed by elaborate ruffs, identical red-robed infants in their arms. Only the colour of their eyes is different. Similarly bizarre is Marcus Gheeraerts' allegorical portrait of Captain Thomas Lee, his torso clothed in an elegant frilled and embroidered grey and white shirt, his legs and feet completely bare, as if he is about to wade through the Irish bog shown behind him. Another kind of personal statement emerges in David des Granges' charming study of the Saltonstall family. Painted in c.1636–7, it shows both Sir Richard Saltonstall's wives, the first, who died in 1630, deathly pale in a white gown and lying in a white bed, the second cradling her new born son on her knee. Far more realistic is Van Dyck's contemporary portrait of a lady in a shimmering blue dress, and only half a century later Jan Siberechts painted his atmospheric view of Henley on Thames, the dramatic sky and the play of light and shadow on the landscape heralding the work of Turner and Constable two hundred years later.

Hogarth, the first British painter to achieve international recognition, is well represented, his charming, intimate portrait of six of his servants contrasting with the much grander, classically influenced productions of Gainsborough and Reynolds from later in the eighteenth century. A Suffolk landscape, with a church tower framed against woodland, shows Gainsborough's earlier, naturalistic style, before he became a fashionable portrait painter, and there is a magical view of Box Hill painted in 1733 by Hogarth's friend George Lambert, the steep scarp slope catching the light of the setting sun, a group of picnickers half hidden in shadow in the foreground. Two canvases – one by Samuel Scott, the other by Richard Wilson – show London's Westminster Bridge, one of the major civil projects of the age, under construction in the mid eighteenth century, and there are characteristic animal pictures by Stubbs, including his powerful enamel of a lion attacking a horse, the pose of the two creatures based on a classical sculpture Stubbs had seen in Rome.

Of the three great geniuses who emerged in the nineteenth century, Turner now has a gallery to himself (see below). The other two, Blake and Constable, the first a mystic visionary, the second a sublime landscape painter, their works linked by a common romanticism, are surrounded by a cluster of lesser figures, among them Samuel Palmer, Edwin Landseer and Henry Fuseli. There are charming, intimate landscape sketches by Cotman and Linnell, characteristic nudes by William Etty, one of which Constable dismissed as low erotic titillation, and

nightmarish visions by De Loutherbourg, his *An Avalanche in the Alps* of 1803 showing a cascade of snow and boulders overwhelming a flimsy wooden bridge, an upflung arm all that can be seen of a figure disappearing into the abyss. Richly coloured, glowing canvases by the Pre-Raphaelites, their work as minutely detailed as an illuminated manuscript, contrast with the grim realism of the artists who depicted the life of the labouring poor towards the end of the century, among them Luke Fildes, whose *The Doctor* was commissioned by Henry Tate, and Frank Bramley, who depicted the Cornish fishing community among which he lived.

From this point, British art is seen as one current in a much wider stream embracing the Continent and America. Impressionism is represented by Monet, the American John Singer Sargent and his compatriot Whistler, whose atmospheric *Nocturne in Blue and Gold* of c.1872–5, as stylized as a Japanese print, is still in its original painted frame, the colours echoing the golden burst of fireworks behind the dark, T-shaped outline of Battersea Bridge and the grey-blue of sky and water. Together with the Post-Impressionists, among them an unusually serene landscape by Van Gogh – a huddle of thatched buildings set among

fields – and a Divisionist clifftop by Seurat, in which the illusion of grass, shadowed rock and sea dissolves at close quarters into hundreds of brushstrokes in complementary colours, these works form a prelude to the Modern Collection, a confusion of 'isms' from Constructivism to Vorticism. In one room you will be looking at cubist paintings by Braque and Picasso, in another at Mondrian's squares and lattices, or at the huge, stark offerings of the minimalist school which emerged in America in the mid 1960s. You may see one of David Hockney's large double portraits, a cartoon by Roy Lichtenstein, or the diptych by Andy Warhol with repeated images of Marilyn Monroe. Sculptures include Dali's nightmarish lobster telephone, like a prop for a horror film, and Giacometti's spindly, stilt-legged *Man Pointing*.

Distorted reality of a different kind appears in the work of Stanley Spencer, whose *The Resurrection, Cookham* is one of several canvases in which he imagined biblical events taking place in his Thames-side village. Spencer has set his picture in Cookham churchyard, where the roses which smother the porch also provide a canopy for a seated Christ, children gathered in his arms. The dead climb sleepily out of their graves, some looking over their tomb chests as if they were leaning on garden gates. A woman tidies up her companion, brushing off the dust of centuries, and the half-seen figure of Spencer's second wife lies in an ivy-covered tomb. Works such as this are equally far from the painful realism of Lucien Freud's nudes, his lumpish, middle-aged women bleakly exposed, as from the abstract work of Hepworth, Ben Nicholson and Victor Passmore. The modern collection is growing all the time, some of the works acquired, one feels, representing sublime acts of faith on the part of the purchasing committee.

The Clore Gallery, a purpose-built extension opened in 1987, now houses the 300 or so oil paintings and 19,000 water-colours and drawings bequeathed to the nation by J. M. W. Turner, perhaps Britain's greatest artist. The works on show are arranged thematically in nine rooms, one containing a group of Venetian scenes, another a series of large, dramatic canvases reflecting Turner's admiration for Titian, Poussin and Salvator Rosa, a third devoted to works executed while the painter was a guest of the 3rd Earl of Egremont at Petworth in Sussex. Some paintings are realistic, among them the view of London from Greenwich in 1809, with the *Queen's House* in the foreground and the dome of *St Paul's Cathedral* visible through the haze across the Thames, or his stormy *Chain Pier, Brighton*, and the Italian views with brilliant blue skies are strongly reminiscent of Canaletto. A moonlit fishing scene, with a lantern illuminating figures on a boat and the ghostly shapes of the Needles off the Isle of Wight just visible through the murk beyond, was Turner's first significant work in oils, exhibited at the Royal Academy in 1796 when he was 21. The later works are more impressionistic, among them his vortex-like *Snow Storm* and the almost transparent *Norham Castle, Sunrise*, in which the blue shape of the fortress on a rock above the Tweed rises out of sun-tinged water, a red cow throwing long shadows as it drinks.

Open: Mon–Sat 10–17.50, Sun 14–17.50; admission free; toilets; guided tours on aspects of the collection Mon–Fri at 11, 12, 14 and 15

THEATRE MUSEUM

Russell Street, Covent Garden, WC2

———— • ————

underground Covent Garden (Piccadilly line)

AN OUTPOST OF the *Victoria & Albert Museum*, the Theatre Museum seems to suffer from the *ennui* which infects some of the displays at South Kensington. The sparkle of the entrance foyer, with its box office and enticing café, is left behind in a series of subterranean galleries which have none of the excitement generated up above. Static, conventional displays in a long curving corridor trace the history of the performing arts from the time of Shakespeare to the present day, including music hall, pantomime and rock and pop shows as well as opera, ballet and the stage.

Programmes, playbills, props, costumes, scores and memorabilia illustrate what are undoubtedly rich collections, among them objects as diverse as Noël Coward's red silk dressing-gown, with his initials embroidered on the pocket, Mick Jagger's grey velvet jump suit, which looks as if it were made for a skeleton, Jenny

Lind's wedding veil, a pair of white silk boots worn by Sarah Siddons, and a draft of *School for Scandal*, marked with Sheridan's alterations and omissions. Some items are more inscrutable. One wonders, for example, why Victor Hugo gave Sarah Bernhardt a human skull inscribed *Cage déserte, qu'as tu fait/De ton bel oiseau, qui chantait?* And what induced Arthur Sullivan to write to Richard D'Oyly Carte, proprietor of the Savoy Theatre, about terms for a two-act piece on mourning paper, his request for a payment of 200 guineas framed in a heavy black border?

Changing exhibitions are staged in adjoining galleries, and the foyer of a small theatre is hung with paintings relating to performances on the London stage, from David Garrick as Romeo in 1750 to Boris Christoff in the 1965 production of Mussorgsky's *Boris Godunov* at Covent Garden.

Open: Tue–Sun 11–19; admission charge; toilets

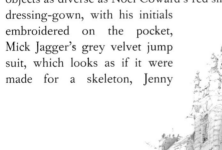

Madame Tussaud's, and The Planetarium

Marylebone Road, NW1, near junction with Baker Street

———— • ————

underground Baker Street (Bakerloo, Circle, Jubilee
and Metropolitan lines)

A T MADAME TUSSAUD's you walk straight into a grand garden party. In a formal garden, with water gushing into a lily pond, clipped box hedges, and Chinese paper lanterns hanging from the trees, a strange company is assembled. Some are dapper in black tie. Others, such as the diminutive jockey Lester Piggott, who is still in his riding clothes, have obviously not been told how to dress. The guests are all celebrities from the world of sport and entertainment – Dame Edna Everage in a yellow sheath dress and flashing glasses stands in a small carpet of gladioli, Paul Daniels is busy with his tricks in a summer-house, Martina Navratilova rests on a bench, Barbara Cartland glimmers in pastel pink. All are arranged so that visitors can easily be photographed next to them.

Through what appears to be a conservatory, the mood changes. Lulled by the sound of harpsichord music, the tiny figure of Madame du Barry, mistress of Louis XV, sleeps on a green couch, one arm protectively cushioning her head, her chest rising and falling rhythmically as if she were breathing. This childlike, small-featured face is the earliest model in the collection, made in 1765 by Madame Tussaud's uncle. Madame du Barry was to go to the guillotine, and there are many other victims of the French Revolution here too: Marie Antoinette and Louis XVI; Marat murdered in his slipper-bath; Robespierre, destroyed by the forces he unleashed. Even more striking is the staring, shrunken face of the Comte de Lorges, modelled shortly after his release from twenty years' imprisonment in the Bastille.

The young Marie Tussaud (1761–1850), then Marie Grosholtz, knew many of those whose bleeding heads were delivered straight from the guillotine, and she is said to have modelled their death-masks through her tears. In 1802, struggling to survive in a France that was still devastated, Marie decided to bring her waxworks to England, leaving her husband, François Tussaud, and one of their sons in Paris. After many years spent touring, her exhibition was settled in a permanent home on Baker Street in 1835. The figures seen today are always being changed, with those whose interest is on the wane being removed to make way for rising stars. Even so, some may find the mix curious, and the waxworks themselves are very variable. Past the display of Hollywood superstars, where a phalanx of flashing cameras greets the glittering form of Joan Collins, is the Grand Hall, where the tired décor does not enhance a mostly sober collection of politicians and other world leaders. A curiously unreal royal family is being photographed by Lord Lichfield at one end of the room. How many, I wonder, stop for long before Disraeli, Gladstone, and Pitt the Younger? And who arranged the curious trio of Picasso, Hockney and Henry Moore, Picasso in slippers, Hockney in trainers, and Moore sober in a blue suit and tie? Generally, artists, classical musicians and writers are poorly represented.

A dark staircase leads from here to the Chamber of Horrors, where Hitler stands just outside the door. The guillotine and the electric chair have a chill about them, but the scene in which George Joseph Smith (1872–1915), the 'Brides in the Bath' murderer, is dispatching one of his wives seems cosily domestic, even though the lady is clearly underwater and the bath tub itself was used for at least one of his crimes. More atmospheric is the smoky, ill-lit cobbled street recalling the haunts of Jack the Ripper.

Next door to Madame Tussaud's is the PLANETARIUM, its large copper dome roofing a round auditorium. A huge Zeiss star projector like a piece of futuristic space machinery, creates the patterns of the night sky, images illustrating the birth of the solar system and a range of special effects, such as the explosion of a supernova. The sequences are linked by a background commentary and there is suitably atmospheric music. The shows, which last 30–40 minutes, are changed annually, but the material I saw seemed curiously old-fashioned.

Open: MADAME TUSSAUD'S daily 10–17.30 (earlier opening at weekends and in summer); PLANETARIUM shows approx. every 40 minutes, starting 12.20 weekdays (earlier in summer), 10.20 weekends, last show 17; admission charge; toilets
NB Madame Tussaud's is one of London's most popular tourist attractions and it is usually necessary to queue for admission at peak times, for up to an hour; those who go to the Planetarium first can obtain admission without queuing

VICTORIA & ALBERT MUSEUM (V & A)

Cromwell Road, SW7

———— • ————

underground South Kensington (Piccadilly, Circle
and District lines)

NO ONE CAN EVER be quite sure they have explored every corner of the V & A. Some eight miles of labyrinthine galleries on several different levels present an interior of maze-like complexity. Just when you think you have mastered the museum, a staircase plunges you into an area you have never seen before. Often, too, many of the less popular galleries are virtually deserted, and I would not be surprised to come upon the skeleton of some forlorn visitor who has failed to find the restaurant or the way out. This sense of geographical complexity may be compounded by a general feeling that you have failed to grasp what the museum is about. The collections here are marvellous, ranging from jewel-like miniatures and an unparalleled display of Constable sketches to Renaissance sculpture, Oriental ceramics and stained glass. But there is no obvious central thread. As its former director Roy Strong once observed, the V & A is like a capacious handbag, into which has been deposited, at various times and by various hands, an assortment of unrelated treasures. Some pins, bits of fluff and the odd piece of string have inevitably lodged in the corners, some of which are very much in need of the present programme of refurbishment.

Like the *Natural History Museum*, the V & A sprang out of the Great Exhibition of 1851 (see p. 16). The brainchild of Prince Albert's friend Sir Henry Cole, it originated in the Museum of Ornamental Art which opened at Marlborough House in 1852, transferring to the South Kensington site a few years later, and acquiring its present title in 1899. Sir Henry was the museum's first director, his declared policy 'to assemble a splendid collection of objects representing the application of Fine Art to

manufactures'. The displays were intended both to instruct and inspire and to play a key role in improving standards of design at a time when Britain was slowly losing her industrial ascendancy over other European countries. A dynamic civil servant, Sir Henry even arranged for the name of the area, which was then Brompton, to be changed to South Kensington, which he thought would attract more visitors. But as the collections grew, and sculpture and paintings were acquired, Sir Henry's original purpose was increasingly disregarded. As a result, what is seen today is both a museum of masterpieces, now housing the national collections of British sculpture, miniatures and watercolours and the greatest collection of Italian Renaissance sculpture outside Italy, and a practical display of the arts of manufacture and design. The V & A excels in early medieval, Oriental and Islamic art, in tapestries and carpets, costume, metalwork and musical instruments, it has the greatest assemblage of ceramics in the world, and the new Nehru gallery displays the largest collection of Indian art and artefacts outside the subcontinent.

The extraordinary range of material on display makes a visit to the V & A especially rewarding, but the museum is much too large to cover in a day; those who have never been here before would be well advised to follow one or more of the introductory tours suggested in the excellent guidebook. The galleries have been devised either to express the style of an age, or to show collections of specific objects or techniques, such as jewellery, silver work, ironwork or porcelain. A historical sweep through the arts of Britain and Europe from the Middle Ages to the present day starts in a display of early Christian art such as would have been produced for monasteries and cathedrals. Here is a medieval treasury of candlesticks, caskets and crucifixes, among them a thirteenth-century Flemish silver hand reliquary, 'windows' in the first three fingers revealing the bones of the saint set inside; a chunky, pocket-sized French book of hours of c. 1300, each page exquisitely decorated; and a cope from the Bridgettine convent at Syon (see p. 150), the linen ground finely embroidered in green and brown silk and golden metal thread.

Much of the northern Renaissance art on display is also religious in spirit, with fluid limewood sculptures by Riemenschneider, and the massive St George altarpiece of c. 1410–20 from Valencia. A strip cartoon in richly coloured tempera and gilt tells the story of the saint, from his taming of the dragon to his martyrdom under the Emperor Diocletian, which apparently involved a series of ghastly tortures. A more secular spirit creeps into the Italian rooms of 1400–1500, where a series of terracotta roundels by Luca della Robbia illustrate the agricultural year, from the hay being scythed in May to the young man gathering olives in November, the length of the day at each season shown on the rim of each roundel. But here, too, Christianity is a dominant theme, inspiring Donatello's low relief marble sculpture of the Ascension, with Christ giving the keys to St Peter as he rises slowly heavenwards.

Unlike these pieces, the inlaid furniture, enamelled snuff boxes and gilded mirrors produced in later centuries were intended for palaces and great houses. Much of what is on display was bequeathed by the former military tailor John Jones (1799–1882), who devoted the fortune he had made in business to acquiring a collection of largely seventeenth- and eighteenth-century French art, cramming boulle furniture, Sèvres vases and paintings by Boucher, as well as works by Guardi and by contemporary English painters such as Turner and

Etty, into his modest bachelor's apartment in Piccadilly. Here, surrounded by riches, he continued to sleep on a military camp bed.

A series of furnished rooms, including Robert Adam's glittering Glass Drawing Room of 1773–4 from Northumberland House and James Wyatt's playful Gothic interior in painted pinewood of c. 1785 from Lee Priory, should be high points of the English collections, but this section is somewhat tired. Even the Great Bed of Ware of 1590, a carved oak four-poster twelve feet wide, looks curiously neglected, perhaps because the frame is bare, with no mattress or coverings.

Much more rewarding is a clutch of galleries which could easily be overlooked. The cast courts, lit from above through barrel roofs, contain over five hundred casts, largely assembled in the 1860s and 70s for the use of design students. A mélange of pulpits, medieval effigies, sculptures and tombs, reliefs and ornaments, including plaster copies of Michelangelo's *David* and *Dying Slave*, is dominated by a reproduction of Trajan's Column of AD 113, the continuous frieze winding up the great pillar now much sharper than the original, which has been badly corroded by pollution. Between these two courts, one of which has been recently restored to its Victorian splendour, runs a display of fakes and forgeries, not all of them, as the V & A catalogue endearingly puts it, 'acquired in moments of weakness'. There are bogus reliquaries and caskets, objects which have been deliberately aged, and pastiche paintings, much of what is here is work of a very high standard. The mosaic floor, described by Sir Henry Cole as another *opus criminale*, was laid by women from Woking Prison.

A sadly silent display of musical instruments, the strings and woodwind either behind glass or stacked in sliding cabinets (the catalogue exhorts us to admire the workmanship), stands above the extensive dress collection, as if a balcony orchestra has been assembled for a great ball. The costumes range from about 1660 to the present day, some curiously timeless, such as the Liberty productions in muted browns and purples of the late 1890s which were inspired by the long gowns of the sixteenth century, others totally of their day, such as

Mr Fish's corduroy rainbow suit of 1968, a flickering pattern of red, orange and green stripes. Nothing here seems to have quite the infectious sense of fun of the brightly coloured ducks paddling on a brown silk kimono in the Toshiba Gallery, or of the Japanese embroidery showing a team of men washing a white elephant, figures dotted about the huge animal like window cleaners on a skyscraper. Nor, with the exception, perhaps, of a pair of French crêpe-de-chine camiknickers fringed with cream lace, is there anything to match the eroticism of an Indian sandstone sculpture of the second century AD, a youthful tree spirit with one arm above her head and a tiny waist curved sensuously in a dance. Also from India is a series of jewel-like gouaches of the Mogul period, of walled cities, elephants, golden birds and a tiger chase, the hunters half hidden in a mesh of grass. Such representational works, characteristic of the Christian west and of the art of Hinduism and Buddhism, contrast with pieces produced in the Muslim world, where realistic depictions of nature were regarded as blasphemous. Cool blue and white tile panels, mosque lamps and perfume burners, an inlaid pulpit from a mosque in Cairo and ornate sixteenth-century carpets are ornamented in geometric patterns or in sinuous stylized plant motifs.

However you choose to spend your time, two sections in particular should not be missed. On the first floor, in three specially protected rooms entered through a turnstile, is the V & A's jewellery collection, with rings, necklaces, bracelets, rosaries, watches, pendants and enamelled portraits studded with every form of precious metal and stone. Some pieces, such as a pair of delicate filigree gold ear-rings, date back to the Etruscan and Greek civilizations; others, such as the huge aquamarine rings with which Edith Sitwell used to adorn her bony fingers, are of the twentieth century. A miniature gold whistle is said to have been Henry VIII's first gift to Anne Boleyn, the vivacious, sparkling girl whom he made his second queen and beheaded three years later. Here too is the Armada jewel of c. 1588, a locket of enamelled gold set with diamonds and rubies and containing a miniature of Elizabeth I by Nicholas Hilliard. The Latin inscription reads: 'Alas,

that so much virtue suffused with beauty should not last for ever inviolate.'

This exquisite piece is part of the best collection of English portrait miniatures in the world, most of them displayed in the six-storey Henry Cole wing housing the bulk of the V & A's paintings, prints, drawings and photographs. Here are miniatures by Holbein (including his *Anne of Cleves* and *Mrs Pemberton*), Isaac Oliver and Samuel Cooper, and what is perhaps Hilliard's best-known work, of a melancholic youth leaning against a tree, caged by briars. At the top of the building is the Constable gallery, the greatest collection of the landscape artist's paintings, drawings and watercolours, most of which were bequeathed by his daughter Isabella in 1888. Both finished canvases and sketches show the development of Constable's style, the later work increasingly expressive and impressionistic. Here are many of the cloud studies he did after he moved to Hampstead in 1819, attracted by the hill village's low horizons and windy skies (see p. 174). Never intended for public display, and often including Constable's notes on the weather at the time, these scraps of paper on which he captured shafts of sunlight through the scudding streamers of a gathering storm, or cirrus clouds high against an ice-blue sky, are powerful and atmospheric. There are Turners here too, and glass paintings by Gainsborough, the back lighting giving a wonderful pink-tinged luminosity to an estuary scene with boats gliding across the water.

Another magnificent inconsistency with the original aim of the museum is housed in a separate gallery immediately behind the shop. Here hang the monumental Raphael cartoons illustrating episodes from the lives of St Peter and St Paul that were commissioned by Pope Leo X in 1515 for tapestries for the Sistine chapel. Cut into strips to be copied by weavers in Brussels, seven of the ten originals were acquired by Charles I for the Mortlake tapestry factory established by his father in 1619 and were subsequently joined together. As tapestries are woven from behind, the designs were reversed, as can be seen by comparing a finished Mortlake tapestry of *The Miraculous Draught of Fishes* with Raphael's original. There are other changes, too. In the tapestry, Jesus's robe is red, but in the painting it appears white, because Raphael used a fugitive pink pigment. Strangely, the colour of the reflection in the lake has not faded, because here the vermilion paint was permanent.

These sixteenth-century cartoons are curiously in tune with the architecture of the museum, a grandiose Renaissance-style palace in brick, terracotta and Portland stone, with an arcaded loggia overlooking the formal Italianate Pirelli garden in the central quadrangle. Built piecemeal over half a century from 1855, the V & A never benefited from a co-ordinated plan, and there was never enough money to complete the decorative schemes, some of which are in any case now hidden behind artificial walls and ceilings. But visitors can enjoy the mosaic- and tile-lined 'Ceramic' staircase and three other remarkable interiors: William Morris's Green Dining Room, with gilded panels and stained glass by Burne-Jones; the gleaming brown-and-white tiled Gamble room, with its lettered frieze formed out of little figures, the 'I' a back view of the designer with his easel; and a Dutch grill with characteristic blue and white decoration. Created to form three interlinked refreshment rooms, these are now treated as exhibits in their own right, and should be imagined crammed with tables and people, the air thick with steam and with the smell of food.

Open: Mon–Sat 10–17.50, Sun 14.30–17.50; voluntary admission charge; toilets; guided tours Mon–Sat

THE WALLACE COLLECTION

Hertford House, Manchester Square, W1

——— • ———

underground Bond Street (Central line)

THOUSANDS WHO VISIT the *National Gallery* never walk the few yards north of Oxford Street to see the outstanding paintings acquired by the Seymour-Conway family, Marquesses of Hertford. Most famous of the many major works here is Frans Hals's *Laughing Cavalier*, its title surely based on the upward flick of his moustaches rather than on the faintest hint of a smile about his mouth and his knowing expression. In the 100-foot first-floor gallery where this picture hangs are also Titian's *Perseus and Andromeda*, originally painted for Philip II of Spain, and several memorable portraits: of a lady with a fan by Velázquez; of Philippe le Roy and his wife by Van Dyck, both dressed in black, she full faced and auburn haired, he fondling the head of a dog as proud and elegant as himself; of Rembrandt's son Titus by his father, painted in about 1657 when the lad was sixteen; of the courtesan Nelly O'Brien by Reynolds, and of the beautiful Mrs 'Perdita' Robinson, whose exceptional looks are here reproduced three times over. The woman in Gainsborough's full-length portrait has the most arresting eyes, but perhaps the heads by Romney and Reynolds are more telling; the face which captivated the ever-available Prince Regent was not matched by sweetness of character.

The collection is also strong in Dutch seventeenth-century paintings and has a room of Canalettos and Guardis,

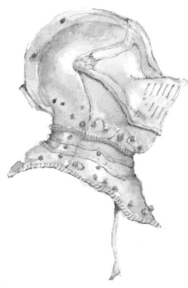

but it is particularly notable for French eighteenth-century canvases, in which it is richer than the National Gallery. Here are sharply-observed Watteaus, works by Lancret and Boucher, atmospheric Fragonards and sentimental female heads by Greuze. The naked figure in Watteau's *La Toilette* sits plumply on a bed, pulling a shift over her head, Fragonard's *Girl in a Swing*, a froth of pink in a sea of green, has a cloying sweetness about it, but nothing mars the misty foliage in his *Garden of the Villa d'Este, Tivoli*. These paintings are all on the first floor, and those whose taste does not extend to the equally fine displays of Oriental and Continental armour, Sèvres porcelain, Limoges enamels, and boulle furniture in earlier galleries can make directly for them up the grand staircase, with its finely-crafted iron and bronze balustrade.

This superb collection is the biggest and most valuable assembly of works of art ever to be given to the nation by an individual. Although the 1st and 2nd Marquesses acquired a number of paintings, it was the next three generations who contributed most, buying with taste and discrimination. The 3rd Marquess (1777–1842), an associate of the Prince Regent, whom he advised on purchases for the Royal Collection, had the wisdom to marry an Italian beauty who inherited two fortunes; both the 4th Duke of Queensbury, 'old Q', and his close friend George Selwyn thought they were

her father and both supported their claims by leaving her enormous sums. Fortunately for all concerned, blood tests had yet to be invented. While the Marchioness retired to Paris, the Marquess lived an increasingly dissolute life in London, providing the model both for Thackeray's Marquess of Steyne in *Vanity Fair* and for Disraeli's Lord Monmouth in *Coningsby*. Nevertheless, he also bought wisely, his acquisitions including *Perseus and Andromeda*, miniatures, Dutch paintings and French furniture. His only surviving legitimate child, Richard Seymour Conway, 4th Marquess (1800–1870), seems to have inherited some of his father's character, siring an illegitimate son at the age of eighteen. Brought up in France, the 4th Marquess settled in Paris, where he purchased a château in the Bois de Boulogne. Here he lived as a recluse, absorbed in adding to the collection. This he transformed, presciently acquiring French eighteenth-century art at a time when, following the Revolution, it was out of fashion, and buying a wide range of other beautiful things: miniatures, tapestries, sculpture, porcelain and furniture. His son,

Richard Wallace, seeing the Prussian army at the gates of Paris, decided to bring most of the collection over to London.

The mansion he settled in was built between 1776 and 1788 for the 4th Duke of Manchester, who owned the square. It was enlarged by the 2nd Marquess of Hertford, who acquired the lease in 1797, and made it his principal residence, often playing host to the Prince Regent, whose attention had perhaps been caught by the ample proportions of the Marchioness. Richard Wallace remodelled the house in his turn to take his collection. After his death in 1890, it passed to the nation, one of the conditions of the bequest being that nothing should be added and nothing lent. This stipulation perhaps accounts for Hertford House's curiously dead atmosphere, as if time has been suspended here and the place is awaiting a handsome prince to bring it back to life.

Open: Mon–Sat 10–17, Sun 14–17; admission free; toilets; lunchtime lecture tours twice weekly on aspects of the collection

SPECIALIST MUSEUMS

The following museums are all centrally located,
but the collections are specialised and of minority
interest only.

THE JEWISH MUSEUM

Woburn House, Upper Woburn Place, WC1

———— • ————

underground Euston (Northern, Victoria lines),
Russell Square (Piccadilly line)

HOUSED IN AN austere and unwelcoming building on the north side of Tavistock Square, this tiny, one-room museum is an introduction to the richness and diversity of Jewish culture. Most of the treasures here, from the circumcision chair to the nine-branched candlestick and the sixteenth-century Venetian Ark, used to hold the Scrolls of the Law, relate to the rituals of Judaism, all of which are explained in an audiovisual presentation.

Open: Tues–Thurs 10–16; Fri, Sun 10–16 (Apr–Sept), 10–12.45 (Oct–Mar), closed all public and Jewish holidays; admission free; toilets; tours for booked groups

THE MCC MUSEUM

Lord's Ground, St John's Wood Road, NW8

———— • ————

underground St John's Wood (Jubilee line)

TWICE DAILY 'LORD'S TOURS' take in the Long Room, with its panoramic view of the pitch, and the real tennis court, as well as a host of photographs, portraits and memorabilia in the museum, among them the ball which Albert Trott hit over the Pavilion in 1899, the bat with which W. G. Grace scored his hundredth century, Donald Bradman's white boots, and the sparrow dispatched by a ball in 1936.

Open: Tours at 12 and 14 daily, except on cricket days, booking advisable (071 289 1611); admission charge; museum also open on cricket days to those with cricket tickets (small additional charge)

PERCIVAL DAVID FOUNDATION OF CHINESE ART

53 Gordon Square, WC1

———— • ————

underground Euston (Northern and Victoria lines),
Euston Square (Circle, Metropolitan lines),
Russell Square (Piccadilly line)

THREE FLOORS OF coolly beautiful Chinese ceramics of the fourteenth to eighteenth centuries, the best collection outside China, assembled by the scholar Sir David Percival. The presentation is academic and erudite, but those who simply enjoy fine craftsmanship can revel in the exquisite shapes and the colours: mustard yellow, brick red, turquoise, delicate smoky green, and raspberry, as well as the more familiar blue and white ware.

Open: Mon–Fri, except Bank Hols, 10.30–17; admission free; toilets; tours for booked groups

5

HOUSES, GARDENS AND PARKS

—— • ——

L ONDON IS A GREEN CITY. In the West End, you are never more than a street or two away from a leafy square, while even in the City, where the ground plan is much more compact, gardens have been created out of former church-yards and the perfect oval of Finsbury Circus even boasts a bowling green and a bandstand, as if it were a seaside resort. Stretching right across the West End is a long corridor of grass, trees and water where three royal parks – former hunting grounds – run almost without a break from Westminster to Bayswater. Here you can walk for miles in an open woodland, fall asleep in the sun, or idle in a deckchair listening to a military band. The oldest and most royal of these royal parks is St James's, almost on the doorstep of *Buckingham Palace* and overlooked by the stuccoed grandeur of Nash's Carlton House Terrace and by the imposing government buildings on Whitehall (see p. 19). Part of Henry VIII's great hunting chase running up to Hampstead, the park was first tamed by James I, who had a menagerie here, with an 'ellefant' which was treated to a gallon of wine every day. His tragic son walked across the park to his execution in Whitehall, one of his dogs desperately running after him; and this is also where Charles II came to exercise his spaniels, chatting to Nell Gwyn over the garden wall of her house on Pall Mall. All paths lead to the sinuous lake at the centre of the park, with its pelicans, black swans and other ornamental birds and much-photographed views from the central bridge: west towards Buckingham Palace, and east over fountains to a strange skyline of turrets and cupolas, as if you had suddenly been transported to St Petersburg.

The rather featureless triangle of Green Park joins St James's to the broad open spaces of Hyde Park and Kensington Gardens, a former monastic estate appropri-ated by the ever acquisitive Henry at the Dissolution. Deer were hunted here until 1768, but now there is nothing wilder than the occasional hedgehog, and the spring and autumn migrants who come wearily down to the long, boomerang-shaped lake inappropriately known as the Serpentine. Picnickers open hampers beneath the trees, and au pairs take their charges to throw bread to the ducks, or to sail their boats on the Round Pond.

When William and Mary forsook Whitehall for *Kensington Palace*, however, this was not a place to wander alone. To deter highwaymen, William had three hundred lamps hung from the trees along the road linking the palace to St James's – his *route du roi*, now transformed into Rotten Row – and a bell would be rung at intervals during the night in the village of Kensington so people out from London for the evening could gather for the dangerous homeward journey. Even so, in 1749, two thugs relieved Horace Walpole of his watch and eight guineas. The writer had been returning from Holland House, the great Jacobean mansion where Lady Holland presided over a literary and artistic salon and the remains of which, now partly converted into a youth hostel, sit in the centre of Holland Park, a curious combination of formal gardens and dense, scrubby woodland about half a mile west of Kensington Gardens.

Less than a mile away to the north is the spacious ellipse of Regent's Park, with the finger of Primrose Hill, purchased by the Crown from Eton College in 1842, pointing north again to the sandy heights of Hampstead Heath, while west along the Thames are the rolling expanses of Richmond Park, more moor than garden, and the tamer grassland and heath around *Hampton Court*. Regent's Park, legacy of Nash's vision for the Prince Regent (see p. 14), is perhaps the most enticing of inner London's open spaces, its large, island-studded lake harbouring a heronry and a bird sanctuary, its eastern side crossed by the Broad Walk, an impressive avenue

continuing the line of Portland Place, and at its heart the secluded beds and pergolas of Queen Mary's rose garden – in flower, it seems, throughout the summer. Here, too, at least for 1992, is London Zoo, where Edward Lear sat patiently painting parrots, and whose furred and feathered creatures with their often disturbingly human expressions inspired Christina Rossetti's descriptions of the little men who tried to seduce Laura in *Goblin Market*:

One had a cat's face,
One whisked a tail,
One tramped at rat's pace,
One crawled like a snail,
One like a wombat prowled obtuse and furry,
One like a ratel tumbled hurry-scurry.

Founded in 1826, and the oldest such institution in the world, the original collection of animals was augmented by the addition of the royal menageries from *Windsor* and the *Tower of London*, which included a hundred rattlesnakes. Since then, generations of children have been brought by their parents and by strings of fond uncles and aunts to get their first taste of a world with rather more to it than pavements, parks and pigeons, while Lord Snowdon's fishing-net aviary of 1963–4 and the arid, ziggurat-like Mappin Terraces designed for bears and goats have come to seem as essential in the panoramic view across the park from the top of Primrose Hill as the distant silhouette of *St Paul's Cathedral* and the fretted outlines of the Houses of Parliament (see p. 19). Current financial difficulties, though, have put the zoo's future in jeopardy, and some of the less popular species are being moved away. No one yet knows how long visitors will be able to enjoy the delights of the penguin pool, where the creatures line up beside the water as if about to take part in a diving competition, and of the artificially created Moonlight World, where ant-eaters waddle in the eerie half-darkness and huge fruit-eating bats creep crablike through the gloom as if practising for a remake of *Dracula*. (Zoo open daily, 10–18 in summer, 10–dusk in winter; admission charge; Camden Town underground (Northern line) and bus 74.)

Where the inner parks are flat and neat, and a gardener with a rake or a pair of secateurs is never very far away, Hampstead Heath still feels like the common it once was, a gloriously open, rolling expanse of meadows and copses set high up above London, the woodland thickening to screen *Kenwood* on the northern edge and half hiding a chain of ponds running down the eastern side: one a bird sanctuary, two used all year round by intrepid bathers, another a boating pool. From the 320-foot hump of Parliament Hill, or from the gazebo in the grounds of Kenwood, you look down on the city in the valley below, and sometimes, on a clear day, right across the basin of the Thames to the hills of Kent and Surrey. There are foxes here, kestrels hover overhead and the woods harbour woodpeckers and tawny owls. There are still

wild blackberries to be picked, but the orchids which John Gerard, the herbalist, found in the 1590s have long since disappeared.

Even wilder is Richmond Park, 2,500 acres of grass and bracken studded with ancient oaks descended from the great forest which once stretched across southern England. The largest of the royal hunting parks, this undulating, breezy upland, with long vistas across rising ground, is still surrounded by the high brick wall built by Charles I in 1637, which runs for 12 miles round its boundaries. Although now crossed by several roads, and harbouring the woodland garden known as the Isabella Plantation, where rhododendrons, camellias, magnolias and masses of azaleas are planted informally round an ornamental stream, Richmond Park is still untamed. Herds of fallow and red deer roam free here, and it would be no surprise to see a royal hunting party trotting smartly down the Queen's Ride, or surveying the ground from the top of the enigmatic tumulus known as King Henry VIII's mound.

Deer are also kept in the royal park at Greenwich, but here they are secreted away in a fenced Wilderness in the south-east corner. Greenwich is the only royal domain on the eastern side of London, its grassy slopes rising sharply to the plateau of Blackheath forming a dramatic backdrop to the Royal Naval College (see p. 22) and the *National Maritime Museum*. The park was a favourite sporting ground of Henry VIII, who loved the great palace which once sprawled along the river here, and it was Charles II who transformed it into a landscaped park, employing Louis XIV's great gardener Le Nôtre to advise on the magnificent avenues which now criss-cross the top of the escarpment.

Other parks and gardens are attached to the many historic houses within the London area: some, such as *Ham* or *Syon*, as grand as palaces; others unpretentious Georgian boxes, such as the house in Doughty Street where Dickens lived early in his career (see p. 127), or the Chelsea terrace where Thomas Carlyle and his wife moved from Scotland in 1834 (see p. 121). Like the royal palaces, the greatest mansions tend to hug the Thames, their faces turned towards the water which once connected their noble owners with the court and carried the barges of their visitors. Most are older than they look. Both *Osterley* and *Syon*, near neighbours sandwiched between the M4 and the Thames, have interiors created by Robert Adam in the 1760s and 1770s, but both are at heart Tudor courtyard houses, the one built by Sir

Thomas Gresham, founder of the *Royal Exchange*, the other the house of the scheming Lord Protector Somerset, who went to the block on trumped-up charges of treason on 22 January 1552. Even *Ham House*, with its sash windows and extravagant state rooms, is at heart an H-shaped Jacobean manor.

Ham lies on one of the loveliest stretches along the river, bordered by the Petersham water-meadows and with the heights of Richmond Park at its back. By the eighteenth century, this idyllic spot within easy reach of London but still surrounded by open countryside was attracting a stream of notable residents, who built small villas set in grounds running down to the river. These were quite different in both style and scale from their grander predecessors. Sadly, nothing remains of James Gibbs's villa for the poet Alexander Pope, built on the profits of his translation of Homer, and Horace Walpole's Gothic Strawberry Hill is now an inaccessible college; but *Marble Hill*, the stuccoed neo-classical box built for George II's mistress Henrietta Howard, survives intact, and only yards away upstream, hidden in a wood, you can see a surviving octagonal pavilion from Gibbs's Orleans House of 1710, the red-brick eighteenth-century remnant with stone dressings now curiously attached to a modern art gallery. Both Pope's villa and Marble Hill reflect the great revival of interest in classical architecture which began in the early years of the century, based on the works and publications of the sixteenth-century Italian architect Andrea Palladio. The high priest of the movement, and its most influential exponent, was the 3rd Earl of Burlington, who had been inspired by what he had seen on his visits to Italy and whose own Palladian villa, like a model for something very much larger, sits a mile or two downstream at Chiswick (see p. 125).

In contrast to these country retreats are several houses which, rather than dancing attendance on the outskirts, are very much of the town. Among them are *Apsley House*, the Duke of Wellington's palace overlooking Hyde Park Corner;

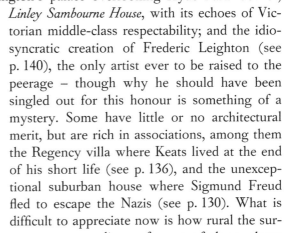

Linley Sambourne House, with its echoes of Victorian middle-class respectability; and the idiosyncratic creation of Frederic Leighton (see p. 140), the only artist ever to be raised to the peerage – though why he should have been singled out for this honour is something of a mystery. Some have little or no architectural merit, but are rich in associations, among them the Regency villa where Keats lived at the end of his short life (see p. 136), and the unexceptional suburban house where Sigmund Freud fled to escape the Nazis (see p. 130). What is difficult to appreciate now is how rural the surroundings of most of these places were: even in the early nineteenth century, there would have been fields beyond the garden.

APSLEY HOUSE

149 Piccadilly, W1

—— • ——

underground Hyde Park Corner (Piccadilly line)

A PSLEY HOUSE, the London home of the 1st Duke of Wellington, has something of the atmosphere of a shrine, with constant reminders of the great soldier's campaigns and his triumph at the Battle of Waterloo in 1815. At the foot of the stairs stands a gross statue of his principal enemy, commissioned by Napoleon himself from Antonio Canova in 1802. Shown as a Greek athlete, the emperor is an embarrassment of white flesh 11 feet 4 inches tall, the strategically placed vine leaf only emphasizing his nakedness. Not surprisingly, Napoleon did not like it, and it languished in the Louvre until bought by the British government and presented to the Duke by George IV. Canova, on hearing that his work had at last found a home, wrote immediately with instructions on how to put it up. Napoleon was also indirectly responsible for the Sèvres Egyptian service in the Plate and China room, with a monumental white-china temple of colonnades, obelisks and inscribed gateways forming the centrepiece. Napoleon had the service made as a divorce present for the Empress Josephine, but she rejected it, as any woman with an ounce of self-respect would have done, and in 1818 Louis XVIII presented it to Wellington.

This china, extraordinary though it is, is outclassed by the magnificent collection of paintings Wellington acquired in the Peninsular War, the campaign which ousted Napoleon's brother Joseph from the throne of Spain. Pursuing the fleeing French after the Battle of Vitoria in 1813, Wellington captured Joseph's coach; inside were two hundred neatly rolled canvases appropriated from the Spanish royal collections. A subsequent offer to return them to the Spanish royal family was graciously declined by Charles IV, who had been forced to abdicate in favour of Joseph. Some of the most prized pictures, including works by Murillo, Velázquez, Jan Brueghel the Elder, Guido Reni and Rubens, hang in the long Waterloo Gallery on the first floor, where the paintings in their gilded frames are displayed two and three deep on red damask.

The room is dominated by three large portraits: Emperor Rudolf II by Hans von Aachen, Mary Tudor after Antonio Moro, and a copy of Charles I on horseback by Van Dyck; but it is some of the smaller compositions which catch the eye. A low light illuminates the deeply-lined face of Velázquez's waterseller as he hands a brimming glass to his customer, his high cheekbones etched in shadow; or there is the quiet composure of Rudolf's young daughter, Ana Dorotea, in the portrait painted by Rubens after she had entered a convent in Madrid. Correggio's *Agony in the Garden*, with a romanticized Jesus praying in a pool of light, was the Duke's favourite picture, but he never liked Goya's great equestrian portrait which now also hangs here, consigning it to a storeroom in his country house, Stratfield Saye. The room itself is very ornate, its high coved ceiling picked out in white and gold and sliding mirrors fitted to the windows to produce a Versailles-like wall of glass at night.

The 90-foot gallery was one of the additions made to the house by Benjamin Dean Wyatt (1775–1850), son of the much more distinguished James Wyatt, when he was commissioned to enlarge the fairly modest three-storey red-brick mansion by Robert Adam which the Duke had bought from his elder brother, Marquess Wellesley, in 1817. Like the Duke of Marlborough a century before, who received Blenheim Palace in 1705 from a grateful nation after his

campaigns against the French, the Duke had been voted £200,000 by Parliament to build an appropriate residence, but his Waterloo Palace, intended to replace Stratfield Saye, never materialised. Instead, Apsley House was transformed. The red brick was encased in golden Bath stone, the entrance façade dignified by a pedimented Corinthian portico, and rooms added both east and west of the main block. The bronze-green iron gates and railings, designed to blend with the adjoining classical entrance to Hyde Park, also date from this time. When first built, Apsley House stood just inside the toll gates at the top of Knightsbridge. Now, it looks out on the mêlée of Hyde Park Corner, marooned on an island between constant streams of traffic. Just across the road is Sir J. E. Boehm's statue of the Duke riding Copenhagen, the chestnut charger which carried him at Waterloo and which was buried with full military honours at Stratfield Saye.

The rooms visitors see are largely on the first floor, a series of interconnected grand apartments circling the staircase. Most of the grandiose and rather oppressive decoration, including the pink and white stripes which make the drawing-room look like the inside of a tent, is by Wyatt, but there are glimpses of Adam in delicate friezes and door surrounds, and in the marble chimney-pieces. A newly opened basement gallery is now used for changing exhibitions on the history of the house and on aspects of the 1st Duke's life and career. Both here and in the Plate and China Room there are many personal mementoes and relics, including the great man's mahogany toilet case engraved with the Wellesley crest, the death-mask taken by the sculptor George Gamon Adams three days after the Duke's death in 1852, the chin as prominent as the hawk-like nose, and orders written at Waterloo on slips of vellum. But nowhere on display is there a portrait of the Duke's wife Catherine Pakenham, daughter of the 2nd Baron Longford. Marrying this pretty but feather-brained creature was Wellington's biggest mistake, and the unsuitability of the match was neatly summed up in the journals of his close friend Mrs Arbuthnot: 'He assured me that ... she could not enter with him into the consideration of all important concerns ... and that he found he might as well talk to a child.' Wellington, it seems, like so many others, felt his wife did not understand him.

Apsley House is closed in 1992 and will reopen in 1993. Telephone 071 499 5676.

CARLYLE'S HOUSE

24 Cheyne Row, SW3

—— • ——

underground Sloane Square (Circle and District
lines); then a 20-minute walk, or bus 11, 19 or 22
along the King's Road and walk down Oakley
Street and into Upper Cheyne Row

EVEN IN THE early nineteenth century, Chelsea was still half in the country, with fields between it and London. Its apparent quietness was one of the qualities which attracted the historian and philosopher Thomas Carlyle (1795–1881), who had come down to London in 1834 to search for a house while his wife wound up their affairs in Scotland. 'Chelsea is a singular, heterogeneous kind of spot,' he wrote to her, 'very dirty and confused in some places, quite beautiful in others ... Our row ... runs out upon a beautiful "Parade" ... running along the shore of the River ... with huge shady trees; boats lying moored, and a smell of shipping and tar.' Jane was worried about damp and bugs, but they took the house at £35 a year and lived here until their deaths. Three years later, the publication of *The French Revolution* established Carlyle's reputation as a literary genius.

The Georgian red-brick terrace house with a tiny back garden which the Carlyles moved into on 10 June is little changed, its small rooms now filled again with their furniture, books, portraits and personal possessions. At the top of the house is the sound-proof study which Carlyle added on in 1853, hoping to escape from the distractions of pianos and the cackling of 'demon fowls'. Here he wrote his epic *Frederick the Great*, a labour of twelve years; the room is now set out as a museum, with cases of manuscripts and other mementoes, among them a letter from Bismarck which Carlyle received on his eightieth birthday, written in a strong flowing script, and a singed scrap of the

original manuscript of *The French Revolution*, lent to the philosopher John Stuart Mill and accidentally used to light a fire.

While Carlyle wrote, Jane received a stream of visitors in the first-floor drawing-room overlooking the street, among them Dickens, Tennyson, Thackeray, Ruskin and Browning. An oil painting by the fire shows her smiling, her long oval face set off by a red dress, and the screen she covered with cut-out prints, portraits and engravings stands by the door, its decoration now faded to a uniform sepia. Carlyle's hat hangs in the passage running through to the garden door, and in the basement is the little flagged kitchen with a scrubbed pine table and a stone sink where he would retreat to smoke.

Jane died suddenly in 1866, the correspondence she left revealing that Carlyle's egotism and irritability had made her very unhappy. While Carlyle's reputation has dimmed with time, his eccentric exclamatory prose seen as increasingly unreadable, her stature has grown: her witty, observant letters are now regarded as some of the best in the English language. Something of her charm emerges in a poem by Leigh Hunt (1784–1859), who lived just round the corner in Upper Cheyne Row:

Jenny kiss'd me when we met,
Jumping from the chair she sat in;
Time, you thief, who love to get
Sweets into your list, put that in!
Say I'm weary, say I'm sad,
Say that health and wealth have missed me,
Say I'm growing old, but add,
Jenny kiss'd me.

Open: Apr–end Oct, Wed–Sun and Bank Hol Mon 11–17; admission charge

CHARTERHOUSE

Charterhouse Square, EC1

———— • ————

underground Barbican (Circle and Metropolitan lines)

MONASTIC GATEWAY beneath a Georgian façade on the north-west side of Charterhouse Square leads to one of the most fascinating places in London, the only surviving example of the great Tudor mansions that once ringed the City. A rambling conglomeration of brick and stone ranges set round three courtyards, the Charterhouse started life as a Carthusian monastery – one of only nine established in England – founded by Sir Walter de Manny in 1371 on the site of a burial ground for victims of the Black Death. A small community flourished here until 1535, when the prior and two others were hung, cut down alive and quartered for refusing to recognize Henry VIII as head of the church.

Surrendered in 1537, the monastery was then transformed into a splendid house by two great noblemen who acquired the property in the sixteenth century: first Sir Edward North, who built a great hall out of the stone and timber of the church, then Thomas Howard, Duke of Norfolk. Both entertained Queen Elizabeth here, poor North having to finance the expense of two regal visits, but Norfolk's tenure came to an abrupt end in 1571, when he was executed for his involvement in the Ridolfi plot to put Mary, Queen of Scots on the throne. This period as a private mansion lasted less than a century. In 1611 the Charterhouse was bought by the wealthy courtier Thomas Sutton, who founded a home for sixty male pensioners and a school for forty boys here. The school, whose former pupils include Thackeray, John Wesley and Joseph Addison, has moved out, but forty brothers, as the old men are known, still live in this idyllic place.

Visitors can see both monastic and Tudor survivals. In the brick arcade which once formed the western arm of the Carthusian cloister is the door to one of the little cells where monks of this contemplative order would live alone, receiving their meals through a dog-leg hatch in the wall. A tower nearby holds what was the monastic treasury, still floored with its original tiles and roofed with a medieval stone vault. A plan on parchment here shows how water was piped to the monastery and distributed to the cells round the cloister via the brick conduit house which can still be seen by the main gateway, while through a squint looking down on the site of the demolished church you can see a slab marking the position of the founder's grave in front of the high altar.

The Tudor great hall overlooking Master's Court rises through two storeys to a hammerbeam roof, its fine interior restored after damage by an incendiary bomb in the Second World War. Carved panelling carries Renaissance strapwork motifs, and the minstrel's gallery at one end, an addition by the Duke of Norfolk, is continued down the side of the room in a kind of open corridor. An echo of splendour here and in the partly Jacobean chapel, formed out of the monastery's chapter house, is quite different from the atmosphere in secluded Wash-house Court, where stone-mullioned windows and diapered brickwork date from the early sixteenth century. These modest rooms are where the lay brothers were housed, and it is likely that Sir Thomas More – who was to die, like the monks, for his beliefs – was accommodated here when he spent four years considering whether to enter a monastery.

Open: Guided tours, Apr–Jul, Wed 14.30 (not 14.45, as the notice in the entrance gateway proclaims); admission charge

CHELSEA PHYSIC GARDEN

66 Royal Hospital Road, SW3

— • —

underground Sloane Square (Circle and District lines); then a 15-minute walk down Lower Sloane Street and along Royal Hospital Road, or take bus 11, 19 or 22 along King's Road, and walk down Flood Street

AN UNOBTRUSIVE GATE in a high brick wall leads into this 300-year-old garden on the banks of the Thames, with areas of woodland, fine specimen trees and a shady lawn softening a formal grid of narrow rectilinear beds. Founded by the Society of Apothecaries in 1673, it was the second physic garden to be established in Britain (the first was created at Oxford in 1621). At that time Chelsea was a riverside village, most easily reached by boat, and visitors would have arrived through the splendid wrought-iron water-gates which now give on to the Embankment.

The 3½-acre site is sheltered and warmed by the buildings which now surround it, enabling rare and tender plants to thrive. The largest olive grown outdoors in Britain spreads over a sunny corner, and there are species from South America and the Far East, including a magnificent golden rain tree (*Koelreuteria paniculata*). The National Collection of *Cistus* is held here and beds of traditional medicinal plants, such as would originally have been grown in the garden,

are still used to supply samples for clinical research, among them patches of feverfew and *Mandragora officinarum*, once used to relieve the agonies of amputation and crucifixion. Another sequence of beds celebrates the many distinguished botanists, gardeners and plant collectors who have been associated with the garden, notably Philip Miller, author of the *Gardeners Dictionary* (1731), William Forsyth, after whom *Forsythia* is named, William Aiton of Kew (see p. 147), Sir Joseph Banks and Robert Fortune. Watching over everything is a statue of the physician and naturalist Sir Hans Sloane, whose collections formed the nucleus of the *British Museum* and who effectively refounded the garden in 1722. Fifty years later the earliest rock garden in Europe was created out of black basaltic lava which Joseph Banks brought back from Iceland.

Open: late March–mid Oct, Wed and Sun 14–17; Chelsea Show week, 12–17 (see p. 180); admission charge; toilets

CHISWICK HOUSE

Burlington Lane, W4

———— • ————

underground Turnham Green (District line); then a
15-minute walk, left down Turnham Green
Terrace, right across Chiswick High Road, along
Duke's Avenue to Great West Road, then via
underpass to Chiswick House

THIS SMALL ITALIANATE stone villa in spacious gardens bordering the approaches to the M4 was built by the greatest patron of the arts and scholarship in Georgian England. The 3rd Earl of Burlington (1694–1753) was born into an immensely wealthy family, whose estates in Ireland and Yorkshire were further augmented by his marriage to the heiress Lady Dorothy Savile. His greatly enlarged London mansion, Burlington House, now the home of the Royal Academy, still dominates the north side of Piccadilly (see p. 96); and Cork Street, Clifford Street, Savile Row and other fashionable Mayfair addresses were first laid out on his instructions. Protégés such as William Kent, Henry Flitcroft, Handel and the sculptor Michael Rysbrack all benefited from his patronage and his close friendship with George II. Indeed, Handel and Kent, together with the poet John Gay, all actually lived for a time in Burlington House.

On his death, the Chiswick estate passed through his daughter to the Dukes of Devonshire, to whom it belonged until 1929.

Fired by the neo-classical buildings he had seen on his visits to Italy, Lord Burlington built a miniature Palladian villa to his own designs at Chiswick in 1727–9. Originally, it was attached to a Jacobean mansion which already stood on the estate, but this was demolished in 1788 and only a linking wing survives. The house is strongly geometrical, built as a square surrounding a central domed octagon. While visitors are now ushered in through a kind of garden door, above their heads a double staircase rises to the grand entrance on the first floor, with fluted Corinthian columns supporting a pedimented portico. Inside,

rooms lead off one another, open doorways and arches giving a bewildering series of vistas across the house. Where the ground floor is plain, that above is richly decorated, with gilded doorways and mirrors, coffered and painted ceilings with panels by William Kent, and wall hangings of green, blue and red which once set off Lord Burlington's art collection. Only the central octagonal Saloon is still hung with the pictures which were here in the eighteenth century, among them Kneller's portrait of the Moroccan ambassador to the court of Charles II, who was famous for displays of horsemanship in Hyde Park.

Lady Burlington, the politician Charles James Fox, who was being devotedly nursed by the 5th Duke of Devonshire's wife, and Prime Minister Lord George Canning, close friend of the 6th Duke, all died in the house, but it is almost without the sort of conveniences and comforts you would expect, apart from a brick-vaulted wine cellar, and there is virtually no furniture. This is a set for *Don Giovanni* or a grand reception, not a place to live in. Here indeed the 6th Duke of Devonshire received Tsar Nicholas I of Russia in 1844, and here Garibaldi was invited when he visited England in 1864. What these two visitors from opposite ends of the political spectrum thought of the house is not recorded, but the 3rd Earl's contemporaries certainly noted its impracticability. 'Too little to live in, and too large to hang one's hat', as one described it. By the time of the 6th Duke, though, there were other attractions to divert his guests. A menagerie he kept here included, at various times, an elephant – probably stabled on the lawns – a giraffe, emus, kangaroos and a Neapolitan pig.

The extensive, well-wooded gardens, though rather unkempt, still reflect Lord

Burlington's romantic design, with classical eye-catchers set off by foliage and water. On the north side of the villa, lines of stone urns frame a view to the *exedra*, a semicircle of clipped yew with undulations to take classical statuary. Beyond, more yew hedges line radiating walks through woodland, but only one of the vistas is now closed by its original Italianate feature, a pedimented rustic house. West of the villa, lawns slope to a long ornamental canal, with more vistas, centred on an obelisk, cutting through the woods beyond. Much of this layout is faintly scruffy, but in its midst is the magical Orange Tree Garden, a deep grassy amphitheatre with broad turfed steps descending to a circular pool. An obelisk rises from the water, a domed temple framed by trees sits on the banks, and plants in brilliantly white tubs form a ghostly audience along the terraces. Sometimes, late in the day, a pair of herons fish in the pool. Quite different in character is the loud formal garden laid out on land bought by the 6th Duke of Devonshire in 1812, with a long glasshouse overlooking box arabesques and a complex parterre filled with garish bedding plants. Beyond, a shady lime avenue leads to the horrors of the Great West Road.

Open: House, daily, Easter – 30 Sep 10–18, 1 Oct – Easter 10–16; grounds, all year, 8–dusk; admission charge to house; toilets; audioguides

DICKENS HOUSE

48 Doughty Street, WC1

— • —

underground Russell Square (Piccadilly line)

THE THREE-STOREY brick house in an unspoilt eighteenth-century street was Dickens's home for less than three years, from April 1837 to December 1839, but it is the only one of his London residences to survive and it marks a crucial period in his early career. In 1837 Dickens was only 25, his reputation just beginning to grow, and it was while at Doughty Street, then a smart, middle-class road attended by liveried porters, that he wrote *Oliver Twist*, *Nicholas Nickleby* and the last instalments of *Pickwick Papers*, works which established his name. By 1839 he could afford to look for something larger.

Apart from the drawing-room, where the furnishing scheme of 1839 has been re-created, the house is now a museum rather than a home, with glass-topped cases where once there were chairs and lamps. But if you can overcome the dusty and faintly chilling atmosphere, letters, portraits, first editions, annotated reading copies and playbills for the amateur theatricals Dickens delighted in conjure up a vivid picture of the man and his times, while in among the display cases are significant pieces of furniture: the velvet-covered desk which Dickens used for his public readings, a favourite plum-coloured armchair, and the table at which he was writing *The Mystery of Edwin Drood* on the day before he died. Fact and fiction are curiously merged. Dotheboys Hall in *Nicholas Nickleby*, where forty wretched boys are starved and mistreated, was clearly inspired by a few chilling lines in *The Times* from July 1829 advertising Bowes Academy in Yorkshire, where there were 'no vacations except by the parents' desire'. And the dining-room where Dickens held his convivial dinner parties contains a grandfather clock that belonged to a Moses Pickwick.

Much of Dickens's life can be pieced together here. A green malachite pendant was a present to his beloved sister-in-law Mary, who collapsed and died in his arms when only 17, and whose clothes Dickens loved to run his hands through in later years. On a half-landing at the top of the house is a photograph of the striking young actress Ellen Lawless Ternan, whose close friendship with Dickens hastened the deterioration of his rather functional marriage. Both Mary and Ellen appear in his fiction, the former as impossibly good characters such as Little Nell, the latter as the strong-willed Lucie Manette in *A Tale of Two Cities* and Estella in *Great Expectations*. Most revealing of all are Dickens's letters. Even a complaint to his publishers is composed with wit: 'When you have done counting the sovereigns received for Pickwick, I should be much obliged to you, to send me up a few ...,' and what clock repairer could resist a request such as this: 'If you can send down any confidential person with whom the clock can confer, I think it may have something on its works it would be glad to make a clean breast of.'

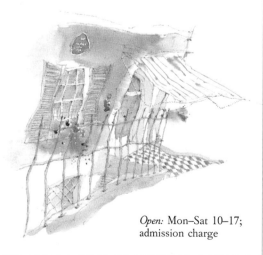

Open: Mon–Sat 10–17; admission charge

Fenton House

Hampstead Grove, Hampstead, NW3

———•———

underground Hampstead (Northern line); signposted
from just outside station

A HIGH BRICK WALL bordering leafy Hampstead Grove hides this two-storey, four-square house of dark red brick and its secluded garden. Four tall chimney-stacks like the legs of an upturned stool mark the corners of the steeply pitched roof, its broad eaves overhanging long sash windows on every façade. Probably built in 1693 for a prosperous city merchant, Fenton House is one of the earliest and largest houses in Hampstead, then just an isolated village on a hill above London (see p. 173), and also one of the best architecturally. Inside, the original pine staircase with ornate twisted balusters has survived, there is William and Mary panelling in several of the rooms, and there are still seventeenth-century closets at the corners of the house.

Some of the rooms, such as the Regency drawing-room with its chintzy upholstery, are furnished as if a family still lived here, but the house is principally a setting for two major collections. The furniture, many of the pictures and the outstanding eighteenth-century porcelain belonged to the connoisseur George Salting, whose niece, Lady Binning, lived at Fenton House from 1936 to 1952. Arcadian shepherds and shepherdesses, begging dogs, crinolined ladies and harlequins from the Chelsea, Bristol and Plymouth factories and from the

German Meissen works, or the rose-encrusted model cottages in the Rockingham Room, are by no means to everybody's taste; more immediately attractive is the cabinet of blue and white Chinese porcelain in the south-facing L-shaped room on the first floor, the ware here typical of the china which inspired the characteristic colouring of Delft pottery.

Quite different in character are the early keyboard instruments from the Benton Fletcher collection which stand in nearly every room and are crammed into the six tiny attics in the roof. There are harpsichords by Jacob Kirckman and Burkat Shudi, the two most prominent makers in London in the later eighteenth century, spinets, virginals and clavichords and what may be the earliest surviving English grand piano. In the south-east attic, where a case-ment window gives a view right across London, figures in Jacobean costume with gaily feathered hats stroll in the landscape painted on the lid of the elaborately decorated virginals of 1664, one of only ten to survive from before the Great Fire and perhaps one of those which Pepys saw being rescued from the flames: 'River full of boats taking in goods ... and ... I observed that hardly one lighter or boat in three that had the goods of a house in, but that there was a pair of virginalls in it.'.

Summer concerts are given in the large drawing-room on the ground floor. Here audiences can gaze at paintings in heavy gilt frames by Sir William Nicholson, among them his *The Golden Valley* of 1910, with tiny figures playing croquet against the heavy summer foliage of a wooded hillside.

A river-scape by Jan Brueghel the Elder, with a primitive bridge arched high above the stream and houses on wooden piles, suggests a village in south-east Asia, and a long panel by G. F. Watts is a dream-like fantasy in white and blue.

In summer, bowls of lavender are filled from the hedge fringing the terrace in the garden. Here, magnolias, pears and a passion-flower cling to the high enclosing wall, mop-headed laurels and hollies frame a small lawn, and brick steps lead down to the orchard at the lowest level. At every turn, there is a well-placed bench.

Open: Apr–end Oct, Sat–Wed 11–18; March, Sat, Sun 14–18; admission charge; toilets.

Freud Museum

20 Maresfield Gardens, NW3

— • —

underground Finchley Road (Metropolitan and
Jubilee lines); then a 5-minute walk, signposted
from station

THIS SLEEPY RED-BRICK house of c.1920 in a leafy suburban road is where the founding father of psycho-analysis, Sigmund Freud (1856–1939), lived in the last year of his life, dying here from cancer of the jaw on 23 September 1939. A refugee from Nazi persecution, he had clung to his Vienna home until the last possible moment, and the working environment he had had in Austria was then re-created for him in meticulous detail in London.

Freud's concern was with the intangible workings of the mind, and although there are all the outward signs that he once lived in this substantial and very middle-class residence, the house seems to lack an essential spirit. His combined study and library, a long room running across the ground floor, is filled with his books and his collection of Greek, Roman, Egyptian and Oriental antiquities. Conspicuous among the otherwise sober furnishings is his famous couch, the gay red and blue rug thrown over it and colourful cushions piled high, as surprising as discovering an august aunt sports bright-red underwear. (His daughter Anna's couch upstairs, in a display devoted to her life and work, is covered with a drab blanket.) Behind the couch is his green tub chair, out of sight of the 'patient'.

Letters, portraits (including a copy of a sinister sketch by Salvador Dali), photographs and newspaper reports help to capture a flavour of one of the most exceptional figures of the twentieth century. Clearly, even when sick and old, Freud made a deep impression on all those who met him. Leonard Woolf reported: 'Nearly all famous men are disappointing, or bores, or both. Freud was neither; he had an aura, not of fame, but of greatness.'

Open: Wed–Sun 12–17; admission charge; toilets; tours for booked groups

HAM HOUSE

Ham, Richmond
British Rail to Richmond (from Waterloo) or
underground to Richmond (District line); or by
boat from Westminster Pier (see page 181); house
is 1½ miles on foot from station along the river, or
take bus 65 (alight at Fox and Duck pub in
Petersham) or 71 (alight at Sandy Lane)

HAM HOUSE SITS ON the edge of the Thames, solid, confident and assured, its entrance front looking over the river to greet the visitors who used always to arrive by boat. The more adventurous can still approach the house this way, coming across the water on the little ferry which still plies back and forth from Twickenham on the opposite bank.

Built of red brick with stone dressings, Ham has remained largely unchanged since the 1670s, when substantial alterations to the original Jacobean house of 1610 were made by the ambitious Elizabeth and John Maitland, Duke and Duchess of Lauderdale. Free to marry only in 1672, when their respective spouses had both died, this rather unattractive couple are captured in a double portrait by Sir Peter Lely

which now hangs in the round gallery; she, well into her forties, is hard-faced and knowing, he, a man in his fifties, was by then both Secretary for Scotland and a member of Charles II's cabal ministry, his features blurred by good living and the onset of disease. Both wanted to transform the old-fashioned house Elizabeth had inherited from her father, William Murray, the 1st Earl of Dysart, into something more appropriate to people of their position and pretensions, but it seems likely that the duchess was the driving force. 'Restless in her ambition, profuse in her expense, and of a most ravenous covetousness' was how

the contemporary historian Bishop Burnet described her, and his description of the Duke has the same flavour: 'his tongue too big for his mouth and his whole manner rough … he was haughty beyond expression to all who had expectances from him, but abject where himself had any.'.

Even in a lavish age, keen to forget the rigours of the Commonwealth, the interiors the Lauderdales created are remarkably luxurious. On the ground floor, mirror image suites for Duke and Duchess such as William and Mary were to contrive at *Hampton Court* and *Kensington Palace* are decorated with ceilings by Verrio, whom Charles II employed at *Windsor*, carved and gilded mouldings, artificially grained panelling, and numerous inset paintings, among them seascapes by Van de Velde the Younger, who was in England briefly to work for the Stuart court. Richly-coloured hangings – gold and purple, crimson and black, black and gold – re-create the precious damasks which once covered the walls, and there is the warm gleam of marquetry and veneer. In her inner sanctum, with its window looking out on to the reconstructed formal garden, the duchess would receive her close associates – one hardly likes to call them friends – measuring out spoonfuls of expensive tea from a small Oriental cabinet. Even grander is the regal state apartment on the first floor which the Lauderdales created for a visit by Catherine of Braganza, Charles

II's Queen, in 1680. Here, the equivalent of the Duchess's closet is a tiny throne room, the ornate parquet floor inset with the Lauderdales' initials and coronet, a throne-like armchair on a platform at one end covered in the same crimson satin that hangs on the walls, gilded plasterwork and a Verrio ceiling. How the duchess must have loved it!

The state rooms, 'furnished like a Great Prince's', as the diarist John Evelyn put it, were part of the extension which the Lauderdales built on the south side of the house, blurring the H-shape of the Jacobean building. The route to them passes through some of the interiors William Murray created in 1637–9, including the white and gold north drawing-room, with overweight cherubs clambering up the baroque chimney-piece, its twisted columns copied directly from the temple gate in one of the Raphael cartoons now in the *Victoria & Albert Museum* (see p. 111). Next door is Murray's evocative long gallery, lit by windows at both ends, the dark, gilded panelling punctuated with classical pilasters setting off 22 portraits in sumptuous gold frames. Here you can see likenesses of the duchess's daughters by her first husband, the elder distressingly plain, the younger a sweet-faced girl whose clear complexion

and red hair recall her mother's earlier beauty. A library off this room, with pulpit-like steps abandoned in the middle of the floor, is curiously empty, not a book in sight.

The duchess resurfaces again in the basement, where what appears to be a bare scullery or wash-house turns out to be her innovative bathroom of 1675, which she reached by way of a little staircase from her bedroom above. A wooden bar once carried a canopy which would have formed a kind of tent over the tub, enveloping the duchess in steam, while an outer chamber was where she relaxed, anointed with herbal preparations and wrapped in a cloth. This great luxury for its age is only yards away from the kitchen and larders, where realistic raised pies stand waiting on the long dresser, goose quills and hens' feathers were used for brushing egg yolk on pastry, and sacks of sugar and flour are open on the floor. The cook received £20 a year during the Lauderdale regime, the chaplain a princely £30, but the wretched scullery maid only £3.10s.

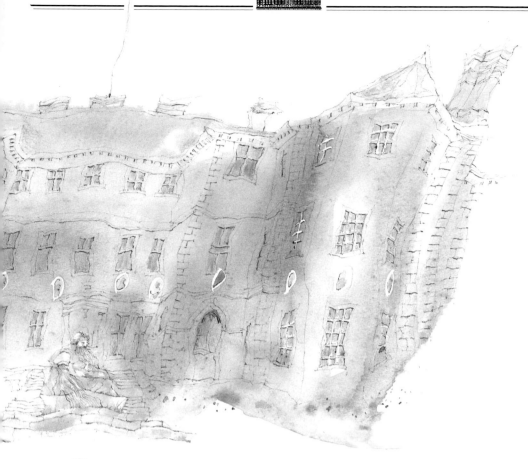

Fortunately, the duchess's descendants did not share her taste for conspicuous consumption and display, and the house was preserved much as she left it. During the regime of the miserly 5th Earl of Dysart, in the late eighteenth century, visitors of any kind were rarely received. The Earl even refused a request from George III, who wanted to come over from Windsor to see the old house, telling the royal messenger: 'Whenever my house becomes a public spectacle, His Majesty shall certainly have the first view.' The Earl married Charlotte Walpole, whose famous uncle Horace lived just across the river at Strawberry Hill. The girl had some misgivings about accepting her conquest, telling her sister, 'If I was but nineteen I would refuse point blank . . . But I am two-and-twenty . . . likely to be large and go off soon.' Her attractive portrait by Reynolds hangs in the hall, the decline she feared apparently still kept at bay. A relationship of two centuries earlier had ended much more tragically. Among Ham's important collection of miniatures is a portrait of Elizabeth I by Nicholas Hilliard,

and visitors can also see a lock of hair cut from the head of her favourite, the Earl of Essex, on the morning of his execution, 25 February 1601.

The formal garden stretching away from the south front is a re-creation of the seventeenth-century layout, with eight grass squares intersected by gravel paths. In the Wilderness beyond, grassy walks radiating from a central clearing divide hornbeam-hedged enclosures planted with maples and studded with delightful cylindrical summer-houses. East of the house, hornbeam arbours frame another reconstruction, with box hedges edging triangular beds of lavender and hedgehog-like clumps of santolina. Sadly, the only original feature from the 1670s, a statue of Bacchus, is now permanently encased in what looks like a green sentry box in the middle of the Ilex Walk, apparently to protect the deity from vandalism.

Ham House is closed for renovation in 1992 and will reopen in late 1993. Telephone 081 940 1950 for further details.

HOGARTH'S HOUSE

Hogarth Lane, Great West Road, W4

— • —

underground Turnham Green (District line); then a
10-minute walk, left down Turnham Green
Terrace, across Chiswick High Road, along
Devonshire Road to Hogarth roundabout; the
house is across the Great West Road, a hundred
yards or so west of the roundabout

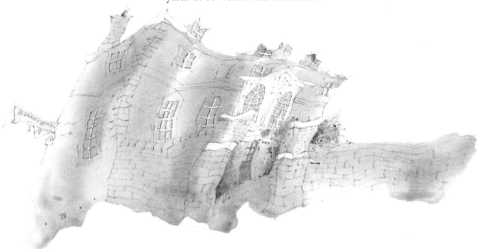

HOGARTH'S TOWN HOUSE was in Leicester Fields (now Leicester Square), just a short stroll away from the streets of Soho and Covent Garden, where he set so many of his moral paintings. This 'little country box by the Thames' was his summer retreat, a two-storey brick Georgian house set on the edge of a riverside village (see p. 171). Although the Hogarth roundabout and the arteries which feed it have now divorced the house from its setting, Church Street on the other side of the junction is still a quiet lane running down to the Thames past the churchyard where the artist is buried.

Here he came to escape his worries, from 1749, when he was 52, until the night before his death in 1764, working in a little weather-boarded studio in a corner of the garden. Despite the popularity of his prints, success had eluded him, neither the large-scale portraits nor the grand compositions of his later career meeting with critical approval. And his relentless campaign to improve the status of English painters seemed to have come to nothing, a particu-larly bitter pill in view of the activities of his neighbour Lord Burlington, who so effectively promoted Italian art and architecture (see p. 125). In what was once the kitchen hangs Hogarth's *The Man of Taste*, portraying Burlington as pompous and absurd.

The house is now a Hogarth museum, its panelled rooms hung with prints and portraits, including well-known series such as *The Harlot's Progress* and *Marriage à la Mode*, and the contrasted *Beer Street* and *Gin Lane*, the latter clearly showing the stepped obelisk-like spire of St George's Bloomsbury in the background. In front of the house, cut off from the roar of the Great West Road by a high brick wall, is a tiny garden. Hogarth's studio has gone, but the fruit of the gnarled mulberry here was used to make tarts for the foundling children entertained by Hogarth and his wife and for whom this compassionate man found homes in Chiswick, perhaps compensating for his own childlessness.

Open: Mon, Wed–Sat 11–18 (till 16 Oct–Mar), Sun from 14; closed for two weeks in Sept and Dec; admission free

Dr Johnson's House

17 Gough Square, EC4

— • —

underground Blackfriars (Circle and District lines),
Chancery Lane (Central line), Farringdon (Circle
and Metropolitan lines)

'MR JOHNSON IS A MAN of most dreadful appearance. He is a very big man, is troubled with sore eyes, the palsy, the king's evil. He is very slovenly in his dress and speaks with a most uncouth voice.' So James Boswell summed up his new acquaintance yet this ill-favoured, melancholic man had enormous creative and intellectual powers, and is remembered for his brilliant conversation and pithy sayings as much as for his writings. The work which established his reputation, the first comprehensive English dictionary, was compiled in the attic of the four-storey, early eighteenth-century red-brick house which closes the west end of tiny Gough Square. Johnson lived here from 1748 to 1759, having chosen the house because it was near William Strahan, the printer of his great work.

Six copyists worked in the garret while Johnson toiled for nine years compiling word lists and the 114,000 quotations with which he illustrates his definitions. His purpose was to produce a dictionary 'by which the pronunciation of our language may be fixed, and its attainment facilitated; by which its purity may be preserved, its use ascertained, and its duration lengthened.' The extent of his achievement can be gauged in the house by comparing what he produced in his first edition with the totally inadequate material previously available. Sadly, his wife Tetty, to whom he was much attached although she was considerably older than him and over-fond of drink, died before the work was completed. Johnson fuelled himself with tea, patronizing Mr Thomas Twining's shop at the west end of Fleet Street.

The house has little in the way of original contents and the small rooms with panelling of American pine, recently redecorated, seem almost clinically fresh. But there are many mementoes of Johnson, including a large black horsehair chair which he found particularly comfortable, and portraits of him and his friends, among them Joshua Reynolds and Elizabeth Carter. There is also a painting of his black servant Francis Barber, the chief beneficiary of Johnson's will, who had arrived in England as a slave from Jamaica. Only the long attic running across the house, watched over by Reynolds' portrait of his friend, has a suggestion of the man who once turned it into the literary equivalent of a sweatshop. Although the area round about is much changed, several small courts such as Johnson would have known still survive, and so does the Cheshire Cheese, one of the many pubs he used to visit as he shambled, bear-like, up and down Fleet Street.

Open: Mon–Sat, 11–17.30 (till 17 Oct–Apr); admission charge

KEATS HOUSE

Keats Grove, NW3

— • —

underground Hampstead (Northern line), then a 10-minute walk down High Street and left into Downshire Hill; or bus 24 from Trafalgar Square to South End Green and then a short walk up towards the heath and left into Keats Grove

'THERE IS NO DOUBT that an English winter would put an end to me, and do so in a lingering, hateful manner.' So Keats wrote to Shelley in the summer of 1820, a few months before he set out with his friend the painter Joseph Severn to winter in Italy. Already desperately ill with the pulmonary tuberculosis which had killed his brother Tom, he died in Rome on 23 February 1821, aged only 25.

The house where he spent much of the last two years of his life lies down the hill from the centre of Hampstead, close to the south-west corner of the heath. When Keats lived here there were fields beyond the garden, and there is still a feeling of the country about the place, with its mature trees and wooden gate. What now appears to be a solid Regency villa was originally two semi-detached houses, the second entered by a door to the side. Keats shared one set of small rooms with his friend Charles Brown, while the other side of the house, from 1819, was occupied by the family of Fanny Brawne, the eighteen-year-old girl with whom Keats fell deeply in love. A long sunny room ending in a conservatory was added by the actress Eliza Chester (1795–1859), said to have been the Prince Regent's last fling, who bought the property in 1838–9 and converted it into one large house.

The extensive collection of Keats' memorabilia now displayed here includes the engagement ring set with a purple almandine which Keats gave Fanny and

which she wore until her death in 1865. There is the portrait which Joseph Severn drew of Keats on 28 January 1821, 26 days before he died; Keats's last letter to Mrs Brawne, written from Naples harbour, with its scribbled postscript: 'Good bye Fanny! god bless you'; manuscript drafts of his poems; and the notebook he kept while a medical student at Guy's Hospital, ornamented with floral doodles. Also shown are some of the hostile reviews he had to endure, *Blackwoods Edinburgh Magazine* of 1818 suggesting 'It is a better and wiser thing to be a starved apothecary than a starved poet . . . .'

The house is no longer as Keats knew it, although there are still original features, such as the knocker on the front door, and the window shutters. The one room the poet would recognise is the small sitting-room looking onto the garden at the back of the house, where he would sit and read all day 'like a picture of somebody reading'. The bookcases are again filled with some of his books, and the furniture has been arranged to reproduce the interior which Severn copied in one of his best-known portraits of his friend (see p. 89), with two chairs placed self-consciously by the French windows. Keats wrote some of his best work at Wentworth Place, including 'Ode to a Nightingale', said to have been composed under a plum tree on the same spot as the one that flourishes at the front of the house.

Open: Mon–Fri 14–18 (13–17 Nov–Mar), Sat 10–13, 14–17, Sun 14–17; admission free; toilets; guided tours for groups booked in advance

KENWOOD (THE IVEAGH BEQUEST)

Hampstead Lane, NW3

———•———

underground Golders Green, Archway (Northern
line), then bus 210 to outside gates; no bus
connects with Highgate underground station, from
which the house is a 25-minute walk

O N 23 JUNE 1887, the 43-year-old multi-millionaire Edward Cecil Guinness, later 1st Earl of Iveagh, strolled into a Bond Street gallery. The partners were at lunch, and the cautious assistant refused to show him the fine paintings he asked to see. Very much put out, Lord Iveagh went straight to Agnews, where he made the same request. The partners were out here too, but the assistant was more perceptive, or more brash, and sold his new customer several pictures. This was the start of a fruitful and exclusive relationship which resulted in one of the most attractive art collections in London. Easily seen in half a morning, the paintings are very much a reflection of Lord Iveagh's personal taste, and you sense that they were all loved. Concentrated on seventeenth-century Dutch and Flemish canvases and late eighteenth-century English paintings, the collection includes a self-portrait by Rembrandt, *The Guitar Player* by Vermeer, and society women by Reynolds, Gainsborough and Romney. The Rembrandt is a late work, painted in about 1665, only four years before he died: the nose is bulbous, the painter gazes out at

us as if he is searching his soul, grey hair escaping from a white turban on his head; every one of his 59 years is etched on his face. Vermeer's guitar player has none of Rembrandt's introspection, the girl plucking the strings caught glancing sideways, as if just called to supper. Among the portraits is Sir Joshua Reynolds' painting of 'Kitty' Fisher, the courtesan who was to die for her beauty at the age of 26, poisoned by the white lead she plastered on her face, and yet another Romney of Lord Nelson's Emma, here shown improbably at a spinning wheel, with a chicken at her feet. Gainsborough's ladies seem more aloof, among them Mary, Countess Howe, her pink dress and grey apron only lightly ruffled by the approaching storm seen behind her.

These paintings hang in the villa which Robert Adam remodelled between 1764 and 1779 for William Murray, 1st Earl of Mansfield, encasing the existing brick building in stucco, adding a third storey and a

new wing, and embellishing the interior with chimney-pieces, cornices, shutters and other unifying details. The house is not large, a country retreat rather than a mansion, but Adam's patron allowed his fellow Scot a free hand, and it is the earliest example of the architect's mature style.

Unlike most of London's great houses, Kenwood shuns the Thames perching high up above the city on the ridge connecting Highgate and Hampstead. Its wooded land-scape park, with a lake in the gentle dip below the house, now merges impercep-tibly with the trees and meadows of Hampstead Heath, as if this too were part of the estate. Approached from this direc-tion, the house is seen at its grandest, Adam's stuccoed three-storey central bay with its shallow pediment and fanciful decoration flanked by a low, many-windowed pavilion on either side. One is the orangery, a survivor from the earlier house and now hung with pictures; the other is the library, Adam's most original contribution to Kenwood. Lord Mansfield had no collection of paintings or sculpture, but he was a bibliophile, and his finest books would have been displayed in the bookcases lining the apses at either end of the room. This was all the book space Adam allowed him. Designed as a double cube with a high barrel ceiling, the library is essentially a huge reception room, with vast French pier glasses between the windows and mirrored recesses on the interior wall to reflect the company and the candlelight. A colour scheme in blue and

brown sets off stucco work by Joseph Rose the Younger and nineteen paintings by Antonio Zucchi on walls and ceiling. In daylight the effect is rather overpowering, but the room probably looks much more effective at night.

The north-facing entrance front with its grand two-storey portico is no longer as Adam intended it, the pilasters he added at either end of the façade now partly masked by the projecting yellow-brick wings added by George Saunders for the 2nd Earl in 1793–6. During these three years the 2nd Earl also commissioned Humphry Repton to improve his uncle's informal park, which was given winding rhododendron walks and a romantically wooded drive. Repton's masterstroke, however, was the little ivy tunnel through which you emerge on the south terrace and suddenly see the natural amphitheatre in which Kenwood lies. And from the windows of the upper floors, it is still possible to look out over London, and to enjoy the view which so enchanted Robert Adam.

David Murray, 2nd Earl of Mansfield, was also 7th Viscount Stormont, inheriting Scone Palace, the family's Scottish seat, as well as Kenwood. Later generations pre-ferred Scone, although the 4th Earl gave a grand *fête champêtre* in London in 1843, with Prince Albert and the Duke of Wellington among the guests of honour. Kenwood again became the setting for glamorous society parties in 1910, when the 6th Earl let the house to Grand Duke Michael of Russia, exiled because of his morganatic marriage. Although the Russian Revolution must have cast a long shadow over his years in England, the dashing duke seems to have lived life to the full, hiring orches-tras and illuminating the grounds for lavish entertainments. But all he has left behind him are two memorial tablets to his dogs in the undergrowth of North Wood. Under threat from developers after the First World War, the house was acquired in 1925 by the 1st Earl of Iveagh who presented it, with his collection, to the nation. The original con-tents, including Adam's specially designed furniture, were all sold in 1922, but pieces are gradually being 'rediscovered'.

Open: Daily 10–18 (till 16 Nov–mid March); admission free; toilets

LEIGHTON HOUSE

12 Holland Park Road, Kensington, W14

———— • ————

underground High Street Kensington (Circle and
District Lines)

N<small>O ONE LOOKING</small> at the street façade of this plain, rather top-heavy red-brick house built for the Victorian painter Frederic Leighton (1830–96) would guess that it contains one of the most extraordinary interiors in London. Opening off the staircase hall, from which it is seen down a cool corridor lined with lustrous blue tiles by William de Morgan is a re-creation of a room from a Moorish palace, like something out of the *Arabian Nights*. A shadowy domed chamber rising through two floors is lined with gleaming aquamarine fifteenth- and sixteenth-century tiles from the Middle East, ornate Damascan window screens shut out the sun, while in the centre glistens a black marble fountain pool, with two candlesticks projecting from the water. Low

divans fill the window bays, and high above is a screened balcony, as if a harem might be hidden away there. Leighton acquired some of the tiles on his travels, others through friends such as the explorer Richard Burton, whose translation of the *Arabian Nights* scandalized Victorian society. Some panels spell out an Arabic inscription, others depict wild tulips, carnations, roses and hyacinths, or brightly-plumaged birds, their throats all 'cut' to accord with Islamic law, which banned the representation of living things.

The hall was a later addition to the orig-

inal house built for the artist in 1864–6 by his friend and fellow Royal Academician George Aitchison, who focused it on a huge north-facing studio with blood-red walls. One corner of the room is still obscured by the skimpy screen behind which models were expected to change or undress.

Although Leighton's original furnishings and collections have been dispersed, the decorative schemes all reflect his designs, with lavish use of ebonized woodwork and rich colours setting off romanticized paintings by Watts, Burne-Jones, Alma-Tadema and Leighton himself. When only 25, Leighton had acquired a reputation overnight when his *Cimabue's Madonna*, which was bought by Queen Victoria, was exhibited at the *Royal Academy*. By 1864, when the house was started, he was 34, and aware that success brought its own pitfalls. For the last few years, he had cut a brilliant figure in London society, frequently gracing the Prince and Princess of Wales's receptions at Marlborough House, but the conflicting demands of his work and his social life had begun to affect his health. Determined to paint undisturbed, he had Aitchison plan his house with only one bedroom.

Open: All year, Mon–Sat 11–5; garden Apr–Sept; entrance free

Linley Sambourne House

18 Stafford Terrace, Kensington, W8

———— • ————

underground High Street Kensington (Circle and
District Lines)

THIS STUCCOED
Victorian terrace
house, disting-
uishable from the
rest in the row
only by the tiny
conservatory attached to
the bay on the first floor,
has changed little since
its first occupants, the
cartoonist and illustrator
Edward Linley Sambourne (1844–1910)
and his wife Mary Anne, moved here in late
1874, shortly after their marriage. Still
crammed with the family's furniture and
other belongings, the crowded, atmospheric rooms give a glimpse of the life of
the upper middle classes at the end of the
nineteenth century and of the work of the
gifted head of the family. Linley Sambourne is known for the drawings he contributed to *Punch* from the early 1870s until
the autumn of 1909, although for most of
this time, until 1901, the magazine's
principal political car-
toonist was John Ten-
niel, to whom Sam-
bourne was in effect
playing second fiddle.
Frequently required to
produce his weekly con-
tribution in only eight
hours, he would sit at his
desk with a watch hang-
ing in front of him while
a messenger waited.
Numerous examples of
his work, including his
appealing illustrations
for *The Water Babies*
(1886) and *Tales of Hans
Andersen* (1910), are

among the photographs,
drawings, prints and pic-
tures which crowd the
walls, many of them part
of the vast store of re-
ference material he ac-
cumulated in his meti-
culous attention to
detail. In the dining-
room, photographs are
hung so closely that they
appear like a sepia wash over the walls,
concealing the William Morris wallpaper.

The artist's easel and his camera on its
sturdy tripod stand in the L-shaped drawing-room running across the house, such
uncompromising objects curiously at home
among the fringed and pleated lampshades,
heavy curtains, plump cushions, and surfaces crowded with books, vases, clocks,
photographs and knick-knacks. Upstairs,
the bedroom occupied by the Sambourne's
son Roy, the eternal Edwardian bachelor,
has signed photographs of Edna May and
other actresses, and
books by Conan Doyle
and Rudyard Kipling.
Roy never married, con-
tinuing to sleep in the
brass bed in this room
until his death in 1946,
but his sister Maud, who
became Mrs Leonard
Messel, was the grand-
mother of Anthony
Armstrong-Jones, Earl
of Snowdon.

Open: 1 Mar–30 Oct, Wed
10–16, Sun 14–17; admis-
sion charge

Marble Hill House

Richmond Road, Twickenham, Middlesex
British Rail to Richmond (from Waterloo), or
underground to Richmond (District line); or by
boat to Richmond from Westminster Pier (see
p. 181); then take any bus going over Richmond
Bridge towards Twickenham and get off at St
Stephen's church, or 25-minute walk over bridge
and left along river

DESPITE THE SPREAD of London far beyond it, the Thames valley at Twickenham is still rural, willow-lined banks framing the river as it winds lazily across the water-meadows below Richmond Hill. Marble Hill, the country retreat of a king's mistress, is one of the few survivors of the string of sumptuous villas built along this stretch of the valley in the eighteenth century (see p. 118), within easy reach of the royal residences at Kew (see p. 14), *Hampton Court* and *Windsor*. Many visitors now arrive here by car, but it is still best approached from the river, by way of the shady path leading south from Richmond Bridge, or across the water in the little open ferry from Ham. The house is then seen as it was intended, set back across a stretch of grass, trees framing the three-storey, cream and white façade, with two dormer windows just visible over the central pediment.

This Palladian box was built in 1724–9 for Henrietta Howard, close friend of George II and later Countess of Suffolk. Henrietta's marriage to the improvident Charles Howard, youngest son of the 5th Earl of Suffolk and thirteen years her

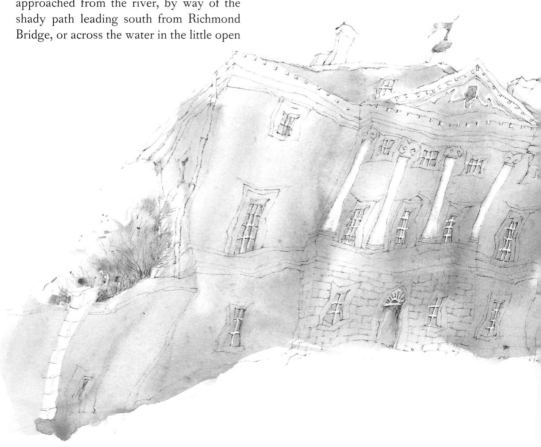

senior, had finally failed several years earlier, and the villa was financed by a settlement from the future king, who from about 1720 had begun to spend 'every evening of his life, three or four hours, in Mrs Howard's lodging'. Probably based on an initial design by Colen Campbell, architect to the Prince of Wales, it was built by Roger Morris under the supervision of Lord Henry Herbert, later 9th Earl of Pembroke, another member of the Prince's circle.

Marble Hill is a curious mixture of ostentation and cosiness, of the lavish and up-to-the-minute and the delightfully old-fashioned, as if Mrs Howard were hedging her bets. Beyond the stone-floored hall on the river front, a carved mahogany staircase rises to the beautifully proportioned Great Room, a 24-foot cube with a high coved ceiling penetrating into the storey above, a direct descendant of Inigo Jones's Single Cube Room of c.1649 at Wilton House in Wiltshire. White panelling sets off gilded plasterwork, golden cherubs loll on the pediment of the chimney-piece, and gold frames outline the views of Rome by Giovanni Paolo Panini, executed for Marble Hill in 1738. Like the staircase, the floor is of highly polished mahogany, some of the impressive boards being almost twenty inches wide. The other rooms are intimate and domestic, and no trace of Palladian grandeur penetrates to the third floor, where a sunny, low-ceilinged long gallery stretching across the house has a Jacobean flavour. Windows looking east over the garden give glimpses of the Thames and of the chimneys of *Ham House* through the trees across the river.

In the wooded grounds, originally designed by the poet Alexander Pope, whose own villa lay a mile or so upstream, and landscaped by Charles Bridgeman, is a rustic grotto, and one of the largest black walnuts in England, planted in the early eighteenth century. A bell tower crowns the elegant ivy-covered stables to the west of the house, and the path running past them to the edge of the estate may perhaps be the one along which the young Horace Walpole used to come to see his elderly neighbour from Strawberry Hill, his Gothic fantasy which survives nearby. A frequent visitor, he spent two hours with Lady Suffolk on 25 July 1767, the day before she died at the age of seventy-nine. She had outlived all those who helped plan the house and grounds.

Open: Sat–Thurs 10–17 (till 16 Nov–Jan), closed 13–14; admission free; toilets in grounds; guided tour on request; audio-tour available

Osterley Park

Isleworth, Middlesex

———— • ————

access from Syon Lane, north side of A4 Great
West Road; *underground* Osterley (Piccadilly line),
then ¾-mile walk

'ON FRIDAY WE WENT to see — oh! the palace of palaces! ... such expense! such taste! such profusion! ... all the Percies and Seymours of Sion must die of envy.' So Horace Walpole described Osterley in 1773, when Robert Adam was busy transforming the existing Elizabethan house for the wealthy banker Robert Child. As at *Syon*, just a few miles away on the banks of the Thames, Adam incorporated his distinctive interiors within the shell of the old building, preserving the ghostly outlines of the great Tudor mansion erected in the 1570s by Sir Thomas Gresham, founder of the *Royal Exchange* and one of the richest merchants of his age. Severe red-brick ranges forming a hollow square carry Gresham's gay corner turrets, their cupolas topped with stone pine cones. On the east façade, an immensely wide flight of steps flanked by the eagles of the Child family crest leads up to Adam's grandiose portico, designed as an open screen to close one side of the courtyard. In contrast to Syon, this paved interior space forms a grand approach to Adam's characteristically glacial hall, and is not hidden from sight at the centre of the house.

Inside, the rooms on show are formal, with none of the domestic clutter which suggests people might actually have lived here. Adam's decorative schemes remain largely unaltered, with ornate plasterwork, cameo-like panel paintings by Antonio Zucchi, French pier glasses, and mahogany and satinwood furniture by John Linnell. In the south wing, a long view through four aligned doorways in the state apartments is focused on two maidens dancing round a tripod – a painted detail in Adam's extraordinary Etruscan dressing-room, where classical urns, spindly trellis work and other motifs in brown and black on a pale blue ground look as if they have been taken straight off a set of Wedgwood china. A hint of candle-light half-way down the enfilade marks the darkened tapestry room, hung with flowery, brilliantly pink Gobelins tapestries of 1775, their claret ground picked up in the upholstery of Linnell's gilded sofas and chairs. The garden theme also features in the state bedroom next door, where the dome of the eight-poster bed is garlanded with realistic silk flowers. Those who find this profusion of pink and gold over-rich, like cream-filled milk chocolate, will probably prefer the coolly classical library on the other side of the house, with pedimented bookcases white against the grey walls. The only vivid colour here is in the ceiling, where delicate plaster arabesques are picked out in red, blue, green and gold.

Adam was preceded at Osterley by his arch-rival Sir William Chambers, who rebuilt the west front and designed the long gallery which now runs its length, an impressive 130-foot corridor that the anglophile Henry James described as 'a cheerful upholstered avenue'. Sadly, the family picture collection

has long since been removed, the paintings which now hang here mostly being on loan.

Chambers also had a hand in Osterley's wooded park, now the largest in the London area, designing the long river-like lake, which could pass for a section of the Thames, and building the little pink and white pedimented temple hidden in the trees beyond Adam's semi-circular orangery. Despite the planes passing low overhead on their way to Heathrow, and the constant roar of traffic on the M4, the open tree-studded grassland still has a feel of the country. To the north of the house is Gresham's red-brick stable block, with hexagonal staircase towers at the angles of the wings. When Elizabeth I came to visit her great subject in 1576, she suggested the courtyard which then linked stables and house was too big, prompting Sir Thomas to instruct his workmen to build a dividing wall overnight. What

the queen said the next morning is not reported, but the hastily erected wall and the turreted mansion show clearly on a seventeenth-century map in Syon House.

Adam's reconstruction was completed only a couple of years before Robert Child died at the early age of forty-three, his untimely end partly caused, it was said, by the behaviour of his only child, Sarah Anne. The little dark-haired girl in a frilly mob cap portrayed in crayon in her mother's dressing room was to elope at the age of 18 with John Fane, 10th Earl of Westmorland. When her mother rebuked her gently, pointing out that there had been much better prospects in view, the high-spirited girl replied, 'A bird in the hand is worth two in the bush.'

Open: House, Mar, Sat, Sun 13–17; Apr–end Oct, Wed–Sat 13–17, Sun, Bank Hol Mon 11–17; park, all year, 9–19.30 or sunset; admission charge to house; toilets; guided tours by arrangement in advance with Administrator

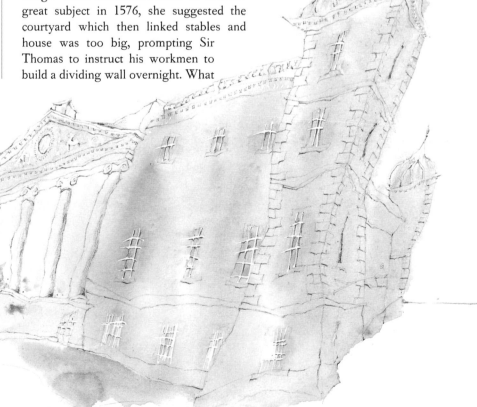

RANGER'S HOUSE

Chesterfield Walk, Blackheath, SE10

British Rail to Greenwich or Blackheath (from
Charing Cross), then a 20-minute walk, up steep
Croom's Hill from Greenwich, on the flat across
the heath from Blackheath; or Docklands Light
Railway to Island Gardens (see p. 181); or by
boat from Westminster Pier to Greenwich (see
p. 181), then a 25-minute walk uphill.

A T ONE SIDE of the plateau-like southern section of Greenwich Park is a cheerful rose garden, from which steps lead up to the back entrance to what was for a time the park ranger's residence. This modest two-storey eighteenth-century house, its red-brick façades crowned with a stone balustrade, was inherited in 1749 by Philip, 4th Earl of Chesterfield (1694–1773), the distinguished statesman and diplomat, who is chiefly remembered for his letters of advice to his natural son Philip Stanhope. Although not intended for publication, his homilies on good behaviour and etiquette became a handbook of manners. Dr Johnson (see p. 135), who had addressed the *Plan* of his *Dictionary* to Chesterfield to no avail, declared that the letters 'teach the morals of a whore and the manners of a dancing master'. Philip Stanhope behaved as any normal person would in the circumstances, marrying in secret a woman whom his father considered beneath him. All would have been well, had not Philip's death in 1768 let the cat out of the bag, the revelation that he had a wife and two children being the cruellest disappointment of Chesterfield's old age.

The grand, bow-fronted ground-floor gallery which Lord Chesterfield added to the house in 1749–50 is now used to display nine full-length Jacobean portraits attributed to William Larkin, his gorgeously arrayed subjects in impossibly extravagant attire all radiating the confidence of the court of James I. Seven – known as the Berkshire marriage set – are of women, perhaps painted to mark the wedding of Elizabeth Cecil, daughter of the Earl of Exeter, to Thomas Howard, 2nd son of the 1st Earl of Suffolk, in 1714. Young Diana Cecil, painted when she was

only twelve, wears the same expensively slashed grey and gold dress as her sister Anne, and both clutch identical lace-edged handkerchiefs. The two men in the series – the Sackville brothers who became the 3rd and 4th Earls of Dorset – are even more magnificent. Richard Sackville, the dissolute, spendthrift 3rd Earl, who was forced towards the end of his short life to mortgage Knole, the family's great Tudor palace, to pay for his gambling debts, is a confection in black velvet, white satin and lace, the huge rosettes on his shoes, as the novelist Angela Carter has described, like 'prize-winning dahlias'. The brothers stand on very similar, richly-coloured Turkey carpets, and the portrait of the 4th Earl is distinguished by strands of black silk hanging from his left ear. To see how fashions changed, look at the portrait of Diana Cecil on the opposite wall, painted in 1638 by Cornelius Johnson when she was in middle age, her low-necked blue satin dress without any of the luscious embroidery that sparkles across the room.

These paintings are the high point of the Suffolk Collection, which hangs throughout the house in a series of mostly small and rather dispirited rooms. Also on show here are the musical instruments assembled by Arnold Dolmetsch, who pioneered the revival of interest in early music and lived nearby. Some of the instruments, such as the Kirckman harpsichord in the gallery, are important examples of seventeenth- and eighteenth-century craftsmanship; others, including the strange rectangular stringed crwth, or Irish harp, were made by Dolmetsch himself. Appropriately, the gallery is now frequently used for chamber concerts.

Open: Daily 10–18 (summer), 10–16 (winter), closed 13–14; admission free; toilets

ROYAL BOTANIC GARDENS, KEW

Kew, Richmond, Surrey

———— • ————

underground Kew Gardens (District line); or by
boat to Kew Gardens from Westminster Pier (see
p. 181)

KEW – AS THE Royal Botanic Gardens are familiarly known – is the Londoner's opportunity to have a day in the country. Once inside the gardens, with inviting tree-lined vistas stretching away in every direction and views across the Thames to the grounds of *Syon House*, only the planes winging their way to Heathrow destroy the illusion that you could be visiting an estate in deepest Norfolk. There is, too, an extraordinary tranquillity about Kew, and it is so large that even on the hottest of summer Sundays it is always possible to find a quiet corner.

The 300-acre botanic gardens originated in the eighteenth century, when the area was divided between two contiguous royal estates: Richmond Lodge, belonging to George II and Queen Caroline, and Kew Palace, the home of their eldest son Frederick and his wife Princess Augusta. In 1759, after Frederick's death, Augusta started a small botanic garden with William Aiton, who had trained at the *Chelsea Physic Garden*, as head gardener. When George III inherited both the Richmond and the Kew estates, he appointed Sir Joseph Banks as horticultural and botanical adviser, and it was during his unofficial directorship (c.1772–1820) that Kew began to acquire the worldwide reputation it enjoys today. Banks and the first official director, Sir William Hooker, appointed after the gardens were taken over by the state in 1841, encouraged a succession of plant collectors who travelled all over the world in search of specimens. In 1876 Amazon rubber saplings were smuggled here and developed before being sent to the Far East to start the plantations which broke the Brazilian rubber monopoly. Explorers too would remember Kew on their travels, both Cook and Darwin returning with 'precious specimens'. Kew's beauty and popularity as a public park tend to disguise the fact that it is still primarily a scientific institution, of international repute, which has unparalleled plant collections and plays an important role in plant identification and in the conservation of threatened species.

Features inherited from the eighteenth and nineteenth centuries add much to Kew's charm. The long lake, with its islands and fringes of water-loving plants, was created between 1856 and 1871, and is now a haunt of mallards, moorhens, coots, tufted ducks and other wildfowl. At one end are the two

Victorian glasshouses by Decimus Burton: his Palm House cascading to the ground in voluptuous curves, his Temperate House, once the largest greenhouse in the world, strung out in a chain of glistening pavilions and octagonal summer-houses like an elaborate sugar model. And dotted about the former grounds of Kew Palace are a series of eye-catchers built for Princess Augusta by William Chambers. Three of his classical temples survive, one crowning a steep, flower-speckled, grassy mound, while his ten-storey pagoda, ringed

with red balconies at every stage, soars above the trees in the south-east corner of the gardens. Kew Palace itself, built in 1631 by a wealthy merchant, is a tall red-brick box with delightful 'Dutch' gables, its modest rooms furnished in the style of the eighteenth century when George III and Queen Charlotte were in residence. Here you can see the black armchair in which Charlotte died on 17 November 1818, her husband's increasing insanity robbing her final years of any tranquillity.

The layout of the gardens, parts of which were landscaped by Capability Brown and William Nesfield, suggests a well-wooded park, with collections of conifers, birches, mulberries, oaks and other trees forming attractive clumps and shading the many walks and glades. There are carpets of bluebells in spring, and brilliant displays of rhododendrons and azaleas along the Hollow Walk. The most formal areas are to the north and east, near the main gate on to Kew Green (see p. 172), with a rose garden in front of the Palm House, bedding schemes along the Broad Walk, and a rose pergola and herbaceous borders in a former kitchen garden. Here too is the curious grass garden, its neatly-edged beds filled with clumps of rank and feathery growth that look to the untutored eye as if they badly need weeding. Kew's most prestigious recent addition is the Princess of Wales conservatory, the angularity of its glass gables contrasting with Decimus Burton's curves. Inside, computer-controlled environments recreate ten climatic zones, from desert to cloud forest. In the steamy heat of the moist tropics, roof sprays drench the leaf canopy in a permanent mist. Through a glass door into the temperate orchid house, the temperature plummets. A sticky black mangrove swamp has been created by a pool, and a desert of small pebbles conceals the fleshy, swollen tips of the extraordinary *Lithops*, or living stones. In winter intrepid walkers can warm themselves up here and in the other glasshouses, but in summer there is nothing better than a long picnic beneath the trees.

Open: Daily 9.30–18.30 or dusk if earlier (till 20 or dusk Sun and Bank Hols); glasshouses 10–16.30 or dusk (17.30 or dusk Sun); Kew Palace, Apr–Sep, daily 11–17.30; Queen Charlotte's Cottage, Apr–Sep, weekends only, 11–17; admission charge to gardens, Kew Palace and Queen Charlotte's Cottage; toilets; guide lecturers can be booked in advance for parties

SPENCER HOUSE

27 St James's Place, SW1

———— • ————

underground Green Park (Jubilee, Piccadilly,
Victoria lines)

THIS EIGHTEENTH CENTURY classical palace sits high up on an arcaded terrace looking out over the trees of Green Park. Newly-cleaned Portland stone gleams white in the sunshine; languorous, drapery-clad statues and a pediment mark the roofline; smooth columns frame the first-floor windows and a frieze of carved ox skulls echoes decoration inside the house. All is symmetrical, assured, balanced. Inside, visitors are shown the sumptuously decorated rooms looking onto the park, all of them newly refurbished. Plasterwork, carved chair rails and door cases glitter with gilding, the colour of a carpet is picked up in velvet curtains, or that of ceiling decoration in a striped wallpaper. Portraits by Gainsborough and Reynolds and heroic scenes by Benjamin West hang on the walls, blue and rust-coloured Imari ware lines a mantelpiece, and period furniture includes a Louis XVI tulipwood roll-top desk, beautifully inlaid.

Spencer House was begun in 1756 by the youthful 1st Earl Spencer and his teenage bride, whom he had married at a secret ceremony at his coming-out ball the year before. Immensely rich, the young earl was able to acquire a prime site for his splendid new house, and to employ the best craftsment of the day to adorn it. His first architect, John Vardy, a pupil of William Kent, had started working for the previous owner and so in a sense came with the house, but in 1758, when the shell of the building and some decorative schemes had been completed, he was replaced by the individual but indolent James 'Athenian' Stuart. Both men have left their mark on the house, Vardy principally on the exterior and the ground floor, Stuart on the state rooms upstairs, although Vardy's schemes have been blurred by the later attentions of Henry Holland, who made alterations for the 2nd Earl in the 1780s and 1790s. Most memorable is Vardy's theatrical palm room, with a deep alcove ringed by columns disguised as gilded palm trees, the fronds arching out over statue-filled niches and a round-headed window, while on the floor above are the lavish main reception room, with a high coved ceiling in green and gold, and James Stuart's most original interior, every inch painted and gilded and with inset panels depicting gambolling cherubs, serene Italianate landscapes and classical deities.

Much of what visitors see, though, is not eighteenth-century at all, but a recreation of the Georgian schemes. In 1942, fearing all would be destroyed in the Blitz, the Spencers removed everything they could to Althorp, the family's Northamptonshire home, even stripping out mouldings, doors and fireplaces. Carved chair rails, skirtings, door cases and other details have been painstakingly reproduced by modern craftsmen, and the marble fireplaces – several of which have still to be completed – are being copied from those now at Althorp. Similarly, only some of the furniture is original to the house, notably the gilded sofas and armchairs in the Painted Room, and a couple of pieces, such as one of the Adam-style wall mirrors in Lady Spencer's room, are modern imitations. This is a splendid copy, not the real thing.

Open: Sun, all year except Jan and Aug, 10.45–16.45, guided tours only, advance booking on 071 499 8620; admission charge; toilets

Syon House

Syon Park, Brentford

———— • ————

British Rail to Brentford or Syon Lane (from Waterloo), then a 1-mile walk; or BR
to Kew Bridge, then bus 237 or 267 to a few yards from entrance; or underground
to Gunnersbury (District line) and bus 237 or 267; or by boat to Kew Gardens from
Westminster Pier (see p. 181) and walk over bridge to buses

EVERYTHING HAS HAPPENED at
Syon. A half-rotten oak stake now
preserved in a glass case just off the
hall was once part of the palisade
with which the ancient Britons
sought to prevent Julius Caesar
crossing the Thames in 54 BC. Catherine
Howard, Henry VIII's fifth queen, spent
her last unhappy months here before she
went to the block in February 1542. Here
Henry lay after his death five years later,
when his body was being taken from Westminster to *Windsor*. His coffin burst open
during the night, and in the morning the
dogs were found licking up such remains as
had fallen to the floor. On the premature
death of Henry's heir Edward VI, Lady Jane
Grey was persuaded to accept the Crown in
Syon's long gallery and was rowed from
here to the *Tower of London*, a fortress
which only too easily became her prison
nine days later when she was ousted by
Mary Tudor. Guy Fawkes came to summon
his accomplice Thomas Percy from Syon on
4 November 1605, and together they set off
for London to blow up Parliament. Charles
I rode over here to see his sons in the
autumn of 1647 while he was detained at
Hampton Court by the Parliamentarians,
and in the same year a historic council at
Syon gave Cromwell the confidence to
march through London to occupy Westminster and the Tower.

Syon is now the last major house in
London still in private ownership. It is a
show place, but it is also the home of the
present Duke and Duchess of Northumberland. Like almost all London's great
houses, it borders the Thames, looking
across the river to the trees of Kew (see
p. 147). Set in 260 acres of parkland and
meadow, where fat cattle graze beneath
clumps of oaks, chestnuts, cedars and

beech, and approached by a long lime
avenue, Syon still feels like a mansion in
the country. It is also one of the few places
where the Thames is not embanked, with a
rich marsh flora along the river.

The house itself could easily be mistaken
for a rather severe boarding school. It is
unexpectedly plain, its long, low ranges set
round an interior courtyard and faced in
yellow-grey Bath stone relieved only by
projecting corner turrets and a crenellated

parapet, and by the two gay, toy-town lodges with classical windows which frame the entrance façade. Inside, however, is one of Robert Adam's most brilliant decorative schemes, described by Sacheverell Sitwell as 'among the greatest works of art in England'. Adam was engaged by the Earl (later 1st Duke) of Northumberland in 1762 to transform the great Tudor house built by the Duke of Somerset, Protector of Edward VI, on the estate of a dissolved Bridgettine monastery. Unlike Somerset House, the Duke's city residence, which was swept away to build the Georgian palace which now houses the *Courtauld Institute Galleries*, the skeleton of old Syon House was retained, Adam's great state rooms being created within the Tudor shell. Each range is two rooms deep, the splendid chambers intended for entertainment and display forming a collar round the more intimate rooms looking on to the courtyard which are now inhabited by the Duke and his family.

Classical statues on delicately stuccoed plinths survey visitors coming into the cool entrance hall with its black-and-white chequered floor and plasterwork by Joseph Rose. Valadier's bronze statue of a dying Gaul, his strength almost visibly waning as he sinks slowly to the ground, lies at the foot of the steps Adam introduced to overcome uneven floor levels. Beyond him is the ante-room, a visual assault of blue and gold, scagliola and plasterwork. Green-grey columns projecting from the walls carry gilded statues, and the highly polished floor, also scagliola, is brilliantly coloured in red, blue and yellow.

There is little ease here, but you could imagine sitting gazing over the park from the drawing-room, where faded crimson Spitalfields silk on the walls sets off a collection of Stuart portraits by Sir Peter Lely and Van Dyck. Here is the canvas Lely painted of Charles I and the young Duke of York when the captive king came over from

Hampton Court, a commission which cost the 10th Earl of Northumberland £20. Charles looks worn and tired, his son, who has inherited his father's reddish hair, destined also to lose the throne. Above them arches the most extraordinary ceiling in the house, with circular medallions painted by Giambattista Cipriani set within a repeated pattern of octagonals and squares in a medley of gold, red and blue. The scale is too small for Cipriani's work to be seen properly; Adam's great rival Sir William Chambers suggested dinner plates had been chucked at the ceiling, but to me it looks more like expensive wrapping paper. Cipriani obviously had a sense of humour: his figures on the ceiling are all free-flying, but those on the coving have their feet firmly on the ground. The colour scheme of the 136-foot long gallery is much more subdued. This light and airy room, with eleven windows looking over the park towards Kew, is decorated in grey-pink, aubergine, soft green and cream. Adam's painted medallions and lunettes, classical pilasters and arabesques of plaster replaced the dark wood panelling of the old house.

Adam worked at Syon for several years, but his grand design was never finished, and the north range was left unaltered until the nineteenth century. Portraits of many of the most notable people connected with the house now hang here, among them Lady Jane Grey, in a white fur stole, Lord Protector Somerset, his wispy red beard only partly concealing the hard line of his mouth, and the 9th Earl of Northumberland, the 'Wizard Earl', thrown into the Tower unjustly by James I for his alleged involvement in the Gunpowder Plot (see p. 37). More unexpected is the weather-beaten, genial face of the 95-year-old William Timms, waterman to George III, George IV, William IV, Queen Victoria, and the 1st, 2nd and 3rd Dukes of Northumberland. Nearby is an extraordinary survival, Moses Glover's map of the Hundred of Isleworth and the Manor of Syon in 1635, with the Thames looping its way through a rural landscape to *Hampton Court* and *Windsor* and a little straggle of travellers crossing the dangerous open common of Hounslow Heath.

As well as engaging Adam to transform the interior of the house, the 1st Duke also called in 'Capability' Brown to remodel the park. Between 1767 and 1773 Brown created the long, gently curving lake which is the focus of the large informal woodland garden, and laid out the sweep of lawn overlooked by a statue of Flora, goddess of flowers, perched on a 55-foot Doric column. The planting includes banks of rhododendrons and azaleas and many specimen trees, among them a superb Pride of India (*Koelreuteria paniculata*) the only sizeable Afghan ash (*Fraxinus xanthoxyloides*) in England, huge swamp cypresses (*Taxodium distichum*), scarlet oaks (*Quercus coccinea*) and a young *Aesculus octandra*. Daffodils and crocuses put on a show in spring. Immediately inside the garden entrance is the gentle arc of the 382-foot Great Conservatory, built in 1820–27 by Charles Fowler, the architect of the market buildings in Covent Garden (see p. 12), who topped the central section with a bulbous dome. There is a small formal garden here with clipped yew cones and a pool, while on the other side of the house, reached through a coin-operated turnstile, is the six-acre rose garden, with a long pergola supporting ramblers, climbers and clematis and shrub roses in open glades. Syon was of horticultural importance long before Kew was established: the first botanical garden in England was created here for the Duke of Somerset in the sixteenth century by Dr William Turner, the 'father of English botany' and author of *Names of Herbes*. Mulberry trees imported by the Duke, probably from Germany or the Low Countries, still thrive in the private gardens on the north side of the house.

Two other attractions border the huge car park area. Most recent is the butterfly house, a collection of all kinds of six- and eight-legged creatures including locusts, stick insects, spiders, scorpions and praying mantis as well as butterflies. Syon is also host to the British Motor Industry Heritage Trust Museum, with serried ranks of gleaming cars illustrating the history of British motoring.

Open: Syon House, Apr–Sep, Sun–Thurs 12–17; Oct, Sun 12–17; gardens, daily 10–18 (dusk in winter); Butterfly House, daily, 10–17 (15 in winter); British Motor Industry Heritage Trust Museum, daily Apr–Oct 10–17, Nov–Mar 10–16; admission charge; toilets; audio tour of house

6

CATHEDRALS AND CHURCHES

— • —

The many-steepled sky
Which made our City fair,
Buried in buildings high
Is now no longer there.

JOHN BETJEMAN'S VERSE – to be sung to Handel's march from *Scipio* – laments what is all too obvious to anyone who looks over the City from the top of the *Monument* or the dome of *St Paul's Cathedral*. The steeples, spires and towers which once dominated the skyline are now dwarfed by skyscrapers of concrete, steel and glass. On the other hand, it is remarkable that so many churches are still there, when so much was devastated in the Blitz or has been swept away since. And from the ground they are much more obvious, appearing unexpectedly around corners, half-glimpsed down alleys, or seen suddenly framed by higher buildings on either side.

Once they were more numerous still. Medieval London was a city of churches in a way that seems almost inconceivable today, with large areas taken up by the spacious precincts of abbeys, convents and nunneries, among them the Carthusian monastery of *Charterhouse* and the Benedictine abbey at Westminster (see p. 165). At the end of the twelfth century, when London's population was some 20–25,000, William Stephen, secretary to Thomas Becket, recorded 126 parish churches, most of which would have been within the walls. Dominating them all was Old St Paul's, started by William the Conqueror and finished in 1315, when it was crowned with a 500-foot lead-sheathed spire, the tallest that has ever been built. The skyline of this ecclesiastical city, delightfully portrayed in early seventeenth-century engravings, was a kind of northern Venice, the brick campanile of the south here translated into Gothic towers and spires. Almost everything was swept away in the Great Fire of 1666, which destroyed Old St Paul's and 88 of the existing parish churches (see p. 13). Only on the fringes of the medieval city did some buildings escape the conflagration, among them the cathedral-like *St Bartholomew the Great*, overlooking Smithfield market, and two very different churches on Bishopsgate: tiny St Ethelburga, the smallest church in the City, its rough stone façade wedged in between offices on either side, and the unusual St Helen's, relic of a Benedictine convent, where two thirteenth-century naves stand side by side, one designed to serve the parish, the other for the community of nuns. Another intriguing building, the Round Church of the Knights Templar, based on the Church of the Holy Sepulchre in Jerusalem, is buried in the Inns of Court (see p. 11). Its restored circular nave dating from 1185 is filled with cross-legged effigies of medieval knights, and entered through an intricately carved Norman doorway. Across the river, tucked away at the south end of London bridge is little visited Southwark Cathedral, Shakespeare's parish church, which harbours a serenely beautiful thirteenth-century retrochoir.

The Great Fire which obliterated medieval London gave the 31-year-old Christopher Wren his great opportunity. The cathedral and the fifty-one churches which he rebuilt to replace those destroyed are the buildings on which his considerable reputation principally rests, although, sadly, only about half still survive complete, together with the towers of half a dozen more. Often fitted into confined and impossibly awkward sites, each one was different. Although mostly classical in spirit, and composed as airy rooms with clear glass windows and prominent pulpits, some had only one aisle, or none at all, some were cruciform, with a central dome, and for some he even re-created a medieval plan. To fit them out he employed the greatest craftsmen of his day, most notably the sculptor and woodcarver Grinling Gibbons, who has left us, for example, the finely-detailed swags of fruit and flowers on the reredos in St Mary's Abchurch, each blossom and pear supported on a fragile stem, and the exquisite font cover in All Hallows by the Tower. The one element lacking in Wren's interiors is a sense of mystery, of a human being in awe of God, and for some this reduces them to architectural exercises. Where his genius comes through unqualified is in his vision of the City's skyline, with the great dome of St Paul's set off by a forest of Portland stone towers, spires and steeples sailing over the red-brick houses round about. From the many-tiered wedding-cake that crowns St Bride's, Fleet Street, to the octagonal lantern and flèche on St Magnus the Martyr in Lower Thames Street, these are the products of a brilliantly creative mind. As Hugh Chesterman's rhyme has it:

Clever men
Like Christopher Wren
Only occur just now and then.

Only forty years before the Great Fire, the first classical church in England had been designed by another genius, Inigo Jones, who started his pedimented Queen's Chapel in 1623. Facing across Marlborough Road to St James's Palace (see p. 20), this rendered building with Portland stone dressings and an innovatory Venetian window at the east end was initially designed for the Infanta of Spain, but when plans for her marriage to Charles I evaporated, it was finished off in 1627 for the king's next fiancée, Henrietta Maria of France. Only a few years later, Jones completed the better-known St Paul's, Covent Garden, with its huge Tuscan portico.

Italianate influence also predominated in the eighteenth

century, when a newly-elected High Church Tory government, swept to power in the wake of Marlborough's victories, celebrated its triumph by promoting several new churches. Although the fifty buildings optimistically provided for under the act of 1710 proved far too ambitious, those that were built included Nicholas Hawksmoor's extraordinary St George's, Bloomsbury of 1720–30, with its curious stepped steeple based on the Mausoleum at Halicarnassus; James Gibbs's St Mary-le-Strand of 1714–17, one of London's most beautiful churches, marooned, like a stately galleon, on an island in the Aldwych; and Thomas Archer's baroque St John's, Smith Square of 1713–28, now a delightful concert hall, its broken pediments and fanciful towers overlooking desirable eighteenth-century brick houses much sought after by Members of Parliament, who work just down the road. As the first of the fifty churches, St Mary-le-Strand was originally designed with a 250-foot column carrying a statue of Queen Anne set 80 feet in front of it, but this plan was happily abandoned when the Queen died in 1714, and the present semi-circular west porch and three-stage tower were constructed instead.

All these churches are comfortably within the ambit of central London, but as the city grew and changed, new buildings had to be provided to cater for the shifting population. The enthusiast will want to seek out the early nineteenth-century Grecian temples lining the New Road built from Paddington to Islington in 1757 (renamed the Marylebone Road), among them one of the few churches by Sir John Soane (see p. 100) – his Holy Trinity, Marylebone, now the headquarters of SPCK – and St Pancras New Church, with its rows of terracotta females. More widely scattered are a number of Gothic Revival buildings by great Victorian architects such as Sir George Gilbert Scott, J. L. Pearson, and G. E. Street, but only one of these, William Butterfield's *All Saints, Margaret Street*, is both central enough to be easily accessible and regularly open.

Alas, church-visiting in London can often be a frustrating business. While *Westminster Abbey* and the great cathedrals have set opening times and frequent services, many other buildings are almost permanently locked, or accessible only during a weekly service. In the City, where the resident population has dwindled away to a fraction of its former numbers, and Sunday services, except in *St Paul's Cathedral* and some other favoured locations, have long been discontinued, churches with enterprising incumbents now come to life during the week, drawing audiences of city workers for lunch-time concerts and talks, but too many remain dark and impenetrable. Others are now used as offices, with the sound of typewriters dimly heard behind screened-off aisles, or the improbable sight of a soberly-suited gentleman conducting an earnest telephone conversation at a desk below the pulpit. The few described at length here can all be visited and have been chosen to cover a range of styles and periods and, of course, to include places of particular historic interest.

ALL SAINTS, MARGARET STREET

Margaret Street, W1

— • —

underground Oxford Circus (Bakerloo, Central and Victoria lines)

No one could be indifferent to All Saints. Some people consider it the ugliest church in London; others that it has an extraordinary emotional intensity; but it is not a place you can ignore. Built between 1850 and 1859 as one of the first essays in High Victorian Gothic, it is the masterpiece of the young William Butterfield, who was only thirty when he designed it.

A Gothic gateway leads into the tiny courtyard flanked by church, vicarage and choir school, all ingeniously packed into a site only just over 100 feet square. All are built of red and black brick, and above soars an astonishing, unbuttressed 227-foot spire, two feet taller than the western towers of *Westminster Abbey* and a prominent feature in the view over London from Primrose Hill. Inside, the dim light filtered through the dark stained glass reveals a riot of colour, with every inch richly decorated with painted panels and tiles, inlaid marble, gilding and stencil work. It is as if a manic artist had been shut up here for years and years and had painfully worked his way round the building, eventually covering even the darkest corners. The raised altar, visible from all parts of the church, stands before a dramatic reredos with tiers of red and blue saints under gilded canopies. Pink granite columns support the strongly-patterned pulpit, inlaid with colourful marbles from Italy, Ireland and France, and a low marble wall across the wide chancel arch is penetrated through playful wrought-iron gates more appropriate to a garden than a church. Four tight keyhole arches divide the nave from the combined baptistery and bell tower, the rope to the bell passing through a painting of the pelican feeding her young on the vault high overhead.

Butterfield produced a building of extraordinary originality, described by the architect George Edmund Street as 'not only the most beautiful, but the most vigorous, thoughtful and original (church) among them all.' It is also an exposition of the Catholic beliefs of the Oxford Movement. Always, there is a whiff of incense, a reminder of the rituals for which it was intended and which are still performed here.

Open: Daily 7–19

SAINT BARTHOLOMEW THE GREAT

Little Britain, Smithfield, EC1

——— • ———

underground Barbican (Circle and Metropolitan
lines)

BLACK AND WHITE, half-timbered gatehouse over a thirteenth-century stone arch marks the entrance to one of London's most impressive churches, saved from the Great Fire of 1666 only because the wind miraculously changed direction when the flames were 300 yards away. A great Norman building with something of the atmosphere of a cathedral, what survives is actually the choir and transepts of a monastery church, part of the Augustinian priory founded here by Henry I's courtier Rahere after a pilgrimage to Rome in the early twelfth century. The gatehouse, from which a path leads through a leafy churchyard, marks the original end of the nave. When the priory was dissolved in 1539, most of the building was pulled down and the chancel became the parish church.

With its flint-faced walls and flint and stone flushwork decoration, part of a major restoration by Sir Aston Webb in the late nineteenth century, St Bartholomew looks as if it has strayed from the depths of East Anglia. Inside, massive unadorned columns of mottled, rugged stone support two tiers of Romanesque arches, which curve gently round the apse at the east end. Behind them is an ambulatory, with glimpses beyond into the Lady Chapel, a suggestion that there may be a mirror-image nave stretching away to the east. The clerestory above is late fourteenth-century Gothic, but the arches are so gently pointed that they do not disturb the essential rhythm of the nave. High up on the south wall of the chancel, looking down on the altar, is a delicate oriel window, installed by William Bolton, prior from 1500 to 1532, so he could participate in the mass without leaving his lodgings. Much of this interior was also restored by Webb, who was faced by a building in a deplorable state of repair. A blacksmith's forge had been established in the north transept, stables in the cloisters – of which one walk still survives – and a printing shop in the Lady Chapel, where the American statesman Benjamin Franklin was employed in 1724.

With the exception of the font, where Hogarth was baptized in 1697, most of the original furnishings have not survived, but there is a fine collection of monuments. From where Prior Bolton sat, he would have been able to see Rahere's sumptuous canopied tomb to the left of the altar, his reclining effigy clad in the hooded black robes of his order and attended by two kneeling monks, both of whom are reading a text from Isaiah, chapter 51. The back wall is pierced, so pilgrims to his tomb could make offerings from the ambulatory. More touching is the monument to John and Margaret Whiting, married '40 yeares & upwards', their memorial curiously showing them naked on a couch. She died in 1680, he about a year later:

Shee first deceasd. Hee for a little Tryd
To live without her, likd it not & Dyd.

Alas, the tablet to Edward Cooke, who died in 1652 aged 39, no longer fulfils the promise of its inscription:

Unsluce yor briny floods, what! can yee
  keepe
Yor eyes from teares, & see the marble
  weepe . . .

In wet weather, water used to condense on the stone, but the modern heating system is so efficient that the memorial has dried out and weeps no more.

Open: Mon–Thurs 8–16.30, Fri 10.45–16.30, Sun 8–20

St James's Piccadilly

Piccadilly, W1

———— • ————

underground Green Park (Jubilee, Piccadilly and Victoria lines), Piccadilly Circus (Bakerloo and Piccadilly lines)

THIS SINGULAR WREN BUILDING, the only one of the great architect's London churches to be erected on a new site, is set back from Piccadilly across a shady courtyard. Apart from the pulpit against the north wall, the red-brick exterior with Portland stone dressings is ordinary enough, but inside there is a vivid impression of light and space, of white and gold plasterwork and of the sun streaming in through the round-headed windows. Here, as nowhere else, the architect was able to work out his ideal church, a quiet and elegant room where every member of the congregation could hear the preacher distinctly. Wren himself was particularly pleased with the design, completed in 1684, and it was to be the prototype for many eighteenth-century town churches.

Although St James's was bombed in 1940, some original furnishings survive, including Grinling Gibbons's festoons of fruit and flowers on the reredos and his enchanting white marble font, its delicate shaft carved to represent the Tree of Life, with the serpent coiled in the branches beneath the bowl and Adam and Eve poised on either side. William Blake was baptized here and there is a monument just outside the west door to the Van de Veldes, father and son, the Dutch marine painters who came to London in 1672 and worked for Charles II.

St James's is now a venue for concerts, exhibitions (in the adjoining Wren Gallery) and lunchtime recitals, and is also known for society weddings. None of these could surely match the occasion in January 1918, described in *Goodbye to All That*, when Robert Graves persuaded his feminist fiancée Nancy, daughter of the painter William Nicholson, to accompany him to the altar. Unfortunately she had only read the marriage service for the first time that morning and was horrified by it, savagely muttering the responses while aunts wept into their handkerchiefs.

Open: Daily 8–19
(Sat from 8.30)

St Martin-In-The-Fields

Trafalgar Square, WC2

— • —

underground Charing Cross (Bakerloo, Jubilee and
Northern lines)

THIS TEMPLE OF a church fronted by a grandiose pedimented portico above a wide flight of steps looks as if it was designed to command Trafalgar Square. But when it was built in 1722–6 the church was hemmed in by 'vile houses' and could only be seen properly a century or so later when the square was laid out on the site of the royal mews and stables (see p. 15). Nevertheless, the architect James Gibbs gave it a monumental classical treatment, ornamenting the sides with great columns and pilasters almost as if he knew the mean streets around his innovative design would one day be cleared away. His Portland stone steeple rising behind the portico must always have been a landmark.

Inside, the church is large and airy, if slightly gloomy, with Corinthian columns supporting a gallery and a wide barrel-vaulted nave leading straight into the chancel. A Venetian window of plain glass almost fills the east end. This is the parish church of *Buckingham Palace* and the former royal 'box' pews, like panelled rooms, flank the altar, looking down on both nave and chancel and on the wineglass pulpit with its elegantly curving steps. Charles II was baptized in the Tudor church on this site, the successor to the medieval building which had stood in open fields, and his Nell, who died in November 1687, aged 37, was buried in the now extinguished graveyard. A font like a soup tureen dates from 1689.

Since the ministry of the Rev. Dick Sheppard, who came to St Martin's after serving on the western front in the First World War, the church has offered succour to the homeless and less fortunate members of society, some of whom may attend the popular lunchtime concerts.

Open: Daily 8–21

ST PAUL'S CATHEDRAL

St Paul's Churchyard, EC4

— • —

underground St Paul's (Central line)

ALTHOUGH CITY SKYSCRAPERS now tower over St Paul's, none of these new buildings has the dignity and presence of Christopher Wren's baroque church, which seems to preside over London like a benevolent spirit. Its dome and twin towers still catch the eye, crowning the view of Ludgate Hill from Fleet Street, half seen down one of the city's narrow lanes, or glimpsed from the river, up the steps of St Peter's Hill.

The only English cathedral built between the Reformation and the late nineteenth century, St Paul's is also exceptional for having been constructed under the supervision of one architect, even though it took 35 years to complete and Wren was already in his forties when his plans were approved in 1675. Nine years earlier the Great Fire had destroyed the huge medieval cathedral which had stood on this site, 'the Lead melting downe the streetes in a streame, and the very pavements of them glowing with fiery rednesse', as John Evelyn graphically reported. Built of Caen stone brought by sea from Normandy, the old cathedral had been one of the wonders of Europe, topped by the tallest spire ever built. Here, in 1501, the fourteen-year-old Arthur, Prince of Wales, was betrothed to Catherine of Aragon, the young Spanish princess who was destined to become the first wife of Henry VIII after her husband's untimely death a year later. Here too Elizabeth I rode in a triumphal procession to give thanks for the defeat of the Armada in 1588. By this time the old church was in a serious state of decay. It was also more of a market than a cathedral, with business of every kind conducted in the nave: 'the south side for Popery and Usury; the north for Simony'. Worse followed. Cromwell's

army used the place as a barracks, stabling eight hundred horses in the nave, and using the aisles as bowling alleys.

Wren produced three designs for the rebuilding which followed the fire. The cathedral he longed to produce was thought too revolutionary by the Commissioners and clergy, and the royal warrant was given to a much more conventional plan. Nevertheless, the finished building, constructed of Portland stone, closely resembles what Wren wanted. Charles II, a shrewd man who well understood the situation, had authorized his architect to make any necessary alterations as work proceeded, a clause which Wren interpreted to the full. And to make sure that there were no later modifications, he arranged for all parts of the building to rise together, rather than working from one end as was usual.

The cathedral is entered from the west end, where an enormously broad flight of steps rises to a pedimented double portico overlooking Ludgate Hill, the towers on either side playfully garlanded with stone flowers. Inside, there is an unbroken vista down the full length of the church. From the back of the nave, you would need a telescope to see what was going on at the marble altar beneath Stephen Dykes Bower's impressive baldachino of English oak, placed here in the 1950s. Huge piers of Portland stone topped with Corinthian pilasters look as if they have been pilfered from a triumphal arch, while a series of shallow domes overhead leads the eye to glittering mosaics in the choir. Added by Sir William Richmond in the 1890s, these depict the creatures of the Earth, with elephants under stylized palm trees and whales spouting silvery jets of water in a deliciously cool, blue and green sea.

A burst of light half-way down the vista

marks the prominent dome over the crossing, supported on eight huge arches, lit by 24 windows and decorated with monochrome frescoes by Sir James Thornhill. A shallow, easy staircase entered from the south aisle leads up to the Whispering Gallery immediately below the windows, thoughtfully provided with a continuous stone seat. A whisper against the wall is said to be clearly audible over a hundred feet away across the void, although the noise level is often too high to hear anything. But this is a splendid place from which to peer down into the church, and there are glimpses of organ pipes and other mysterious objects tucked away in the arches of the crossing. Thornhill's paintings, illustrating the life of

St Paul, are perhaps better seen veiled by distance. When the great man was working on them, on a platform over a hundred feet above the ground, he stepped back to judge the effect and stood perilously close to the edge of his support. With great presence of mind, his assistant started to smudge the still wet composition; Thornhill sprang angrily forward, thus saving his life.

Much steeper stairs and a tight spiral

staircase lead from here to the Golden Gallery, just below the lantern crowning the dome, from where there is a panoramic view over London: to one side, the Gothic outline of St Pancras Station looms over the gilded figure of Justice on the Old Bailey, the wedding-cake tower of St Bride's signals Fleet Street, and office blocks shroud the Houses of Parliament (see p. 19) in the distance; to the east, there are glimpses of the *Guildhall* and of the *Tower of London*, with the strong silhouette of *Tower Bridge* straddling the river and the flaming urn on Wren's *Monument* glinting in the sun. Green patches suggest leafy squares and churchyards. From up here you can also see how Wren built a dome within a dome: the outer shell, rising sixty feet above Thornhill's paintings, is supported on a brick cone built over the inner dome.

Like Robert Adam a century later, Wren assembled a team of outstanding craftsmen to work on his masterpiece, commissioning Grinling Gibbons to carve the swags of fruit and flowers on the choir-stalls, and the French iron-master Jean Tijou to provide the wrought-iron screens framing the altar and closing the chancel aisles which form an ambulatory round the east end. No monuments were allowed in St Paul's until 1790, when overcrowding in *Westminster Abbey* caused this ruling to be relaxed. Now there is a clutch of grandiose memorials. Field Marshal Earl Kitchener, drowned off Orkney in 1916, lies deathly white in a chapel dedicated to the dead of the First World War, his effigy fully kitted out as if he had fallen asleep in his dress uniform. Nearby is a classical arch commemorating the Duke of Wellington, with his recumbent figure almost invisible on top of a massive sarcophagus and a statue of the great man on a prancing horse high above. More naval and military heroes, Nelson among them, crowd the south transept, where there is also a monument to the artist J. M. W. Turner, shown sitting on a rock with a piece of chalk in his hand. More surprising is the statue of the lexicographer Samuel Johnson which stands at the end of the north chancel aisle. The good doctor, whose physical appearance in real life always drew comment (see p. 135), is depicted as a Roman, his physique impressive and his feet enormous. Some have sug-

gested that the muscles are those of a retired gladiator, others that the toga might be taken for a bathing towel and that Johnson is off for a dip in the sea. No such ambiguities surround the effigy of John Donne, the only monument from the old church to survive the Great Fire intact. Dean of St Paul's from 1621 until his death ten years later, and the most celebrated preacher of his age as well as an outstanding poet, Donne is depicted standing on an urn with his shroud clutched around him. As Izaak Walton's biography unforgettably relates, the pose is taken from a painting done when Donne was still alive, the Dean sitting to the artist naked in his winding sheet.

Fittingly, Wren himself is buried in the crypt, his grave marked by a plain black slab and the Latin inscription: *Lector, si monumentum requiris, circumspice* (Reader, if you seek a monument, look about you). Many other artists lie near him, among them Millais, Turner, Reynolds, Holman Hunt and Van Dyck, and the walls round about are covered with memorials. Unusually, the crypt extends right under St Paul's rather than just being confined to the east end, and the two most famous burials are beneath the dome. Lord Nelson, hero of Trafalgar, lies right in the middle, his slight figure encased in a huge black marble sarcophagus originally carved for Cardinal Wolsey. Confiscated by Henry VIII, the tomb lay unused at Westminster until resurrected for England's best-loved admiral. Just to the east is the imposing tomb of the Duke of Wellington, a pink and black, marble and porphyry sarcophagus resting on four sleeping lions and surrounded by candles. The Duke's funeral on 18 November 1852 was one of the most elaborate ever staged in England. The funeral carriage was made of metal from guns captured at Waterloo, and an enormous crowd watched the bier, drawn by twelve black horses, process from Horse Guards to the cathedral. St Paul's was blacked out for the occasion, and a four-hour service held by gaslight.

Open: Daily 7.30–17; ambulatory, crypt and dome, Mon–Fri 10–16.15, Sat 11–16.15; admission charge for ambulatory, dome and crypt, and for nave except for services; tours Mon–Sat at 11, 11.30, 14 and 14.30

St Stephen Walbrook

Walbrook, EC4

— • —

underground Bank (Central and Northern lines)

THIS WREN CHURCH, hidden away behind the Mansion House (see p. 47), once stood on the banks of the Walbrook, a stream which runs down to the Thames but is now confined deep underground. Built between 1672 and 1679, it was designed while Wren was involved in the early stages of *St Paul's Cathedral* and is a variation on the theme of his great cathedral. Outside, apart from the fragile stone spire perched on a sturdy ragstone tower, it is nothing much to look at, but the interior, reached by climbing a steep flight of steps which once went down to the water, is one of Wren's most dramatic. Sixteen ingeniously placed Corinthian columns subdivide what is basically a large rectangular room, indicating nave, aisles and sanctuary and outlining a central octagon roofed by a top-lit coffered dome.

Newly decorated in cream and white and lit by windows of clear glass, the church seems wonderfully light and airy, the decorative plasterwork crisply outlined and the columns apparently shifting and regrouping as you walk around. The reredos, the carved pulpit, with cherubs dancing on the tester, and the tiny stone font, its wooden cover encrusted with urns overflowing with fruit and flowers, are original furnishings; but the high-backed pews have been stripped out and replaced by low benches of pale wood arranged around a central altar, a lumpen mass by Henry Moore. At the back is a telephone in a glass case, the first to be manned by the Samaritan organization, which was started here in 1953 by Rev. Chad Varah. John Betjeman singled out St Stephen Walbrook as being one of the most characteristic of Wren's churches, 'comparatively unmolested by Victorian restoration'. I wonder what he would think of it now.

Open: Mon–Thurs 9–16, Fri 9–15

WESLEY'S CHAPEL AND HOUSE

47/49 City Road, EC1

— • —

underground Moorgate (Circle, Metropolitan and
Northern lines), Old Street (Northern line)

THE FIRST HEADQUARTERS of the Methodist church was established in 1739 in a disused foundry just north of the line of the old City wall. Here, for almost forty years, John Wesley preached to his followers, ran a free medical clinic and dispensary and a school for sixty pupils, and administered a refuge for women and children. When the dilapidated premises could no longer keep out the weather, he rented part of a large bare field being used to dump the earth excavated for Wren's *St Paul's Cathedral*. On 21 April 1777, his new chapel was begun.

This unpretentious little building is set back from City Road down a short avenue, a classical porch on stubby Doric columns marking the centre of the yellow-brick façade. Although substantially renovated, the large airy interior has many echoes of the original chapel, among them the Adam-style plaster ceiling and the horseshoe gallery, originally supported on ships' masts presented by George III. Set prominently before the altar is the mahogany pulpit – the top tier of what was once a three-decker – from which Wesley harangued his congregation, while the simple pulpit from the foundry is now exhibited in the Museum of Methodism in the crypt. Wesley himself is buried directly behind the building.

The narrow, yellow-brick late eighteenth-century house to one side is where Wesley lived for the last twelve years of his life, dying in 1791 in the bedroom on the first floor. With its cramped hall and bare floorboards, the house seems bleak, but it is very evocative of the man who started the largest Protestant church in the world. A tiny, cupboard-like room, simply furnished with his chair, kneeler, and candlestick, is where Wesley prayed every morning at four o'clock, before going next door to conduct a five o'clock service. On show are the black coat, three-cornered hat and buckled shoes in which he set out on his annual travels round England, often journeying five thousand miles a year on terrible roads; and a mahogany bookcase is filled with his annotated, leather-bound books, including a Greek New Testament. Among the many letters and other documents is a note Wesley wrote on 22 January 1791, only a couple of weeks before he died, beginning: 'I am half blind, and half lame; but by the help of God I creep on still.' Neither he nor his brother Charles, who helped him with his ministry, seem to have been plagued by uncertainties, Wesley's steadfast belief in the Almighty and in his life's work stemming back to a traumatic incident in his childhood, when he was rescued from a burning house only moments before the roof fell in. And anyone who doubts that Methodism is fuelled by tea has only to look at the splendid gallon teapot presented to Wesley by Josiah Wedgwood.

Appropriately, Wesley's House looks out over the burial ground of Bunhill Fields, London's principal Nonconformist cemetery from 1665 to 1852. The tomb of John Bunyan, with a laden pilgrim sculpted on the side of the chest, is conspicuous to the left of the central path; a simple headstone commemorates William Blake, 'the poet-painter', and an obelisk marks the grave of Daniel Defoe. Across the graveyard is Bunhill Row, where Milton spent the last years of his life, working on *Paradise Lost* and *Paradise Regained*.

Open: House and Museum of Methodism, Mon–Sat 10–16; chapel, daily 9–17; admission charge; toilets; guided tours

WESTMINSTER ABBEY

Broad Sanctuary, SW1

———— • ————

underground Westminster (Circle and District lines)

THIS GREAT MONUMENT is Britain's answer to Reims or Amiens, a soaring Gothic cathedral anchored by flying buttresses, with rose windows lighting the transepts and an apse at the east end ringed by an ambulatory and radiating chapels. At its heart is a medieval shrine which drew pilgrims here for centuries, the tomb of the saintly Edward the Confessor, whose death in 1066 precipitated the invasion of William the Conqueror. At lower levels, the lines of the original building are now obscured by a thick encrustation of monuments, and many of the side chapels are stacked with chairs, benches and other paraphernalia, but neither this clutter nor the milling tourists and the constant background murmur of voices has destroyed the atmosphere of the place. Where *St Paul's Cathedral* can seem like a temple to reason and intellect, Westminster Abbey still inspires awe as well as admiration.

This is also the church most closely associated with a national consciousness. Just inside the west door is the tomb of the Unknown Soldier, one of the thousands who died in the First World War on the battlefields of north-west France, and who was brought here to be buried on 11 November 1920. French soil fills the grave, a slab of black Belgian marble covers it and a frame of Flanders poppies is like a splash of blood on the floor. Round about are the tombs of statesmen and generals, musicians and scientists, the great, the good and the now forgotten forming a kind of national biography in stone. There is a regiment of kings and queens here, too, the effigies of the wraith-like Plantagenets with their tapering fingers walling in Edward the Confessor, and a phalanx of Tudors surrounding Henry VII and his consort. This was also the church where most of them were crowned. Ever since the coronation of William the Conqueror, on Christmas Day 1066, all British monarchs except Edward V, one of the Princes in the Tower, and Edward VIII, have been crowned in the abbey. These ceremonies have not always gone smoothly. During the five-hour service for Queen Victoria, the proceedings were interrupted by a discussion about the ring, which had been designed for her little finger but which the Archbishop of Canterbury insisted on painfully forcing on to the fourth, and the Bishop of Bath nearly ended the service prematurely by turning over two pages at once. At the rehearsal for George VI's coronation in 1937, the orb had to be retrieved from the six-year-old Princess Margaret, who was playing with it on the floor.

The first church on this site, built on a gravel island in the marshes bordering the Thames, is lost in the twilight of the Dark Ages, but legend has it that it was constructed by the Saxon king Sebert on the orders of St Peter himself, to whom the cathedral is dedicated. With the noise of traffic in Parliament Square always faintly discernible, it is difficult to imagine how lonely this spot once was, isolated from the little Saxon trading settlement developing along the river to the east. Nothing remains of the Saxon church, and very little of the Benedictine monastery established by the Confessor, who died eight days after his new church was consecrated on 28 December 1065. The cathedral seen today was built over 250 years from 1245, with a remarkable adherence to the original cruciform Gothic plan. As a result, unlike most other English cathedrals, the abbey is a work of great unity. Moreover, although there have been no monks here since 1540, when

Edward I's foundation was dissolved, the ghost of the former monastery still persists. To the south of the church are two cloisters ringed with stone arcades; the thirteenth-century octagonal chapter house is little changed; the abbey library fills part of what was once the monks' dormitory; and other monastic remains survive in the houses and offices of the precincts.

The current restoration programme which started in the mid 1970s has revealed the beauty of the Caen and Reigate stone, seen white against the gold of the Houses of Parliament behind (see p. 19). White too are the two towers at the west end, completed in 1745 to designs of Christopher Wren and Nicholas Hawksmoor, their pinnacled outlines adding a much needed vertical accent to the bulk of the cathedral. Erupting out of the east end, like a butterfly from a chrysalis, is the fairy-tale fantasy of Henry VII's chapel of 1503–19, an extravaganza of pepperpot turrets and statue niches, with gargoyles clinging to the buttresses and glinting weather-vanes.

Inside, a gilded screen of 1834 by Edward Blore blocks the view of the high altar, but nothing interrupts the procession of soaring Gothic arches rising from cluster pillars of purple Purbeck marble to the vaulted roof 102 feet above, the ribs of the vaulting delicately outlined in gold and pinned by a series of brooch-like bosses. Cranmer is said to have preached from the early sixteenth-century pulpit with linenfold panelling; and beside it is Rysbrack's effigy of Sir Isaac Newton, a celestial globe balanced above the great scientist showing the comet of 24 December 1680 following Newton's predicted path. All the monument lacks is Alexander Pope's intended epitaph:

Nature and Nature's Laws lay hid in Night:
God said, 'Let Newton be!', and all
   was light.

Another nineteenth-century gold screen, by Sir George Gilbert Scott, backs the high altar, which is framed by medieval canopied tombs and set on a priceless pavement. Laid down in 1268 by one of the Cosmati family from Rome, this piece of *opus sectile* work was copied almost three hundred years later by Holbein, who included a section of it in *The Ambassadors* (see p. 83). More Italian work also distinguishes the shrine of Edward the Confessor, reached by a curious bridge over the ambulatory, as if his chapel were an island in the sea of the cathedral. Despoiled at the Dissolution and again under the Commonwealth, the tomb is now without the bejewelled golden shrine which once held the saint's coffin, but the original marble and mosaic base still survives, even if pitted and scratched, its sides pierced by three uncomfortably small recesses where the sick knelt in the hope of a cure. Graffiti also mar the Coronation chair beside the tomb, a battered Gothic throne incorporating the legendary Stone of Scone beneath the seat. Traditionally said to be the stone described in Genesis 28.18 on which Jacob rested his head, this lumpish white boulder was thought by the Scots to have mystical properties and was used for the coronation of Macbeth and a line of other Scottish kings until 1277, when Edward I seized it and brought it to England. Scottish nationalists tried to carry it off again in December 1950, but it was recovered a couple of months later. Of the effigies which surround it and the saintly Edward, seek out the Pre-Raphaelite features of Eleanor of Castile (c.1244–90), with her long golden hair and gentle fingers, her body slipping out of sight behind a pillar, and the bearded Edward III (1312–77), accompanied by recumbent angels and beautifully preserved bronze images of six of his fourteen children, visible from the south ambulatory. An unadorned marble box, like a piece of luggage, holds the remains of Elizabeth Tudor, Henry VII's daughter, who died in 1495, while across the shrine lie Richard II and his much-loved wife Anne of Bohemia, whose death provoked such a storm of grief that the king pulled down the palace at Richmond where she died. Before their arms were lost, the effigies lay here hand in hand.

To the east, past the sad, log-like effigy of Henry V, is the magnificent Henry VII chapel, with the banners of the Knights of the Garter like brilliantly coloured flags above the elaborate canopied stalls. The stone figures of almost a hundred saints line the walls, among them the hirsute St Wilgefortis, whose beauty was so great that God granted her a beard to discourage her many suitors. There are other memorable details here too, such as the dragons and dogs climbing the fluted pillars, but initially every eye is drawn to the fan vaulting high overhead, a triumphant swirling web that is no more than a façade, the tracery supported on the ribs of a groin vault which you can see vanishing behind it. Henry VII and his consort Elizabeth of York lie behind the altar; their gilded effigies, for which the king left minute instructions, were the work of the Florentine Pietro Torrigiano, and the first Renaissance sculpture produced in England. Shielded by a black iron screen, the figures are quite difficult to see. More easily visible is Torrigiano's effigy of Henry VII's mother, Lady Margaret Beaufort, whom he movingly modelled as an old woman, with sharp features and wrinkled face and hands.

Lady Margaret lies in the chapel's south aisle, beside the grandiose tomb which James I erected for his mother, Mary Queen of Scots. An effigy of Mary's cousin and rival Elizabeth I is in the north aisle. This is Gloriana in old age, her face beak-nosed and proud, her long fingers grasping the sceptre she was so reluctant to relinquish. Beyond her is a little clutch of royal children. James I's daughter Mary, who died in 1607 at the age of two, is propped up on her elbow gazing at her little sister Sophia, who died the year before, aged only three days. Sophia is in her crib, turned away from us, her chubby face, eyes closed as if peacefully sleeping, only visible in a mirror. A casket between the babies holds the bones of Edward V and Richard, Duke of York, the young princes murdered in the Tower. How strange that England's greatest queen, who chose to remain unmarried rather than compromise the throne, should here lie with the children she never had. How strange, too, that her tomb should also contain the bones of her half-sister Mary Tudor, as staunchly Catholic as Elizabeth was Protestant.

These monuments are just a few of the

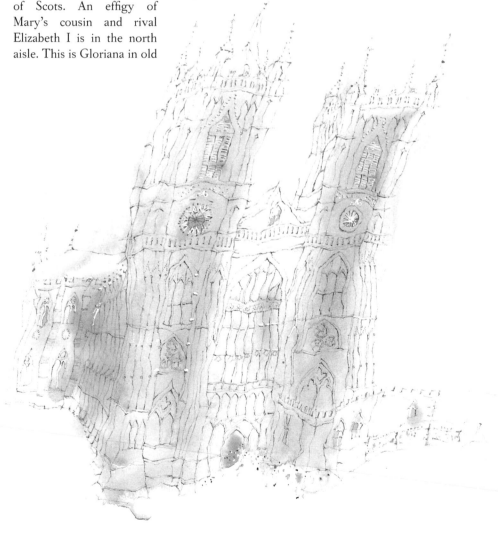

hundreds in the abbey. Some memorials are brightly coloured Jacobean tombs, with effigies in orange leggings and scarlet ribbons; some include graphic tableaux, such as the bas-relief showing Wolfe's troops scaling the Heights of Abraham above Quebec, or the panel recording the murder in the Haymarket of Thomas Thynne of Longleat, who was shot in his coach by hired killers in 1682; others are simple stone slabs. Standing effigies of a group of statesmen line the route to the north door, as if part of the Commons has been turned to stone, and a few musicians cluster by the high altar nearby. Across the abbey is Poets' Corner, crammed with monuments to men of letters. The first to be buried here was Chaucer, in 1400, but he had the added distinction of once being a clerk of the king's works. Tennyson was immured with the book of Shakespeare's poems he was reading at the time of his death, presumably so that he would have an opportunity to finish them, and Ben Jonson, who lies across the abbey in the north aisle, was buried upright at his own suggestion, so he would not take up too much space. But many of those commemorated are in fact buried elsewhere, as successive deans regarded their unconventional lifestyles with disfavour, and the memorials postdate their deaths by many years. Shakespeare, for example, had to wait until 1740, Blake for the bicentenary of his birth in 1957, while Milton was excluded on political grounds for over sixty years.

Effigies of a different kind are displayed in the twelfth-century undercroft off the Great Cloister, once probably the monks' common room. It now houses a collection of the startling figures which used to be on show at state funerals as a substitute for the decomposing body, the earlier ones of wood, those dating from after 1660 with faces of wax. The lifelike images of Edward

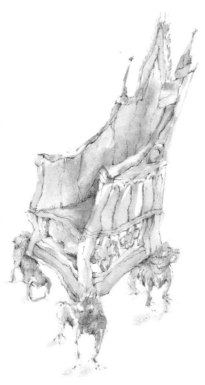

III and Henry VII are said to have been modelled from death-masks, Edward's drooping mouth and flattened left cheek the result of his fatal stroke. Nelson is here, the hair above his deeply-lined face said to have been arranged by Lady Hamilton; and in a case to one side is the ring which Elizabeth I is supposed to have given to her impetuous favourite, the Earl of Essex, 33 years her junior, and which he tried to return to her, as an appeal for clemency, when he was arrested for treason. The ring never reached the Queen, and the boy she had loved was executed.

Nearby is the chapter house, one of the largest in England, with a single, central shaft spreading out into the vaults of the roof like a huge stone umbrella. There are red, thirteenth-century tiles on the floor, decorated with centaurs, lions, ferocious fish and other beasts, and traces of the original murals on the walls, a frieze of delightful creatures including a dromedary and a 'kameyl'. Eighty monks could sit on the stone benches against the walls, and this resonant chamber is where Parliament met in the late fourteenth century.

Much of the abbey is grand, but the atmosphere changes in the intimate Little Cloister, seen on the way to the College garden. Much smaller than the cold and austere Great Cloister, this secluded court with a fountain playing in the middle has domestic façades of brick and stone above the round-headed colonnades. Ferns, ivy and a fig-tree creep from the central garden, and milk bottles stand outside doors.

Open: Nave and cloisters, Mon–Sat 8–18, subject to services; royal chapels, Poets' Corner, choir and north transept, Mon–Fri 9–16.45, Sat 9–14.45 and 15.45–17.45; garden, Thurs 10–18 (till 16 Oct–Mar); library, Wed 11–15; chapter house and undercroft, Mon–Sat 10–18 (till 16 Oct–Mar); admission charge except to nave, cloisters, garden and library, but free admission to whole abbey on Weds, 18–19.45; guided tours (charge); audio guides

WESTMINSTER CATHEDRAL

Ashley Place, SW1, at the west end of Victoria Street

———— • ————

underground Victoria (Circle, District and Victoria lines)

AN UNEXPECTED OPENING in the brutalist modern architecture lining Victoria Street suddenly reveals the west front of this unique Byzantine church, its bold red and white façade echoed in the orange and white pavement of the fronting piazza. There are no traces of medieval England here, but rather an echo of Italy and the Orient: the horizontal bands of stone and brick seem to conjure up the zebra-like face of Siena Cathedral, while the domes and minarets are reminiscent of St Mark's, Venice or St Sophia in Istanbul. On the left, a rocket-like campanile soars 284 feet into the sky, the prominent gilt cross at the top said to contain a relic of the True Cross.

London's most important Catholic church, intended to crown one of the thirteen sees founded in 1850 after the emancipation act of 1829, Westminster Cathedral was started in 1895 to designs by John Francis Bentley (1839–1902). The Byzantine style, unique amongst major English cathedrals, was deliberately chosen by Cardinal Vaughan so as not to compete with *Westminster Abbey* just down the road. But the cathedral has never been finished. Inside pillars and arches faced with over a hundred varieties of richly veined and coloured marbles – dark green, black and wine red, white, pink and cornflower blue, some with flowing veins like running water, others streaked with

dark lines like fossilized Stilton – and glittering golden mosaics contrast strangely with the rough bare brickwork of the upper part of the building, the three shallow domes roofing the nave seen only dimly in the gloom above. The result, a mixture of opulence and primitive starkness, is strangely compelling, and you could believe this was what Bentley intended. Twelve small windows in a fourth dome over the sanctuary light the eight golden-yellow marble columns supporting the baldachino over the high altar, like a temple within the cathedral.

Each of the side-chapels lining the nave has an individual decorative scheme. In St Patrick's chapel, shamrocks of mother-of-pearl glisten in the reredos of black Irish marble, and more are carved in the white marble screen bordering the nave, a reminder that the saint used the three leaves of this little clover-like plant to expound the doctrine of the Trinity to the pagan Irish. The next chapel is dedicated to St Andrew, the fisherman who became a 'fisher of men' and the patron saint of Scotland. A pinkly-glowing lobster, skate, eel and starfish, and a rosy crab with grey claws are among the sea creatures inlaid in the marble floor, and the bright mosaic overhead is like a canopy of golden fish-scales. The altar is of Scottish granite, and the elongated lines of a severe row of inlaid ebony and

ivory choir-stalls suggest that their designer, Ernest Gimson, was fired by the spirit of the Scottish architect Charles Rennie Mackintosh. The Lady Chapel to the right of the High Altar, every inch covered in mosaic or marble, is the most sumptuously decorated, an indication of what the cathedral as a whole will look like if it is ever completed. By contrast, Eric Gill's bas-reliefs of the fourteen stations of the cross on the piers of the nave, executed during the First World War, are low-key and restrained, like line-drawings in stone.

Westminster Cathedral is not to everybody's taste, but I find it one of London's most memorable buildings. And in summer a lift takes visitors to the top of the campanile, where the view reveals a quite different city from that seen from the *Monument* or the dome of *St Paul's Cathedral*. This is a spacious place, its streets broken up by leafy squares and the wide green corridor of the royal parks. To the south, the piers of the Albert and Battersea suspension bridges signal the line of the Thames; to the east, canyon-like Victoria Street leads the eye to the Houses of Parliament (see p. 19) and *Westminster Abbey*, brilliantly white where the stone has been newly cleaned. *Buckingham Palace*, to the north, half hidden by trees, looks down the avenue of planes along the Mall, with the shaft of Nelson's Column visible above the buildings in Trafalgar Square at the far end.

Open: Cathedral, daily 7–20; campanile, Easter–Oct. Wed–Sun 9–13, 14–17; charge for campanile; guided tours by arrangement with Cathedral Clergy House, 42 Francis Street, SW1P 1QW

7

LONDON'S VILLAGES

—— • ——

THERE ARE NO VILLAGES IN LONDON. A vast urban sprawl has swallowed up the little communities which were once dotted around the capital, but here and there, in among the brick terraces and the twentieth-century villas, you come across the heart of what was once a Thames-side fishing settlement or a farming hamlet, or an attractive cluster of Georgian houses built as country retreats within easy reach of the city for the prosperous middle classes of the late eighteenth century. Most of these places would have been surrounded by fields and market gardens well into the nineteenth century, the amorphous development which joined them all together prompted only by the growth of a railway network. Even in 1801, Barnes was a remote village isolated in a great meander of the Thames, reachable only by water or on foot across the common, while Dulwich, $4\frac{1}{2}$ miles south of Whitehall and separated from the river by a low ridge of hills, was a tiny hamlet surrounded by woods and farmland. With an expanse of park and common bordering its long main street, weatherboarded cottages and hand sign-posts, Dulwich still feels like a place in the country; and Barnes, now a much sought-after residential suburb, is still centred on a leafy green and the former village pond.

At Chiswick, the village that Hogarth knew can still be sensed in the lane that winds down to the Thames from the ghastly Hogarth roundabout, the traffic almost immediately left behind in a quiet street of cottages and solid Georgian houses, focused on the bulk of St Nicholas's church. Round the corner is prosperous Chiswick Mall, where mellow seventeenth- and eighteenth-century façades overlook gardens on to the river. Walpole House, about half-way down, opposite the island of Chiswick Eyot, was the home in the seventeenth century of Charles II's mistress Barbara Villiers, said to be the 'fairest and lewdest' of all his attachments. Later it was a boarding school, which Thackeray attended, and which he is thought to have drawn on for Miss

Pinkerton's Academy in *Vanity Fair*. This pretty stretch of riverside was also the place that Sir John Thorneycroft chose to test the weapons that led to his invention of the torpedo, his success fortunately leading to the relocation of the works on the south coast in 1906.

Other attractive areas first grew up round the great houses of the nobility, or the residences of the sovereign. Henry VIII's chancellor Thomas More put Chelsea on the map in 1520 when he built himself a country house within easy reach of Westminster in what was then a tiny riverside hamlet, surrounded by meadows and wooded hills. After More's execution, for refusing to recognize his sovereign as head of the church, Henry had a manor here and the place became known as a 'village of palaces'. Nothing remains of these great mansions, but More's chapel, with its Renaissance capitals and original wooden roof, miraculously survived the bombs which devastated the rest of the old parish church in the Second World War.

Ever since More's day, Chelsea seems to have attracted more than its fair share of scholars, writers and painters, some of them living up to their raffish image on the houseboats linked by a swaying catwalk of gangplanks at the western end of the Chelsea embankment. Along the river curves Cheyne Walk, with elegant Queen Anne houses set back behind elaborate gates and protected by a thin strip of greenery from the traffic which now streams along the Thames. No. 4, built in 1718, is where George Eliot died just before Christmas in 1880; Dante Gabriel Rossetti kept a small zoo at No. 16, where he lived with Algernon Swinburne from 1862; Whistler, the painter, occupied No. 96 from 1866 to 1878; Mrs Gaskell was born at No. 93 in 1810; and Turner, by then a recluse who had adopted his landlady's surname in an attempt to escape attention, lived out the twilight of his life at No. 119, yards away from the river which he had captured so evocatively.

Royal connections are more obvious at Kew and Richmond in London's western suburbs. With its large shady green, bordered by attractive cottages and houses and with a duck pond at one end, Kew seems to be like a prime example of the traditional English village, but in fact, although courtiers were residing here in the sixteenth century, what we see today is mostly no more than two hundred years old. Kew mushroomed to house the supporters and satellites of the Hanoverian monarchs who resided in what is now Kew Gardens (see p. 147), and St Anne's church in the middle of the green dates only from 1714 when the Queen after whom it is named gave the site for the building. Thomas Gainsborough is buried in the churchyard here, and so is the fashionable society portraitist John Zoffany, who settled in London from his native Germany in 1758.

Richmond is grander, more town than village, and here, with wooded river banks stretching away on either side, the country seems not too far away. From the graceful, five-arched eighteenth-century bridge,

with its elegant balustrades, one road sweeps up the hill to the main gate into Richmond Park, while another bears north into the principal shopping street past Quinlan Terry's grandiose 1980s development, a neo-classical mélange of red brick, stucco, pediments and Venetian windows overlooking terraced gardens above the river. The heart of Richmond lies on the site of the old Tudor palace (see p. 21), bordering the lime-fringed grassy sweep which was once a jousting ground. On the west side of the green, near Henry VII's gatehouse, a clutch of stately, three-storey red brick houses, built in 1723 for the maids of honour of Caroline of Anspach, George II's consort, are surrounded by other seventeenth- and early eighteenth-century developments, some destined for courtiers dancing attendance at Kew, others taken by rich Londoners seeking to escape the smoke of the city. In Old Palace Yard is Trumpeter's House of 1701, its façade here pleasingly off centre and its main frontage, with an imposing portico, turned towards the river. Georgian dignity disappears on the other side of the green, where the Edwardian baroque theatre by Frank 'Matchless' Matcham shouts across the grass.

For the energetic, there is a pleasant walk from the green down Old Palace Lane and south along the river, climbing the hill through the gardens which run steeply up just beyond the bridge. The view over the Thames valley from the Terrace Walk following the summit of the ridge is everything it is said to be, but at its best on a misty summer evening, when you seem to be looking over a vast forest stretching away into the distance, its canopy broken only by the glistening river. Far below, cows graze in water-meadows fringing the Thames, there are glimpses of *Ham House* and *Marble Hill* through the trees, and, on a clear day, the romantic silhouette of *Windsor Castle* can just be seen etched on the horizon. You can walk on upstream from Richmond, through some of the most rural scenery London has to offer, to Petersham and Ham. The former, with its beautiful red-brick houses and ancient church, is ruined by the main road to Kingston, which cuts right through it; the latter is village-like, around an extensive green, with ducks on a willow-fringed pond, an avenue leading to the great house overlooking the river, and a wide corridor of common sweeping up to Richmond Park.

Where Richmond was for centuries dependent on the Thames, one-eighth of the population in 1700 making their living as watermen, Hampstead to the north of London is an airy hilltop town, clambering up the side of the heath that divides it from Highgate. Once an isolated Middlesex village on the old road heading north out of London from Charing Cross, Hampstead developed rapidly in the late seventeenth and early eighteenth centuries, when medicinal springs discovered on the slopes of the hill became the basis for a fashionable Georgian spa. Londoners flocked to take the waters in the Pump Room and to patronize the attendant coffee-house and tea-shops. The spa soon faded, but the wealthy continued to live here, bringing up their families away from the fumes and disease of the city, and a community of artists and writers injected the faintly Bohemian atmosphere which Hampstead still retains.

This is one of the most attractive parts of London, as enticing to wander round as a hilltown in France or Italy. Away from the main thoroughfare of Heath Street, where the traffic backs up almost to the top of the hill from the traffic lights outside the underground station, is a warren of narrow streets, hidden corners, courts and alleys, with flights of steps where the hill is at its steepest. Unspoilt late seventeenth- and eighteenth-century houses sit back behind brick walls and wrought-iron gates and form elegant Trollopian streets; while hidden away above a deep pond in a fold of the heath is the incongruously named Vale of Health, a higgledy-piggledy scatter of early nineteenth-century houses which attracted such diverse figures as the poet and critic Leigh Hunt and the crime writer Edgar Wallace, and where D. H. Lawrence was living in 1915 when his novel *The Rainbow* was denounced as obscene. Keats would walk over from his rooms in Wentworth Place (see p. 136) to see Leigh Hunt, who came to Hampstead in 1815 after a spell in prison for libelling the Prince Regent. In Well Walk, where a little Victorian fountain is the only sign of the former spa, Constable lived at the end of his life at No. 40, painting the meticulous cloud studies which are now on show in the *Victoria & Albert Museum*, and No. 14 is where the birth-control pioneer Marie Stokes endured the disastrous first marriage that inspired her best-selling *Married Love*.

Down Flask Walk and across the High Street from here is Church Row, a wide thoroughfare of sedate early Georgian houses with roof-line parapets and original wrought-iron railings, and with the tower of St John's rising out of the trees at the far end. H. G. Wells lived here (at No. 17), as did Lord Alfred Douglas (No. 26), a poet of very minor talent whose association with Oscar Wilde led to Wilde's arrest for sodomy in room 53 of the Cadogan Hotel. Constable and his wife are buried in the overgrown old churchyard which falls away below St John's and which also contains the graves of the architect Richard Norman Shaw and of Jane Austen's aunt Elizabeth; while in the neater extension up the hill the Labour politician Hugh Gaitskell lies next to Kay Kendall, 'deeply loved wife' of Rex Harrison.

A shady lane bordering the graveyard leads to Holly Place, once an enclave of émigrés escaping the French Revolution, and via the mysterious corridor of Mount Vernon to a tiny green on Holly Hill, surrounded by eighteenth-century houses on two sides. A white, weatherboarded bay bulging gently over the street is the end of Romney's House, where the artist lived for a couple of years before returning to Cumbria and the wife and children whom he had deserted 37 years before; while across the grass are the elaborate wrought-iron gates to the magnificent *Fenton House*, with its large walled garden. Nearby, left from Hampstead Grove running on to the crest of the hill, is the top-heavy Admiral's House, with a rooftop balcony resembling the quarterdeck of a ship. The Gothic Revival architect Sir George Gilbert Scott lived here from 1856 to 1864, and the house next door is where John Galsworthy completed his interminable *Forsyte Saga*. Hampstead's more recent residents have included John le Carré; the novelist Jack Trevor Story, who lived in a haze of whisky and nostalgia in East Heath Road; and Richard Burton and Elizabeth Taylor, who resided briefly in Squire's Mount.

Highgate, a mile or so along the ridge to the east, is a very different proposition. Here there are elegant streets and eighteenth-century houses as fine as those in Hampstead, but the old centre is not as extensive as that across the heath, its heart is more disrupted by traffic pouring through, and it has not made the best of its position. Highgate sits primly on the crest of the hill rather than tumbling down its slopes, with none of the steps and steep inclines which lend such charm to Hampstead. It is at its best around the grassy triangle at the end of South Grove, where the soaring Gothic spire of St Michael's forms a suitably dramatic backdrop to a picturesque village-like grouping of ancient pub and mellow red-brick houses, among them the elegant late seventeenth- and early eighteenth-century mansions lining The Grove. Pond Square to the east is surrounded by some delightful cottagey dwellings, but has been ruined by the harsh coating of asphalt over what should be a central garden; and Highgate High Street, poised on the lip of the hill, has almost lost the country-town atmosphere it once had. At the north end, where Hampstead Lane sets off west across the top of the heath, the Gatehouse Tavern marks the site of a medieval toll-gate, original focus for the tiny community which clustered here in the Middle Ages and which was swelled from the sixteenth century onwards by

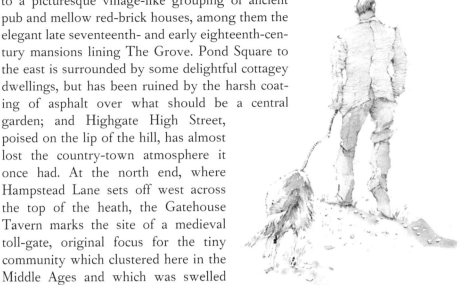

wealthy and aristocratic Londoners escaping the dirt and disease of the rapidly expanding capital. Highgate has never been as literary as Hampstead, but Samuel Taylor Coleridge lived at 3 The Grove from 1819 to 1834, and Byron Cottage at 17 North Road is where A. E. Housman wrote *A Shropshire Lad*, the nostalgic ballad which he published at his own expense in 1896. Being a poet proved something of a liability; a new cook refused to work for Housman on the grounds that Mr Swinburne down in Chelsea had given her nothing but trouble.

Where Hampstead's slopes are enjoyed by the living, Highgate's are given over to the dead, sleeping soundly in a jungle-like cemetery which is one of the most unexpected and astounding places in London. Laid out from 1838 as one of seven new burial grounds ringing the city to relieve overcrowding in the existing graveyards, the cemetery was available for paying customers only, who financed the extraordinary display of Victorian funerary art now seen here. To the west of the steep gulley of Swain's Lane is the older, western section, where elaborate tombs smothered in ivy are buried in a forest of sinister luxuriance. High on the hill, reached by a slippery path, an Egyptian avenue with obelisks and columns flanking a Pharaonic arch climbs steeply up to the catacombs ringing a giant Cedar of Lebanon. The wealthy paid dearly for the privilege of interment in one of these chambers, but now the pedimented doorways are cracked and crumbling, bird droppings cake the ledges, and the air is heavy with decay. However bright the sunshine, there is the sense of a silent, watchful company hidden among the trees. Highest of all is the pyramidal mausoleum of the wealthy German immigrant Julian Beer, proprietor of *The Observer* 1870–80, who took his revenge on the establishment that rejected him by ensuring that his tomb looked down on them all. Apart from a few open days, when visitors can wander freely, access to this part of the cemetery is only by guided tour, when you are unlikely to see the graves of D. G. Rossetti, Charles Dickens, Sir Edwin Landseer and John Galsworthy, all of whom are buried here; but there is unrestricted entry to the newer, eastern extension opened in 1857 on the other side of Swain's Lane. Here the terrain is not so steep, the vegetation still just about under control, and a constant stream of visitors beats a path to the grave of Karl Marx in the north-east corner, crowned by an enormous, bearded bust and inscribed: 'Workers of all lands unite . . . . The philosophers have only interpreted the world in various ways. The point however is to change it.' (Guided tours of western cemetery Mon–Fri at 12, 14, 16 (15 winter); Sat, Sun, 11–16 (15 winter), but advisable to check on 081 340 1834; eastern cemetery open 10–17 summer, 10–14 winter; admission charge to both; access from Swain's Lane)

8

ESSENTIAL INFORMATION

— • —

The *London Tourist Board* (LTB) is an excellent source of all kinds of information. The central office at *Victoria Station* (open Apr–Oct, daily 8–20.30; Nov–Mar, Mon–Sat 8–19, Sun 8–17; telephone information service on 071 730 3488) is manned by knowledgeable staff, is stacked with leaflets, most of them free, and has an extensive bookshop. Here you can get maps, a monthly events sheet and useful publications. The LTB has outposts at *Harrods* (open Mon, Tue, Thurs–Sat 9–18, Wed 9–19), *Selfridges* (open Mon–Wed, Fri, Sat 9.30–18, Thurs 9.30–20) and the *Tower of London* (open Apr–Nov, daily 9.30–17), but none of these operates a telephone service. The *City of London Information Centre* (St Paul's Churchyard, EC4, open Mon–Fri 9.30–17, Sat 9.30–17 (12.30 Nov–Apr), Sun, May–Oct 9.30–17; telephone 071 606 3030) has information on lunchtime concerts and other events, and there are also useful information centres by the quay at '*Greenwich* and in the Old Town Hall in the centre of *Richmond*.

BANKS AND CURRENCY EXCHANGE

Banks are usually open Mon–Fri 9.30–16.30; and some are now open on Saturday mornings 9.30–12. Banks generally offer the best exchange rates. Bureaux de change, which can be found at major rail and underground stations and dotted all over central London, tend to stay open much longer hours, usually Mon–Fri 8–21; some operate 24 hours a day and several are open at weekends. But do check commission rates and other charges before making any transaction. Reputable dealers operate in branches of Thomas Cook (1 Marble Arch branch usually open daily 8–20), Harrods (open Mon–Sat 9.30–17, Wed 18), and at some other large stores.

EATING AND DRINKING

There is an abundance of places to eat and drink in London, and the recent changes in licensing regulations mean that it is now possible to have a meal at almost any hour of the day. Apart from patronising one of the hundreds of little sandwich bars and cafés, some of the cheapest food in the city is to be found in pubs. Once you were lucky to find anything more than a cheese roll and crisps in these establishments, but what is on offer has improved enormously in recent years, many pubs now providing a range of hot and cold fare. Pubs can now open 11-23 Mon–Sat, and 12–15 and 19–22.30 or 23 on Sunday, but many still choose to close in the afternoon. By law, no one under the age of 18 can

be served with alcoholic drinks, but children between the ages of 14 and 18 can go into a pub if accompanied by an adult. Of the drinks on offer, beer is the best buy, and many pubs now offer at least one real ale as well as keg beer; some even brew their own. Beer should never be cold, and is sold in legal measures. There are no such regulations governing the sale of wine, which pubs may sell in any size of glass and often at exorbitant prices. Those keen to seek out places offering live music, or fringe theatre, or other special features should buy the excellent Nicholson *London Pub Guide*, which gives information on some five hundred pubs and bars.

The pub's principal competitor, the wine bar, is now liberally scattered across central London, with concentrations in the City and Covent Garden. Here you are likely to find a fairly relaxed, often candle-lit setting, with food and eating arrangements one step up from pub grub. Since the change in licensing laws, which allows customers to drink through the afternoon provided they are having a meal as well, some wine bars in central areas now stay open all day. Good places will offer a range of quality wines, as well as a reliable house number, which can be drunk by the glass or bottle. At roughly the same level are the self-service eateries found in large museums and galleries such as the *Victoria & Albert Museum*, the *Tate*, the *Imperial War Museum* and the *National Gallery*, and the crypt restaurants at *St Martin-in-the-Fields* and St John's Smith Square.

The choice of restaurants, bistros and brasseries is almost overwhelming, with places offering every kind of cuisine and catering to every taste and pocket. Like wine bars and pubs, some are now open all day. New establishments are constantly opening, some to close only months later, and it is wise to check out a few before making your choice. The densest concentrations are found in the Covent Garden/Soho rectangle and in Chelsea and South Kensington. Every restaurant must display a copy of its current menu at the door, on which the prices must include Value Added Tax (VAT). The menu must also state if there is an obligatory cover charge – which may be as much as £2 – and if a service

charge of 10–15 per cent is automatically added. Such extras can make a significant difference to your bill. If a service charge is not included, it is usual to leave a 10 per cent tip. Aim to eat in the evening between 19 and 22, unless you are going somewhere which caters for an after-theatre trade. The most difficult night of the week is Sunday, when many places are closed. It is always wise to book.

For all-day service and a wide choice under one roof, it is difficult to do better than Harrods. There are eleven restaurants, bars and cafés here, catering for every taste and pocket, and ranging from the ice-cream parlour in the Food Halls, where you can choose from an imaginative range of milk shakes, sundaes and ice-creams, to the elegant Georgian Restaurant, named in 1911 in honour of George V's coronation, where lunch is served to the gentle accompaniment of a grand piano. The nearby Terrace Bar offers breakfast from 7, and Harrods even boasts its own pub, The Green Man, suitably entered through the menswear departments.

American The Hard Rock Café at the west end of Piccadilly (150 Old Park Lane, W1, 071 629 0382) still attracts long queues; or there is the unique ambience of Joe Allen (13 Exeter Street, WC2, 071 836 0651). Both venues are open in the afternoon.

English Good British cooking is not too easy to find. To sample it at its best in wonderfully old-fashioned surroundings, visit Rules (35 Maiden Lane, WC2, 071 836 5314, open in the afternoon), where you can eat rich casseroles and pies, game and oysters. Similarly filling, but cheap and cheerful, is the nearby Porters (17 Henrietta Street, WC2, 071 836 6466, open in the afternoon), with its pies, puddings and crumbles, or go to Simpson's in-the-Strand (100 Strand, WC2, 071 836 9112), for traditional roast beef and saddle of lamb carved at your table.

Ethnic Indian and Chinese restaurants are found just about everywhere; for the best Chinese cooking visit Soho's Chinatown, based on Gerrard Street, and for a taste of imperial India, take in the Bombay Brasserie (Courtfield Close, Courtfield Road, SW7, 071 370 4040), where the set buffet lunch is particularly good value. Greek establishments are clustered in and around Charlotte Street, W1. For Jewish cuisine, go to Bloom's in the East End on a Sunday, when it is packed with family parties (90 Whitechapel High Street, E1, 071 247 6001, open Sun–Thurs 12.30–21.30, Fri 12–15).

Fish For seafood addicts there is the upmarket Bentley's chain of oyster bars and fish restaurants, or try informal Manzi's (1 Leicester Square, WC2, 071 734 0224), or the Café Fish (30 Panton Street, SW1, 071 930 3999, open in the afternoon). For the best fish and chips in town visit the Sea-Shell (49–51 Lisson Grove, NW1, 071 723 8703).

Italian Almost every other street in central London has an Italian trattoria, most featuring quarry-tiled floors and strategically placed pot plants and offering almost identical menus; one of the best is San Frediano (63 Fulham Road, SW3, 071 584 8375). The Pizza Express and Spaghetti House chains are good value if you are looking for something cheap and cheerful; for a more sophisticated and expensive evening try one of the Covent Garden establishments, such as Bertorelli's (44A Floral Street, WC2, 071 836 1868), Luigi's (15 Tavistock Street, WC2, 071 240 1795), or Orso (27 Wellington Street, WC2, 071 240 5269).

Vegetarian and Health Food These are particularly congregated in the Covent Garden area, where there are two branches of Cranks (one in the central market) and Food for Thought (31 Neal Street, WC2). Neal's Yard, off Neal Street, is a vegetarian and health food gourmet's delight, with an excellent cheese shop and eateries in converted warehouses.

Last, but not least, is the traditional *English afternoon tea*. The larger museums and galleries, and historic houses such as *Osterley*, *Ham* and *Kenwood*, cater for those with weary legs by offering tea, scones and cakes. More elegant and pricey spreads can be found between about 15.30 and 17.30 in many large hotels and stores, among them Harrods (in the Georgian restaurant), Heal's (196 Tottenham Court Road, W1), Fortnum & Mason (181

Piccadilly, W1), Brown's Hotel (Albemarle Street, W1), the Ritz (Piccadilly, W1), the Savoy (Strand, WC2) and the Waldorf (Aldwych, WC2). Some offer a groaning help-yourself buffet, others waitress service. At Harrods (Sat only), Fortnum & Mason and the Savoy you eat and drink to a piano accompaniment, at the Ritz you may find a pianist or a harpist, and the Waldorf offers a tea dance on Fri, Sat and Sun. Where bookings are not taken, arrive early if you want a good table. Less expensive are a number of patisseries and tea-shops, among them Maison Bertaux (28 Greek Street, W1) and Patisserie Valerie (44 Old Compton Street, W1), both in Soho; Maison Sagne (105 Marylebone High Street, W1); Daquise (20 Thurloe Street, SW7), a good antidote to the Science Museum; and the much-patronized Louis in Hampstead (32 Heath Street, NW3).

Events

Beating Retreat A grand display of massed bands, pipes and drums held on Horse Guards Parade, Whitehall, in late May or early June, with some performances floodlit. For tickets write to Household Division Funds, Horse Guards, Whitehall, London SW1A 2AX, enclosing stamped addressed envelope and giving date on which required (details are given in national press or ring 071 873 6173).

Boat Race Fiercely competitive teams from Oxford and Cambridge universities race over a $4\frac{1}{2}$-mile course on the Thames from Putney to Mortlake on a Saturday in March or April.

Changing the Guard There are ceremonies at *Buckingham Palace*, Whitehall (Horse Guards Parade) (see p. 19), the *Tower of London* and *Windsor Castle*. The Buckingham Palace ceremony takes place daily from April to the end of July and every other day from August to the end of March, but is cancelled in bad weather. The guard is actually changed outside the palace, with bands playing, between about

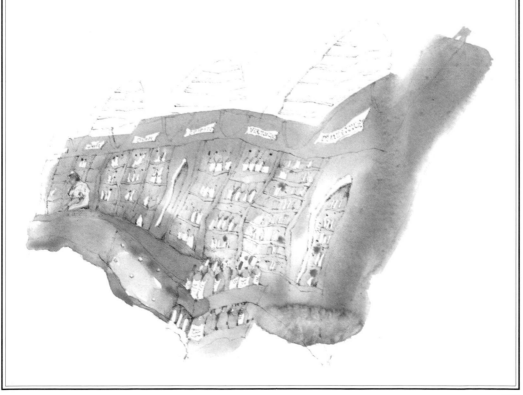

11.30 and 12, but a detachment of guards lines up at 11 in Friary Court in St James's Palace before marching off to music down the Mall, and the crowd here is usually smaller; outside Buckingham Palace itself it is often impossible to see anything for people. The Whitehall ceremony (at 11 weekdays, 10 Sundays) has no accompanying music and is shorter. The ceremony on Tower Green takes place at 11.30 when the court is at Buckingham Palace. Similarly, there is a ceremony, with music, in the Quadrangle at Windsor when the Queen is in residence; otherwise the changing of the guard here is on Castle Hill (summer) or outside the Guard-room (winter), daily at 11 in summer, alternating with the guard change at Buckingham Palace in winter.

Chelsea Flower Show Held in late May in the grounds of Christopher Wren's Royal Hospital, Chelsea, SW3, this massive four-day horticultural display is a must for all garden-lovers. Entrance on the first day is restricted to members of the Royal Horticultural Society. Information on 071 834 4333.

Lord Mayor's Show This colourful annual procession showing off the newly-elected Lord Mayor to the citizens of London is usually held on the second Saturday in November, starting at 11. The Lord Mayor processes through the city in his gilded coach (brought out of the *Museum of London* for the day), accompanied by magnificent floats. Consult LTB or City of London information centre for date and route.

State Opening of Parliament A royal pageant to mark the start of the new Parliamentary year in late October or early November. The royal procession starts from Buckingham Palace shortly after 10.30 – with the Imperial State Crown in its own carriage preceding the Queen's state coach – and moves down the Mall, across Horse Guards Parade, down

Whitehall and to the Lords' entrance of the Houses of Parliament, arriving at 11.15. The ceremony inside the Houses of Parliament is not open to the public. Information on 071 219 4272.

Trooping the Colour Staged to mark the Queen's official birthday, this colourful ceremony usually takes place on the second Saturday in June. At 10.40, the Queen rides in a carriage down the Mall from Buckingham Palace to Horse Guards Parade, where there is a birthday parade. Tickets are allotted by ballot: apply, for two only, by the end of January, enclosing a stamped addressed envelope, to The Brigade Major (Trooping the Colour), Household Division, Horse Guards, SW1. Ballots are also held for tickets for two full dress rehearsals, which occur on the two previous Saturdays.

Wimbledon Lawn Tennis Championships This major event in the British social calendar takes place over a fortnight in late June and early July. To enter the ticket ballot, send a stamped addressed envelope before 31 December of the previous year to All England Lawn Tennis and Croquet Club, Church Road, SW19 (recorded information 081 946 2244), or queue on the day.

GETTING AROUND

London is a huge city, and cracking the transport system is essential. The fastest way to travel is by the *Underground*, or tube, which runs from about 5.30 a.m. to midnight. You will see more by bus, but risk crawling along interminably in heavy traffic. Both bus and underground fares are based on a zone system, with six bands stretching 12 miles from the centre of the city. The cheapest way to use the system, if you are going to be constantly on the move, is to buy a daily, weekly or monthly

Travelcard. These are available in different combinations of zones and can be purchased from all underground stations and from railway stations that fall within the zones (a passport-size photograph is needed for the weekly and monthly cards). Free bus and tube maps, and information, can be obtained from the Travel Information Centres at Victoria Station and at Euston, King's Cross, Piccadilly Circus and Oxford Circus underground stations, and from many underground ticket offices – it is always worth asking. The redeveloping docklands area east of the City is now crossed north to south by the *Docklands Light Railway*, an unmanned, raised overground system which runs from 5.40 to 21.30 from near the Tower, or Stratford, to Island Gardens on the Isle of Dogs, from where you can cross to Greenwich via a pedestrian tunnel running under the Thames.

Taxis, or cabs, will take you direct to your destination, and are obliged to take the shortest route. They have most of the disadvantages of buses, but can be very useful at night, or if you are laden with luggage. Those available for hire display a lit yellow sign – there is no point hailing a cab whose sign is not lit. The charges are displayed inside and the meter starts clocking up the cost from the moment your journey is agreed. A tip of between 10 and 15 per cent is anticipated, but is voluntary.

Last, but not least, are the *riverboat services*. Speedy riverbuses ply between Charing Cross Pier (Embankment underground) and Greenwich every 20 minutes between 7 and 20, with stops at Festival Pier (for the South Bank Centre), Swan Lane near the Monument (for the City), London Bridge City Pier (south bank), West India Pier (for the docklands) and Greenwich. An hourly service operates Mon–Fri, 8–18, between Chelsea Harbour (Lots Road, SW10) and Swan Lane Pier, calling at Charing Cross Pier, and there is also an hourly service, Mon–Fri, 7–18, from Charing Cross Pier to London City Airport, calling at Swan Lane Pier (ring 071 512 0555 for details). Westminster Pier, by the Houses of Parliament, is the principal starting-point for river cruises, downstream to the Tower (20 mins), Greenwich (45 mins) and the Thames Barrier ($1\frac{1}{4}$ hours); upstream (summer only) to Kew ($1\frac{1}{2}$ hours), Richmond ($2\frac{1}{2}$ hours) and Hampton Court (3–4 hours, only one a day). Check sailing times on 071 730 4812 (recorded information) or on 071 930 2062. If you can, it is best to travel at high tide as you will have a better view. Also, if you buy a return ticket, remember to check the time of the last boat back.

You can also travel on London's canals. The London Waterbus Company runs a scheduled service on Regent's Canal from Little Venice (Warwick Avenue underground) to Camden Lock (Camden Town underground), where a lively street market operates at weekends. The canal cuts through the north side of Regent's Park and the zoo, where passengers can alight (Apr–Sep daily, Oct–Mar weekends only, 071 482 2550 for information).

NIGHTLIFE

The West End is the place to look for nightlife. Apart from the Barbican Centre, home of the London Symphony Orchestra, and the Mermaid Theatre on the river at Blackfriars, the City dies in the evening. London's most lively area for pleasure-seekers stretches across Soho and Covent Garden, in both of which there is a rich concentration of theatres, cinemas, restaurants and wine bars. But

there are many outposts. On any one evening the range of entertainments on offer may include an open-air concert in Holland Park (see p. 116) or the grounds of *Kenwood* on Hampstead Heath, pub theatre at the King's Head in Islington or above The Bush on Shepherd's Bush Green, folk music in the Half Moon in Lower Richmond Road, Putney, and open-air theatre in Regent's Park (see p. 116). The only way to be fully informed about what is going on is to scan the comprehensive entertainment listings in the weekly *Time Out*, *City Limits* or *What's on in London*, all published on a Wednesday. London's evening paper, the *Evening Standard*, published Monday–Friday, lists major theatres and cinemas, and principal concert venues advertise in the Sunday quality press, with details of imminent attractions. For shows and concerts, it is best to book in person from the box office (most open at 10), which can be done by phone with a credit card, or by arrangement to pay on collection. Tickets can also be obtained from ticket agencies, but check the booking fee before making a firm commitment.

Ballet and Opera Both the Royal Ballet and the Royal Opera are based at the Royal Opera House in Covent Garden (Bow Street, WC2, 071 240 1066), London's greatest theatre but not the most accessible. Seats for productions at the Coliseum by English National Opera are easier to get hold of, in a season that runs from August to May (St Martin's Lane, WC2, 071 836 3161).

Concerts The most important concert venues are the South Bank Arts Centre (Royal Festival Hall, Queen Elizabeth Hall and Purcell Room; box office 071 928 8800, general information 071 928 3002); the Royal Albert Hall in South Kensington (071 589 3203), venue for the Henry Wood Promenade Concerts from mid July to mid September; the Barbican Centre in the City (071 638 8891); the delightfully cosy Wigmore Hall north of Oxford Street (071 935 2141), where many young artists make their débuts; and St John's Smith Square (071 222 1061), near the Houses of Parliament, with its excellent crypt restaurant. But there are many other venues, and those who enjoy church music should attend choral evensong at St Paul's or Westminster Abbey, or some other major church, when the singing is often of a very high standard (times of services usually appear on the Court page of the quality newspapers).

Jazz Visit Ronnie Scott's (47 Frith Street, W1, 071 439 0747) in the heart of Soho, one of the oldest and best-known jazz clubs in the world. Jazz also features in the evening at two pizza restaurants: Pizza Express (10 Dean Street, W1, 071 437 9595) and Pizza on the Park (11 Knightsbridge, Hyde Park Corner, 071 235 5550).

Nightclubs Most of these are aimed at the young and trendy, and tend to come and go with astonishing rapidity. The smart and starry, such as Annabel's and Stringfellows, are for members only. If keen to sample what is on offer, consult the *Time Out* listings.

Theatres London is a world centre of theatre, with a wide choice of venues ranging from the huge London Palladium, which seats over 2000, to the King's Head, Islington, a theatre in the back room of a pub, and the tiny Cockpit off Lisson Grove. Most are concentrated in and around Soho and Covent Garden and this tightly-packed rectangle running south to the Thames from Oxford Street includes the oldest and most elegant houses. Although the present building is Regency, by Benjamin Wyatt, there has been a theatre on the site of the Theatre Royal, Drury Lane since 1663, and it was here that Nell Gwyn made her debut. The theatre is also known for its ghost, which seems to have a preference for matinées. Similarly evocative is the Regency Theatre Royal, Haymarket, built by John Nash in 1820–1, its classical portico neatly closing the view down Charles II Street opposite; while London's grandest theatre is perhaps the Palace at Cambridge Circus, a triple-decker Victorian opera house currently being restored to its former glory by Andrew Lloyd Webber, whose long-running *Jesus Christ Superstar* was staged here.

The London Palladium, a home of light entertainment and popular variety almost from the day it opened, was designed as a lavish Edwardian theatre by Frank 'Matchless' Matcham in 1910, his luxurious fittings even including box-to-box telephones. Nothing could be further from the stark outlines and bare concrete of the National Theatre complex on the south bank, projected since 1949 and finally opened in 1976, with Peter Hall as artistic director. Of the three auditoria here, the Cottesloe is largely devoted to fringe theatre, the Lyttleton has a traditional proscenium arch, and the Olivier is built round an open stage. Just down river, a small, Tudor-style theatre is being reconstructed on the site of Shakespeare's Globe.

London's theatres usually offer everything from musicals to Restoration drama, often with star names in the cast. Tickets for musicals tend to be the most expensive, and these in particular are what touts will try to sell you at vastly inflated prices. Most theatres offer twice-weekly matinées, which may be cheaper than the evening shows, and a limited number of half-price tickets for some West End productions can be obtained from the excellent Society of West End Theatres (SWET) ticket booth in Leicester Square on the day of the performance (maximum of four per person, cash only, open from 12 for matinées, 14.30–18.30 for evening performances). If you want to go to the National Theatre, 40 tickets per auditorium (Olivier, Lyttelton and Cottesloe) are sold on the day of performance from the box office (071 928 2252). However you buy your ticket, always check on sightlines so you can be sure you are not sitting behind a pillar or that the top half of the stage will be cut off.

Public Holidays

Britain has fewer public holidays, known as Bank Holidays, than most countries in Western Europe. Banks and many shops will be closed and public transport services are reduced, but many tourist attractions stay open on the holidays that fall within the summer season and it is worth checking if you want to visit them. The crucial dates are 1 January (New Year's Day), Good Friday, Easter Monday, first Monday in May (May Day Holiday), last Monday in May (Spring Holiday), last Monday in August, 25 December (Christmas Day), 26 December (Boxing Day).

Public Lavatories

It is best to use the facilities available in most museums, art galleries, historic houses, large department stores and railway stations, but some good public lavatories exist, notably in the City: in Paternoster Square near St Paul's Cathedral, and just off Basinghall Street near the Guildhall. Using the dalek-like, coin-operated superloos now dotted all over London is a gamble – the facilities may or may not be acceptable. Lavatories in hotels, restaurants and pubs should only be used if you are a customer.

Shopping with a Difference

London is known for its big *department stores*, concentrated in Knightsbridge and along Oxford Street, Regent Street and Piccadilly, and all offering a huge range of goods under one roof. With some 300 departments and a staff of several thousand, Harrods is one of the world's largest, its displays a unique combination of the exotic and the everyday, the glamorous and the down-to-earth. In the famous Food Halls, still decorated with their original Doulton tiles and with wall-mirrors reflecting tiers of chocolates and pink pyramids of prawns, this blend of showmanship and the genuinely useful is seen to perfection. Here you can buy a humble banana or a loaf of bread, but also carry off a crystallised pineapple, such as must surely grace a banquet of the gods, or choose from some 500 cheeses, among them white ricotta from Italy, earthy sheep's-milk cheeses from Corsica. Tête de Moine (monk's head) from Switzerland and the little-known milleen from Ireland. In the bowels of the building, Harrods runs a unique range of services, among them a ticket agency, an estate agent, and even a bank, where you can cash a cheque up to 17 every day of the week, except Sunday. A significant proportion of sales are to overseas customers, and the seven-language store guide, written in Japanese, Arabic, German, Italian, Spanish and French as well as English, looks like an advertisement for some specialist, multi-lingual dictionary. Other stores in the House of Fraser group, for which Harrods is the flagship, include D. H. Evans of Oxford Street, Dickins & Jones of Regent Street, Barkers of Kensington, and the Army and Navy Stores in Victoria.

No visitor to the West End could miss these elephants of the shopping world, but London also has some less obvious attractions which it would be much easier to overlook.

Arcades To get a flavour of Regency London, and to stay warm and dry when the weather is bad, wander down one of the shopping arcades off Piccadilly. On the north side, near Bond Street, is the prototype for them all, the Burlington Arcade of 1815–19, patrolled by a top-hatted beadle. Almost directly opposite, running down to Jermyn Street, is the feminine Piccadilly Arcade, with hanging baskets of flowers and narrow bulbous shop windows like rows of giant jars, the pink and green colour scheme contrasting with the tasteful coffee and brown décor of Prince's Arcade just to the east. Much more sober is Nash's Opera Arcade linking Charles II Street and Pall Mall, still lit by its original elegant lamps but now the least fashionable of them all. Exclusive Jermyn Street running parallel to Piccadilly is lined with delicious specialist shops. Both Paxton & Whitfield, at No. 93, an Aladdin's cave of succulent ham and cheese and pies in ornate pastry cases, and Floris, at No. 89, an exotic perfumery, can be smelt before they are seen. Also here are hatters, shirt-makers and tobacconists catering for the clientele which patronizes the clubs in St James's and Pall Mall.

Auctions You do not have to be a potential purchaser to enjoy these free entertainments or to inspect the exhibits on viewing days. At both Christie, Manson and Woods (8 King Street, SW1) and Sotheby's (34/5 New Bond Street, W1) you can stroll in and watch an auction in progress (do not be intimidated by the official-looking men on the door or the ranks of earnest bidders ticking off their catalogues: walking in and out while a sale is in

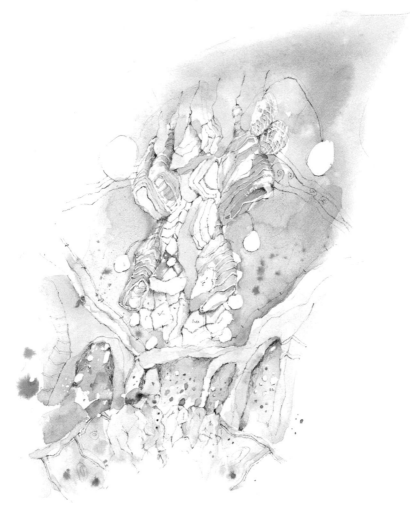

progress is accepted practice). Also good value are Bonham's (Montpelier Street, SW7), Christie's South Kensington (85 Old Brompton Road, SW7) and Phillips, Son & Neale (7 Blenheim Street, W1).

Street markets There are any number of these, from the fruit and vegetable traders in Berwick Street in the heart of Soho to the stalls selling pricey knitwear, leatherwork and other craft goods in Covent Garden. Apart from Covent Garden, where the Victorian market arcades make an unusually attractive setting, colourful venues include the Saturday bric-à-brac and antique market in the Portobello Road, W11 (it begins at 8 a.m. – get there early if you are hunting for something special); the Sunday morning Petticoat Lane Market in the East End (Middlesex Street, E1), where fashion goods usually include an impressive array of leather; the weekend crafts and clothes market (10–18) at Camden Lock, NW1, attractively set among former warehouses occupied by potters, jewellers and other craftsmen on the edge of Regent's Canal; and the stallholders selling silver, jewellery and knickknacks who congregate on Wednesdays and Saturdays outside the antique shops in Camden Passage, N1.

Tours of London

By bus There are any number of tour companies operating in London, and it is best to shop around to find the package you really want. A wide selection of half-day and full-day tours is available, some incorporating three-course lunches and entry to major sights such as The Tower and Westminster Abbey. The cheaper tours will often have taped commentaries which can be unsatisfactory; the best – and more expensive – will offer trained London Tourist Board Blue Badge Guides. Most companies offer a number of pick-up points in central London. The LTB has brochures on those tour companies it recommends and all the following offer a variety of packages:

Evan Evans, 27 Cockspur Street, SW1 (071 930 2377)
Frames Rickards, 11 Herbrand Street, WC1 (071 837 3111)
Harrods Luxury Tours, Knightsbridge, SW1 (071 581 3603)
London Transport Sightseeing Tours, Wilton Road, Victoria, SW1 (071 227 3456)

On foot You can take your pick from a riverside pub walk, a journey through the London of Dickens, a walk on the trail of Jack the Ripper and many more. For details, contact LTB or the following:

Citisights, 213 Brooke Road, E5 (081 806 4325)
City Walks and Tours Ltd, 9/11 Kensington High Street, W8 (071 937 4281)
Historical Tours, 3 Florence Road, South Croydon (081 668 4019)
Perfect London Walks, PO Box 1708, NW6 (071 435 6413)
Tour Guides, 2 Bridge Street, Westminster, SW1 (071 839 2498)

INDEX

——— • ———